MW01674194

OMNEC ONEC

AMBASSADOR FROM VENUS

By Omnec Onec

GLOBAL COMMUNICATIONS

Omnec Onec: Ambassador From Venus
By
Omnec Onec

Additional Material By Col Wendelle Stevens (Ret)

Copyright © 2008 - Timothy Green Beckley
DBA Global Communications, All Rights Reserved

EAN: 978-1-60611-051-5
ISBN: 1-60611-051-9

Nonfiction

No part of this book may be reproduced, stored in retrieval system or transmitted in any form or by any means, electronic, mechanical, photocopying, recording, without express permission of the publisher.

Timothy Green Beckley: Editorial Director
Carol Rodriguez: Publishers Assistant
Sean Casteel: Associate Editor
William Kern: Editorial Assistant
Cover Art: Tim R. Swartz

If you are the legitimate copyright holder of any material inadvertently used in this book please send a notice to this effect and the "offending" material will be immediately removed from all future printings. The material utilized herein is reproduced for educational purposes and every effort has been made to verify that the material has been properly credited and is available in the public domain.

Printed in the United States of America

For free catalog write:
Global Communications
P.O. Box 753
New Brunswick, NJ 08903

Free Subscription to Conspiracy Journal E-Mail Newsletter
www. conspiracyjournal.com

Omnec Onec

Contents

Dedication.. - 7 -
Acknowledgements.. - 9 -
How She Came To Be Here.. - 11 -
An Autobiography.. - 23 -
Chapter One From Venus I Came.. - 25 -
Chapter Two Laws of The Supreme Deity............................ - 47 -
Chapter Three Tythania Canes of Age.................................. - 61 -
Chapter Four In The Womb.. - 75 -
Chapter Five The Venus Plane.. - 97 -
Chapter Six Teutonia... -105 -
Chapter Seven The Creative Life.. -123 -
Chapter Eight Earthward Bound... -137 -
Chapter Nine Brotherhood of Planets.................................... -171 -
Chapter Ten Again Des... -183 -
Chapter Eleven Sheila.. - 201 -
Chapter Twelve My Earth Family.. - 209 -
Chapter Thirteen Compared to Venus.................................... - 239 -
Publisher's Comment... - 249 -
Postscript By Publisher.. - 253 -
Special Comment... - 265 -
Appendix I Other Venusians.. - 267 -
Appendix II Bell-shaped Spacecraft...................................... - 271 -
Why My Interest in the Case.. - 277-

Dedication

I dedicate this book with love to my children, Joe Don Tobea Lynn, Zandar Onath, Jason Prron and Sharon Yvonne, and to everyone everywhere who also seeks a more balanced Universe and love for the Supreme Deity, as well as to all mankind.

Omnec Onec

A major assumption which goes into discussions of space colonization and inter-stellar communication is that [Earth] biological intelligence and societies represent the supreme example of organization and complexity of matter. We have to face the fact that we may only belong to a transient stratum in a whole hierarchy of levels in organizational development.

Dr. Paul Davies, Kings College, London

Teutonia, A Temple City on Venus

Acknowledgements

I wish to thank three men who have been instrumental in making this book possible. Their help and encouragement contributed greatly to the success of this effort.

The first is Ranier Luedtke, the author of my biography. Without his three years of dedication, research, perseverance and hard work, this book and my mission on Earth could have gone unfinished. I believe he almost knows more about me than anyone. He asked me things I would never have thought of or remembered otherwise, and from our taped sessions he kept the contents in the personal expressions of my own nature.

The second is Stanley, the father of two of my children, who always shared his dreams and helped it to become a reality, who never let me down and always encouraged me. I always loved his ability to dream and his love of art and beauty. I feel he really appreciated me on all levels.

The third is Wendelle Stevens who, with faith, set about to seek me out after hearing an audio tape of a radio interview done in Chicago a number of years ago, and whom I know very well on the soul level as a very aware individual. I admire his faith and honesty. This we all need as we race ahead in this very technical world fraught with dangers. He gave me this opportunity to reach out to you by publishing these details of my origin. He helps me fulfill a chosen mission to help all mankind everywhere to understand by answering some very important questions about one's true origin and destiny, and to return the birthrights to each one of you, to trace your heritage and its roots to the beginning as soul, and to its physical origin somewhere in our vast Universe.

My special thanks to many more friends everywhere who have also lent their advice and assistance so generously.

I can once more regain my true identity and share these truths which have been such a well guarded secret on Earth. Perhaps you can now join the brotherhood of planets to which so many others belong. Perhaps you call catch up with the balance of life and being that is so uniquely yours.

With love and respect.

Omnec Onec (once Sheila)

Everyone connected with this book was chosen by my people for their part. They contacted me to let me know who was acceptable. That is why I personally contacted each one of them individually.

Omnec Onec

"The subject of UFOs cannot be dismissed as mere nonsense. To a person who does not study the subject it may always be rejected as nonsense... a person who studies it cannot possibly come to that conclusion."

Prof. J. Allen Hynek

How She Came To Be Here

This unique book is the personal account of a living human being who was, with her full consent and active cooperation, transported to Earth in a spacecraft from her home planet. She arrived in the company of her paternal uncle and was carefully prepared and conditioned to live here and grow in the physical society of our native life wave of our own planet.

Her own mother on Venus died shortly after her birth and she was taken into the childless family of her natural mother's sister and raised as her own. When her uncle accepted a mission to the denser life wave of Earth she chose to come along in order to make up some lapses in her own experience in the denser physical realm and to balance some unfinished Karma, both physically and with other personalities here.

She was carefully conditioned to our density and became physically manifest in an Earth-body equivalent to a 7 year old girl. Her uncle and the crew who brought her here introduced her into a Tennessee family who had just lost their own 7 year old daughter, Sheila, in a terrible bus accident enroute to her grandmother's home to go to school. The grandmother, having seen little of the granddaughter, was not aware of the substitution, and sent the Venusian to school as her own kin. Years later Sheila's adopted mother was made aware of the substitution by the Venusian uncle, who explained everything to her, and she agreed to raise Onmec Onec in place of her own daughter Sheila.

Although Omnec had the appearance of a 7 year old girl she had the Venusian wisdom and knowledge of her 210 Earth-year equivalent at the time of her arrival here in 1955. This enabled her brilliance in school and she excelled in almost everything, which she tried to conceal so as to protect her real identity.

This then is her story of her early life on Venus, her arrival here in the middle of our first modern excitement over UFOs, her preparation and adaptation to Earth living and its peculiar problems, unknown to her on her home planet.

But how is this possible? How can we reconcile this report with the severely inhospitable conditions perceived and measured by science as surface conditions of Venus?

Omnec Onec (Sheila) makes reference in this book to land and water separation, and to bases and structures on her home planet Venus as well as on Mars and our Own Moon. We see no evidence of structures or of artificial organization on either Venus or our Moon or Mars, two of which have been completely photographed with high resolution cameras. We also fail to see the seas and rivers and bridges and port facilities that certainly would have shown up within the camera resolution available.

This seems to be an irreconcilable problem on the face of it and casts the rest of the story into serious doubt for much of our unenlightened Earth humanity. But is this a necessary situation? There are very broad-based beliefs in earth society that have been with us through all our history, that easily accommodate the seeming conflict between this account and our contemporary view of our reality.

Some Eastern beliefs allow for an unseen astral world that coexists in time and space with us, which has form and structure and is peopled with beings, both good and bad, that are aware of us and can and do influence us. The theosophists studied those concepts with a scientific fervor and attempted to explain them in technical terms and to relate this underlying nature to the physical sciences we thought we knew. "The First Principles of Theosophy" by Jinradasa, originally published in Adhyar, India, provided one of the most authoritative early treatises on the nature of being for Earth humanity. The Freemasons originating in Europe propounded similar ideas in great secrecy. The Rosicrucians shared a common origin with Freemasonry but published their ideas more openly. In a volume called 'The Cosmoconception' by Max Heindel, many of the great mysteries of being were described in contemporary western language, and again was related to science. There are many such references in metaphysical literature. Eduard Schare in France and Rudolf Steiner in Germany wrote extensively on such metaphysical concepts and understanding.

All of these great schools of thought divided the nature of being into several planes of existence, the lowest and densest for us being the physical plane. They divide the physical plane into 7 levels of density; solids, liquids, gasses, plasma state (a sort of supergas) or 4th etheric, 3rd etheric, 2nd etheric and 1st etheric. All of these states, we are told, are still of the physical plane making up the form world, and they all have density, form, rigidity, mass, weight, inertia and other properties of physical plane matter appropriate to the nature of their state. There is for most of us an apparent major division among these 7 states of matter. The lower three are called, for the sake of convenience, the form world, or the 3-dimensional world, or the third density, the only world to us as denizens of that realm. Though we really occupy all of those states of the plane simultaneously, we are only <u>aware</u> on the lower 3 planes. Another with a greater awareness may not be familiar with our limitations because they "see" more of the total reality. We cannot see the additional reality that they see because of our own limitations in perception and we reject that part of existence. This does not make it any less real however, and as our awareness improves we will be able to "see" more.

We have evolved very sophisticated instruments to extend our perceptions and have made high resolution images of the Moon and Mars from which we may study the <u>lower 3 states of matter</u>. A complex of buildings or a planned structured facility on these levels would surely show up. And, much as we would like to believe it, <u>all</u> scientists are not in on a "cover-up." We have a complete file of Moon photos, tens of thousands of them, all automatically numbered by the cameras as the pictures were taken. The same goes for Mars. They are all here, including the mis-shot frames — and still no cities on the Moon; no oceans and ports on Mars. Others can study these files and come up with the same conclusions. In 5 or 10 years more, low level orbiters will photograph every inch of Venus, and whatever they find will similarly be made available to researchers. Those are not expected to "see" much more than already revealed on the Moon and Mars.

Until our awareness increases however, and we evolve new instruments to extend our awareness, we still will have only the lower form states to study, which may not be where the action is at present time. If, however, the primary existence, structures and appurtenances of that place are on a different level of the form (physical) world, and we have evolved our senses and instruments to perceive it, we may very likely find exactly what Omnec sees and describes in her book. Because she does not suffer from all of our limitations, her perceptions are real and natural to her. Because she does not experience the greater limitation that we do, she may not even be fully aware of the severity of our limitation. That limitation is ours and nobody else's. Only we can overcome it.

I have studied a different extensively documented UFO case where the often returning extraterrestrial visitors involved described other human life in our solar system and civilizations with cities and structures on Venus and Mars and even other local planets, and also described an intercommunication among these planets. As far as I can determine, neither Omnec nor the other witnesses have ever heard of each other. In both cases, the extraterrestrials have to make a change to be tangible to us.

Omnec describes other planets of being above or beyond the physical also, which she calls the Astral, Spiritual, etc. These terms agree with our own metaphysical literature on the subject because they have a common origin, and have now become a part of our language. Omnec's description of the astral plane quite agrees with our own metaphysical concepts of the same.

It is now easy to see that Omnec's birth and early life on Venus took place on the next plane of being. On several occasions she traveled to higher regions for a special purpose, such as her initial preparation for coming here, again returning to a level at which she was normally living.

When she and her uncle made final preparations for departure to Earth, they first changed state to more dense level on Venus, where they used a bubble car for convenience until they arrived at that state, about equivalent to our lower astral here. There they changed vehicles and used a "metallic" disc-shaped, more intricately structured form of vehicle. The nature of everything, all matter, including the clumsiness of her body and the density and restriction of the medium in which they existed, changed. The city of Retz on their native plane had become the city of Retz on their now denser plane of reality. A considerable difference between the two cities was immediately apparent, though they actually coexisted in time and place on two separate planes of reality.

There was an oppressive heaviness to everything on the now lower level, but it was from here that they departed for Earth. The cumbersomeness of the body was very difficult until Ormec learned to get used to the new density.

This was still not equivalent to our physical plane. They remained here until their departure from Venus for travel to Earth. There is no dense physical counterpart of the City of Retz, and no evidence of life to be seen in the dense natural state familiar to us that would be equivalent to Earth.

Upon arrival here, they entered the upper physical or etheric levels of Earth physical being and proceeded to the etheric counterpart of a temple here, like Retz, having a dense physical level where they underwent more conditioning to prepare them for the slow-down into our matter. Again there was an abrupt and frightening further restriction that she had to very carefully learn at the temple in the Himalayas. The disc-shaped ship was also further densified to carry them to their destination here, where Omnec remained to this day.

An extraterrestrial visitor in still another direct contact case once pointed out the difference in levels of consciousness unfoldment, the density levels they occupy, and our apparent inability to "see" the life-waves on even our most adjacent planets. According to him, our senses and awareness evolve from our immediate environment outward as our consciousness unfolds in any particular embodiment in time and space. We first become aware of self and then our immediate surroundings, evolving senses to perceive and comprehend what most immediately affects and concerns us. This is very local at first but slowly expands according to need.

Our early awareness is of our own home and our very small place in time and space. At that point, to us, nothing else exists. It is all there but outside of our consciousness-awareness and consequently <u>not there</u> to us at our level. To another, more experienced, it may all be there and more. As our consciousness unfolds we become aware of more and it then becomes existent to us. From our immediate home and family we grow into awareness of other families, then a community of families and nations, and our new awareness gives us unlimited new possibilities within the limits of our evolving sense perceptions. Instrumentation is designed to enhance the senses but we have not yet designed new instruments to give us new senses, or horizons beyond our native world. When we look out into space we perceive only what vibrates to these same limited senses.

The extraterrestrial said that when we become aware of all the nature of our own planet, we might be said to have Earth planetary consciousness, which is still very limited. A further expansion of consciousness would pick up adjacent levels of reality in adjacent realms of being that vibrate nearer our own rate and we would become aware of them. We might then be said to have extra-planetary consciousness-awareness. This can further expand to include full awareness of the next nearer planets to us in a vibratory sense, and even others, until we have achieved Solar consciousness where we would have full awareness of all life and being at all levels in a solar system. Until then we can perceive only what vibrates to the highest levels of consciousness unfoldment we have achieved up to now, and to most of us this is only what vibrates to the spectrum of our earth physical materiality, which may not even border into the vibrational rate of reality tangible to other life waves on other planets — even in our own solar system.

We are then told by that same source that there are other life waves in evolution in our solar system, and even co-existing with us in other realms of vibration on our own and other planets.

Suddenly we are confronted with a great universality of extraterrestrial and extra-dimensional life and being entirely beyond our sense of perception at this time. Just as we can grow to awareness of them, some of them have already become aware of us and have learned to control their realities into ours in specially designed vehicles. They have become tangible to us in our own native reality by a form of control exercised by them. They can become tangible or intangible to us according to their own will. Different societies have different modes of emerging into our reality or transcending out of it again, and they are seen by us as either densifying slowly, or suddenly, in place and evaporating out again in the same way; or as emerging from a point that grows, slowly or suddenly, into our reality and disappears again the same way.

Now, strangely, all of these phenomena are abundantly reported in the UFO literature. Our extraterrestrial visitor went on to tell us that Mars and Venus have lifewaves that vibrate near enough to ours to have discovered and made contact with us. They also mentioned an Earth lifewave beyond us that we would have to call inter-dimensional because they do not vibrate directly to our physical-chemical world of being. They nevertheless are considered Earth beings, and some of them are in contact with equivalent levels of Mars and Venus and other planetary life as well as with our own, and they do use vehicles of convenience for such contacts. When we look out at any of these heavenly points with our own Earth eyes, even aided by instrumental extensions of the faculty, we perceive only that part that vibrates to our Earth physical-chemical rate, and that may appear to be entirely lifeless and quite inhospitable to us. In fact it is a very small part of the reality that actually exists.

Considering this statement of the case, it is not impossible that some of these exotic UFO vehicles, which undoubtedly exist, could in fact come from Venus or Mars as some of the occupants have alleged.

The winged serpent is common to many of our mythologies, including the Aztecs, the Toltecs, and even some Asian sects, and they are usually associated with stories of white men who bring wisdom and knowledge, who are believed to came from Venus, or else Venus figures prominently in the story. This does seem to conform to the statement in this report that the Venusians coming here are from the single white race that makes up that lifewave. Why winged serpents, since we have no counterpart in reality? What do the needle-shaped silvery, shiny metallic 'vimanas' (space craft) of the Sanscrit epic mythologies such as the Mahabarata, the Ramayana and the Mahavira, seen high in the sky look most like? Serpents of course, and they are flying in the air — winged serpents. The Vedas of ancient India describe several sizes and varieties of vimanas, the flying silver serpents, such as the Agnihotra Vimana with two engines, the "Elephant Vimana" with more, and other types named after birds such as the "Kingfisher Vimana," "Ibis Vimana" and others. King Ashoka of Northern India was said to have ridden in a "Pushpaka," an auxiliary vehicle launched from a vimana. The Ramayana describes the Pushpaka as follows: "Bhima flew along in his car, resplendent as the sun and loud as thunder.., the flying chariot shone like a flame in the night sky... it swept like a comet... it was like a second sun shining in the heavens ... then the chariot rose up higher and all the heavens brightened." The Mahavira reads: "An aerial chariot, the Pushpaka, conveys many people to the ancient capital of Ayodhya. The sky is full of stupendous machines—flying machines, dark as night but picked out by lights with a yellowish glare." And there are many other such accounts.

The vimanas were understood to come from Venus and they visited other parts of the world as well, including ancient Atlantis, South America and Africa, but their widest contact with Earth humans was reported in Central Asia. In this respect it is curious to note in Omnec Onec's story that she was taken to a temple in the Himalayas for a time for special conditioning to enable her to live here in our Earth density.

One of the greatest bodies of recent metaphysical information in our time, in some ways eclipsing the "Seth Material" received by Jane Roberts, is that received by Don Elkins, Carla Rueckert and James McCarty in Louisville, Kentucky, known as "The Law of One," books one, two, three and four. This highly erudite material was trance-channeled directly from "Ra," a "fifth density mind/body/spirit complex" similar in a sense to "Seth." The "Ra" complex took its third density physical experience on Venus in our solar system before that humanity emancipated from third to fourth density. Second density experience is in natural forms of flora and fauna, lacking rational consciousness in the physical vehicles.

According to "Ra," there was a time in the past in our solar system when Venus was a flourishing third density planet having a humanity with polarized conscious life form very similar to our present form here on Earth now. They were in their later stages of development and were approaching emancipation in our later Atlantean and Early Egyptian days of glory, some 12,000 to 15,000 years ago. The Venusians, having matured their third density evolution and sciences, had developed marvelous technologies and to us, unbelievable machines and devices, and they travelled freely in space and to this planet, Mars and others.

They brought new ideas, a belief in one Supreme Creator, advanced spiritual knowledge, and a promise of our eventual salvation or emancipation from third density also.

They came physically from Venus in the great vimanas of Vedic and Atlantean literature, and some of them also took physical incarnation on this planet.

They claim to have designed and constructed, or guided the construction of several of the great pyramids of the world, some of which still remain undiscovered. They introduced or were responsible for the introduction of many of the religions of this world today. They designed the 22 highly symbolic pictures painted on the walls of the chamber of initiation (the king's chamber) in the great pyramid at Ghiza, which later became the court cards of the Egyptian Tarot, and the foundation for all other tarot systems known today.

Their third density level of evolution, similar to ours now but more advanced, emancipated on their planet and graduated to fourth density being. Some of their already advanced fourth density mind/body/spirit complexes (not in physical bodies) graduated to fifth density. The third density manifestation, a bi-polarized evolution like ours today, had used up much of the third density material and resource of their planet, and that technology had polluted all third density nature to the degree that it underwent cataclysmic cleansing, as we may be about to do, which also served to accelerate third density experience for those left and expedited them out of body to move on.

According to "Ra" the graduates moved on to fourth density being, roughly equivalent to our spirit or astral/spiritual level, and continued their evolution and that of their planet there. Advanced beings already working in fourth density moved to fifth and continued there also. Most of the third density failures, who were not ready to emancipate, were transferred to Earth for third density recycling here. They died out of their bodies there and were incarnated in earth physical bodies here with conscious memories of their past sealed so as to allow them free-will activity in this bi-polarized third density reality. Hence the number of Earth mind/body/spirit complexes in physical incarnation here now who have vague memories of their Venusian physical experience before the change.

We are told that fourth density experience on Venus now is almost Eden-like because the third density physical manifestation was, as here, more an imperfect crystallization of fourth density reality, which is now freely expressed in fourth dimension without the third density crystallization limitations. We of third density can of course see and perceive only third density manifestation, even with our best instrumentation, and therefore see only the result of something like a runaway greenhouse effect and planetary physical convulsions combined, which do not carry over into fourth density being.

We are told that fifth density Venusian spirits have the advantage of fifth density evolution, also and simultaneously, in the Venus system, and that there is some cross-communication between the fourth and fifth densities there.

Some of this sounds very much like the Eckankar philosophy propounded a number of years ago, and which was in point of fact advanced knowledge brought here by Venusian emigre spirits. It also sounds like the Sanskrit Vedas.

We have had reports of UFO visitors from Venus from the oldest histories in the world to date. There are extended accounts in the Upanishads, in the Tau Te Ching, and in modern UFO history. A number of UFO contactees were told that their visitors were from Venus. Among the ones who released extensive accounts of these visits are George Adamski, Howard Menger, Kevin Rowe, Bill Clenden, the Mitchell Sisters, Frank and Tarna Halsey, Dr. Wilbert B. Smith, and more. Some of these have received unfavorable publicity, but that does not change the real facts in the matter.

Ron Card has been contacted by a Venusian team who arrive in a bell-shaped ship since he was a college student in Miami more than 15 years ago. He has carefully documented these contacts, and they now fill a whole book. These various stories are consistent in their nature and content though some of these contactees never heard of any of the others. Consider the account listed as Appendix I in the back of this book.

Albert Coe has been in contact with humans from outside our solar system who have Venusian and Martian crew members aboard their ship. He published his report in a private volume titled, 'The Shocking

Truth" 20 years ago and the contacts continued, off and on, right up until he died of cancer in 1984.

This is of special interest here because the Venusians who brought Omnec Onec here were met by a Martian human who assisted them upon arrival.

Our visitor in this book claims conscious physical transfer from Venus, in her Venus body, here to Earth in the same physical body which was, according to her description, densified by stages to live in third density physical. She did not come alone, and she came in a ship which was also densified by stages so as to be physical in third density reality in order to operate here. She and her party, and the densified ship, are all brought to Earth together, in company with others, in a large cigar-shaped transport ship.

Final densification took place here on Earth at a temple in the Himalayas that extends into fourth density reality and has served such cross-density (cross-dimensional) operations before.

So when you read this account, do not discount it as science fiction, or another spiritual nut seeking attention. You will be reading the conscious recollection of one of those fourth density personalities adjusted back to third density on a benevolent mission for her people and the Venusian spirits taking the grade over again among us, and to us for our own benefit as hosts to the spiritual émigrés.

Considering these statements of the case, is it so impossible to believe that some of these exotic UFO vehicles could in fact come here from Venus as sate of the occupants have alleged, and may even have left representatives here among us as our witness here claims?

I leave that for you to judge for yourselves. Here then is the story of Omnec Onec from Venus.

Col. Wendelle C. Stevens
(Retired)

An Autobiography

Venus person becomes physical —

Venusian lifewave different —

Venusian past history —

Relationship to Earth —

Past life relationships —

Karmic relationslnps —

Human life is universal —

Many inhabited planets —

Modes of transportation —

Special preparation —

Venusian spacecraft —

Home and family there —

Adaptation to Earth —

Adopted home and family on Earth —

Difficulties of Earth living —

Contact with Venus family —

Chapter One
From Venus I Came

1. I land in the Nevada desert
2. Many others from neighboring planets here
3. People's images of the planets are false
4. Earth is colonized
5. Their involvement throughout history
6. Government learns truth — TOP SECRET
7. Telescopes do not reveal all
8. Why our people continue to visit
9. Earth, the negative planet
10. Karma brought me here
11. Why I was chosen and my life on Earth
12. People s consciousness higher today
13. Interest in spiritual unfoldment
14. Laws of the Supreme Deity, Venus and Earth
15. Venus
16. What the book will do
17. Imagination

It was in the deep of night, among the remote mountains and desert wilderness of Nevada, that the glowing spaceship touched down. The odd humming sound steadily became fainter and fainter. Then, as if from nowhere, a round opening appeared in the circular craft and several figures stepped down into the headlights of an approaching car. One was a tall, handsome man with his long blond hair neatly tucked away under a hat. Beside him stood a little girl and the ship's pilot.

Minutes later, the tall man and his little blond niece were on their way down the bumpy desert road, while the mysterious spaceship sped off into the starry sky.

The most earthshaking revelation of the twentieth century will be that since Earth was first colonized, human beings have been arriving from the planets in this very solar system — planets which most people today believe cannot possibly have advanced human life. Their ships land secretly in remote parts of the world where they are met by friends who have already been absorbed into earth society. Most of the newcomers do become involved in life here, something that has been going on for a long time; but the people who know about us, or even suspect we exist, are very few in number.

Today, after almost three decades of silence, the truth about that chilly desert night can be told. Until this moment, for what has sometimes seemed like an eternity, I have lived the life of Sheila. But Sheila was to be my name only until the time was right for me to tell Earth's people who I really am, and where I really come from. That time has arrived.

My real name is Omnec Onec (also Echo Leia). I was the little blond girl of that night in the desert, and the stately man beside me was Odin, my loving uncle. Both of us had arrived from Tythania, the planet you call Venus. As a child I had made the decision to spend the rest of my life on earth, as a matter of destiny more than anything else.

I am one among thousands of people from the neighboring planets who make Earth their home. Some of our people stay only long enough to complete special missions, but many have made the courageous decision to spend the rest of their lives here. Scientists, doctors, educators, artists, engineers, and ordinary citizens from these advanced planets live and work secretly among the people of Earth.

The idea that Earth cannot be the only planet in the Universe with intelligent life is pretty well accepted today. Millions of people believe that among the UFOs are spaceships from distant planets more advanced than earth. The bold and adventurous will go a few steps farther, to wonder about this story of my life, and to put aside for a while all the canned truths about the planets in this solar system.

My fondest hope in writing about my life on Venus and on Earth is that people will be awakened to the truth, as incredible as the truth may seem. It's sad that for so many years, images of barren and hostile planets have been drummed into people's minds. Hardly a child finishes school without learning about the extremes on Venus and Mars. Telescopes and space probes all say the same thing, so it seems. When Earth's astronauts arrive on our neighboring planets, the one thing they will not find is human life. So it is no wonder that people today hardly have an original thought about what really does exist out there.*

I know from personal experience that most of the popular ideas about our planets are far from being true. The greatest government secret of the century is that advanced human civilizations have been discovered on many of the planets in our solar system. And the physical spaceships which are seen in the skies every day are from some of them. Governments of the world know as well that people like myself, living secretly within the earth's population, number well into the thousands.

For their own very good reasons, as I shall explain later, governments and military powers on Earth are doing all in their power to suppress any evidence that may leak out from UFO witnesses, space probes, astronauts, astronomers, and anyone else who may know of us. (I am not saying that all astronauts and astronomers know.) Meanwhile, most of the public hears from unsure astronomers and government sources and is satisfied.

No wonder the truth is so unbelievable! I can understand why people like myself are called crackpots. It is much easier to believe the latest evidence from the space probes than to suspect there might be some grand secret.

In reality, Venus and the rest of our twelve planets† are very much alive. More than half the planets in our solar system do support human life. The civilizations that I know of are all spiritually and technologically much more advanced..., and wore ancient than any race living on Earth today. And beyond this family of planets are countless more solar systems, most of which also support human life. Man is truly a universal species.

The story of men on Earth will clear up many questions that need to be

---

* Human life at our level of reality.

† Twelve planets are mentioned here because to Omnec the number is the twelve that they detect with more vision.

answered about our people before I go on with the story of my own life. Lately, more and more people are reconsidering the conventional stories of man's past. Archeologists are admitting that advanced civilizations may indeed have existed on Earth tens and hundreds of thousands of years ago. There is also enough evidence indicating that during prehistoric times, man had technologies superior to today's. There is also evidence showing that throughout history, Earth's civilizations have been visited and helped by people from other planets. I have known this for a long time. It is true.

In every age, visitors from outer space have had an influence on the culture and technology of people around the globe. Sacred literatures of the world speak of flying spaceships and man-like beings descending from the sky, bringing great wonders. Legends and myths also mention man-like beings landing on Earth and living among the people. Ruins of cities exist, whose architecture cannot be duplicated by modern technology, and whose rock engravings speak clearly of the extraterrestrials who built them. Unexplainable things scattered around the world all seem to tell the same story. Ancient man was much smarter than people admit, and he was never entirely alone.

The Venusian village where I was born and raised is called Teutonia, which means "descended from Germany." It was named in memory of a brilliant German scientist who came to Venus and contributed to our people's growth there. As a child, I learned the story of man on Earth in Teutonia's Temple of History, a place of learning that is more like a time machine than a school.

Millions of years ago, our first expeditions landed on Kal Na-ar (Earth), the youngest of the planets. The space scientists of several planets had watched Earth undergo evolution, every so often sending ships to investigate. The planets of a solar system, I should mention, are not all created at once. They are constantly forming, maturing, and dying. New planets are continuously being colonized and dying planets are being abandoned.

Our expeditions found Earth to be the greenest, most lushly vegetated planet in this solar system. But, as beautiful as it was, the entire planet was soon considered unfit for colonization; and it was without doubt very dangerous for any of our people to settle here. As word spread, Earth became known as the hostile, negative planet. It was then that it was called Kal Na-ar., meaning "negative child." After those explorations, nobody stayed there any longer than was absolutely necessary.

A problem with Earth was that it had only one moon. Planets in the physical universe usually have two or more moons, so that each can help balance the other's influence. For a planet to have no moons also is fine, but to have only one can unbalance a planet. In this solar system, Earth is therefore unique.

As the Moon revolves around the Earth, its gravity slightly stretches the Earth itself, causing tides. If these tides would have been the only problem, our early explorers should have rejoiced. The Moon also has an effect on any human being who decided to live here, or throughout the ages has been born here. Partly because of the water in our bodies, the Moon has just as definite an influence on us as on the oceans. It adversely affects our minds and emotions, a condition that has existed throughout history, and will exist as long as there is only one moon.

One of the problems is the flaring of negative emotion in masses of people, which is actually a self destructive force in man. Mental illnesses are also related to the phases of the Moon. The word lunacy comes from this effect. Visitors to Earth are often advised to drink plenty of water during times of the full noon, to help adjust to their lives here.

Not only does the Moon play with man's emotions, but the whole unbalancing effect also reduces people's life-spans. And because the planetary vibrations are coarser or denser than on Venus or Mars, there is much more illness and depression. With good reason, Earth became an unpopular planet in its early years, and was not colonized until life on Venus and its neighbors had changed drastically.

Social and cultural reforms on Venus were very slow for many thousands of years. Life was troubled much like it is on Earth today, even worse, and the common people decided to do something about it. The breaking point was a planetary revolution the likes of which Earth has not seen, which bloodlessly destroyed money and the class structure forever. The consciousness of Venus's people changed to a point where the once wealthy and powerful had no choice but to change or leave the planet. In the time for each, the other planets underwent the same kind of growing pains.

Earth happened to be the nearest planet that could be colonized, so those who left took their chances here. But they were well equipped when they arrived, with advanced technologies that included antigravity spaceships, electricity, solar and nuclear power, and many powerful gadgets not yet rediscovered by modern man.

The governments and the way of life they established were very much the same as what had been overthrown on the home planet. They were designed in such a way that a few benefitted at the expense of many and slavery was a common thing. Civilizations flourished for a while.

The inevitable happened. Already immersed in such passions as greed, vanity, and anger, these newcomers succumbed to the negative influences of this unbalanced planet. People's emotions flared, life-spans shortened, and natural disasters turned life into a nightmare.

Earth became a planet of ups and downs, very much like it is today. It was doomed to repeated cycles of war and destruction unless the people could grow spiritually, which has not yet happened. The original colonial civilizations expired in nuclear wars and natural holocausts, and also the slow death of losing knowledge and culture generation after generation. Battling the elements just to survive took so much of the people's time, that education of the young suffered and precious knowledge was lost. The stronger survivors in every age lost no time in conquering the weaker.

Before the age of Lemuria, the land of Mu, two major races thrived on Earth. None of these peoples learned the lessons of war and progress in peace, as the home planet had done. Ancient history is an endless tale of one great civilization following another in dominating the choice regions of Earth.

Lemuria rose and fell as all the others, although it was one of the most advanced civilizations to develop here. The capital city Kharahota now lies beneath the sands of the great Gobi desert. Once again there had been the almost total suppression of the poor at the hands of the greedy and powerful ruling class. A vast area of the land suddenly sank into what is now the Pacific Ocean, leaving few traces for the survivors to find.

Atlantis was a great island continent that existed in what we know as the Atlantic Ocean. In many ways the Atlanteans were technically superior to modern men, but they too experienced technology racing ahead of their spiritual maturity to control it. Thanks to nuclear testing and many other misuses of their technology, the continent broke up and the last islands sank beneath the sea in a single day, leaving very few survivors.

Through all these turbulent years the Brotherhood of the Planets looked upon Earth as an immature child who needed guidance. As civilizations rose and fell, spaceships from Venus, Mars, Saturn, and Jupiter came here, and our people continued to come here to live. Those are the four planets responsible for colonizing Earth, and each is today the home of one of the four original race types evolving here.

One white race, known by many people as Aryans, came from Venus. We are the tall "angelic beings" so often spoken of in your UFO contacts. Normally we are seven to eight feet tall, and are well known for our long blond hair and blue or green eyes. Our hands are broad, with long and slender tapering fingers. The outer fingers curve in toward the straight middle finger, making each hand look almost like the flame of a candle. Very noticeable are our unusually high foreheads, large and wide-set eyes, and high cheekbones. Our temples are more sunk in than most, and barely visible are small, bony ridges on each side of the forehead, hidden by the way we wear our hair.

A yellow race is from the planet Mars. These are a slender people, small in stature, with golden or dark brown hair and olive to yellow complexion. Their large, slanted eyes are anywhere from grey to dark brown in color. Martians are known for their secretive nature and the futuristic many-leveled elaborate cities we see in science fiction illustrations. (The Martian lifewave is not in our physical density either.) Martians are associated with the histories of the Oriental and ancient Spanish peoples.

A red race came to Earth from the Saturn system, although it first evolved on Mercury. A change in the orbit of Mercury took it closer to the Sun and as living conditions deteriorated, the people migrated to Saturn. Saturnians are known to have red to brown hair and a ruddy complexion, with yellow to green eyes. A tall and stocky people, they are known in our solar system for their athletic nature. The Atlanteans and American Indians are among those who can trace their heritage back to Saturn. The Egyptian and Aztec peoples, among others, were very much influenced by the Saturnians.

A black race evolved in the Jupiter system. These are a tall, royal-looking people with broad faces and square jaws. Their hair is a deep, glistening black, and their eyes are from purple to violet. The Jupiterians are also known for their beautiful voices and open sharing nature *of* being. Descendents are in Africa and other parts of the world.

In all the centuries of struggle, Earth has never been forgotten or neglected. Compassionate people from the home planets have always been here to help their races. There were times when the people of Earth remembered their true heritage, and visitors from space and those of us who lived here were openly welcomed and known. During the more barbaric times and in recent years, the extraterrestrials have been more cautious in making their presence known.

During the times of Lemuria and Atlantis, we were recognized for our concern about the spiritual, cultural, and technical progress of Earth men. The people of Saturn, for example, were helpful in the rise of Atlantis. In ancient Egypt, a good relationship existed between extraterrestrials and the Pharaohs. Then, as in the time of Atlantis, scientists from other planets brought spiritual and technological knowledge to Earth. Among the engineers constructing the pyramids were people from other planets. Egypt's surge in culture was due to this influence.

The so-called dark ages of the past were not unusual, and space travelers were also here during those times, but instead of being seen for what they really were, they were looked upon as Gods. Much of the world's sacred literature and legends speak of them and their work here on earth.

The visitors also learned their own lessons in this process. They learned from experience the Earth's peculiar nature, and how new technology was quickly exploited in the struggle for power and domination, and the disasters that resulted. They became very wary of man on Earth, and as a consequence, refused to share their knowledge freely. Since this withholding of knowledge began, the civilizations of Earth have been little aware of their true heritage. Spiritual leaders were sent more often, and any technical help was given in small safer doses.

During your biblical times, space people exercised a greater influence over the spiritual growth of Earth men. Many of the prophets and spiritual giants were extraterrestrials. Your Old Testament contains many references to spaceships, heavenly beings coming from the sky, and leaders going off to speak with God. Many other parts of the world also experienced visits by the 'Gods from the heavens' with spiritual truths for the people.

Never again was technology given freely and completely to Earth. Instead, scientists were infiltrated into societies to secretly help mankind, making sure that the knowledge they brought was not misused. The very same thing is being done today.

Meanwhile, the sciences and technology have experienced a new surge of growth on Earth. Electricity, steel, engines, aircraft, nuclear power, and much more has been rediscovered. Wars continue and become more deadly, and most of the people know nothing of the inspiring kind of life on Earth's many neighbors in space.

In the later 1940s, UFOs began to be reported in surprising numbers, and many people were amazed to discover that they outmaneuvered and outran man's most sophisticated aircraft. Governments and military forces around the world were puzzled, but very much interested, and also very quiet.

Few people were at that time aware of the sudden interest in Earth. In their continuing experiments with Radar, scientists had generated radar beams which eventually reached Venus. Monitoring stations there received what seemed at first to be distress signals from Earth. A reply was sent. Experts on Earth of course could not decipher the signals, but they did correctly calculate that the signals came from a near point.

Ships were sent to investigate. What they found was frightening; a planet inventing and exploding ever more powerful nuclear weapons. The last fifty years on Earth has been a time of tremendous technical growth, but at the same time relatively little spiritual growth. It was the same sad pattern we had seen on Atlantis end Lemuria before this. The rebirth of the dreaded atomic sciences became of grave concern to scientists and spiritual leaders of the Brotherhood of Planets. No longer would the problems of Earth be entirely her own. With this awareness of nuclear power, this planet has become a menace to the entire solar system.

Nations of the world began to notice the mysterious UFOs over capital cities, industrial sites, military bases, research centers, and nuclear testing grounds as well. Now there was little doubt that these ships were manned or controlled by a superior technology. Military officials began to worry.

Being mystified was bad enough, but learning the truth about them was worse. Leaders weren't quite prepared for the shock of learning that advanced human life exists elsewhere. This all came to a head when representatives of the Brotherhood contacted key leaders with enough proof as to who they were. More than one U. S. President has learned the startling truth firsthand! Our messages wore ones of advice and persuasion, but never coercion.

Over a number of years, and through many exchanges of views, much was learned about the planets and their people. Our representatives explained that even with our advanced powers, we would not think of interfering in Earth's affairs. If we wanted to, we could have conquered Earth very easily at any time, but this was not in line with our spiritual belief allowing each individual the freedom to make his own decisions and accept his own experiences.

If a nuclear war were to develop, which imperiled our representatives or our ships, even then we would not interfere. We do not kill, even in self-defense anymore, either as individuals or as a people.

Nuclear power and its dangers were the highlight of these talks. Both the leading powers were advised directly of the danger and futility of such confrontation. Our scientists made it clearly known to top military leaders and to nuclear scientists that to continue their testing would be self-destructive. Instruments aboard our ships and space laboratories, we explained, had detected damages unknown to Earth scientists.

Raised eyebrows and objections came when we turned our attention to political systems. Our own experience has been that the two or three party system causes untold problems because a large part of the population is always unhappy with what the party in power does, and none have ever been truly benevolent. Corruption, unjust practices, and destructive competition are built right into the system. We stressed that this was not theory, that other planets had the same problems before Earth was colonized.

We pointed out how the daily power struggles are nothing more than destructive, and that quarrels between nations are so often petty children's games. And that democracy, including representative democracy, really exists nowhere on this planet. Nations of this world are ruled by Oligarchies of wealth. Their bloodstream is money. You people have no idea how complete this control of the world really is. The true picture is as shocking and unbelievable as the truth about our nearby planets.

What was the outcome of these talks? Eventually the two superpowers and a number of nations agreed to end nuclear testing in the atmosphere, and to depart from the "massive deterrent" concept certain to ensure mutual annihilation in the foreseeable future. But most of our people's ideas were rejected, and at the same time an age of secrecy was ushered in. Too many people have too many personal interests at stake to allow the truth to become known. If our existence became common knowledge, it would signal the end to the widespread corruption and exploitation on planet Earth.

Here, a very small percentage of the people own most of the resources, land, factories, and money in the world and money is the tool by which the control is exercised. As difficult as it may be to understand, we have learned to live without currency or money on Venus. The direct result is no hoarding, no accumulation and no weapon of exploitation. The difference in life is mind-staggering.

Also Venus has no central or national governments, and nothing resembling a class structure. The wealthy and powerful people of Earth who are aware of us do not want the masses to learn of our way of life. Secrecy is a matter of survival.

People with financial interests in the energy industries are very anxious to suppress anything to do with the UFOs or their occupants. Magnetic and solar power provide the energy needs of technically advanced planets. Being unlimited and costing little, introduction of such technologies here would put the other energy industry out of business. Magnetic power is also used to run our flying discs and the larger mother-ships. If everyone had such a craft, whose cost of operation is almost zero, autos, jets, and trains would no longer be needed. Neither would there need to be highways, railroads, airports or a hundred other inconveniences of our modern life. People wouldn't need to live in cities any longer, because commuting a thousand miles every day would be simple, speedy and inexpensive. Consider the losses to vested interests in such a case. Their position is clear. Technology from Earth's neighboring planets would bring change, unwanted change, into the lives of selfish people who seek to preserve the system.

Today we have a number of enemies here, and although the common man might welcome us with open arms, we do consider Earth to be a hostile planet. Our ships have been shot at by the military, by police, and by frightened citizens. Our ships are hunted down when spotted even though we show no hostility. This is one good reason for avoiding populous areas.

The Brotherhood is wary of Earth's immaturity, which happens to be only a reflection of the young age of this planet. People all too often react in a negative way to something as unexpected as one of our ships and as completely foreign to their concepts. Man on Earth has gone through so many wars and disasters that the idea of life on other planets is not too comforting. Your science fiction movies of creatures invading Earth have not been of any help.

Our ships are elusive because they are flying over enemy territory, but they are not considered really enemies by the people themselves. Besides treating us to undeserved hostility, governments and militarists have done a thorough job of clamping down a lid of secrecy over actual sightings, landings and contacts. Books have been written showing how the military and intelligence agencies have consistently controlled the press, silenced witnesses, issued false statements, and confiscated valuable evidence. This is unfortunate. A great number of people are aware of the censorship, but an even greater number of people would be utterly shocked to learn how serious and thorough the censorship really is.

Despite the harassment, our spacecraft continue their operations here. With the expanding technology our observations have grown to the greatest level in centuries. More of our convoys patrol your skies, land, and contact people on earth than ever before in your recorded history.

Those of us who live here are more and more making our presence known to trusted friends.

Before going on, I must advise that all UFOs are not from our Brotherhood of Planets, or even from our solar systems. Some are actually astral lights and inter-dimensional entities, and some are unknown to us. Some come from great distances. The whole picture is very complex, but there have been a great number of landings and contacts by our people.

In all parts of the world our ships are active, watching Earth's atmosphere, lands and oceans. The serious effects of continued nuclear testing are of special concern, as well as natural events such as earthquakes, climatic changes, and axial tilt of the earth.

Seeing all this activity, more and more people are becoming convinced that some of the UFOs actually do come from more advanced planets, and are slower to laugh at somebody else's experience with UFOs or their occupants. But the connection to your neighboring planets has not yet been made public, and may not be for some time.

It may be of interest to report that the gravity of Saturn and Jupiter are not as great at the surface as your scientists suspect, and that neither Uranus, Neptune, Pluto or the planets beyond are ice cold. With the exception of Mercury, distance from the sun does not control any planet surface temperature. It is true that Pluto and the planets beyond are affected by another asteroid belt between Neptune and Pluto that increases the energy of the sun's radiation, by acting as an electrical grid. The belt between Mars and Jupiter does the same for Jupiter, Saturn, Uranus and Neptune.

Since the blossoming of the U. S. and Russian space programs, probes have been sent to the nearby planets. Here have been the first opportunities to penetrate another planet's atmosphere and take photos at close range but considering the censorship, I doubt that any surprises will be made known soon. Most of the data sent back to earth has never been released. Carefully selected proof that human life is impossible on the other planets is accepted by the public. After all, space probes sent directly to the surface can not lie. But those in control of them can.

Our people who have decided to live on Earth are very quiet about it, especially those of us who have important jobs. For them to do any talking at this time is out of the question. They have too much to lose, a mission on Earth, or possibly their lives. What if a respected scientist at a U.S. nuclear research lab suddenly admitted that he was a scientist from Venus? Or what if a high government official did the same? He could be either ridiculed or believed, neither of which is very comfortable.

Why my people continue to help this planet, not to mention living here, probably is not easy to understand. Why leave a peaceful and comfortable life to live in such a negative environment here on Earth? People have asked me the same thing. Why did I leave Venus when life was so much more pleasant there? The answer lies in the design of the Universe, and also in Earth's unique place in our solar system.

For thousands of years our space travelers have been exploring the physical Universe, everywhere finding the most exacting order and regularity. Not only atoms but also planets and solar systems follow natural laws that existed even before this galaxy was formed. Cosmic plans and laws exist, of which man on Earth knows very little. The design of the physical universe is meaningful to those who have discovered its secrets.

The Universe was designed with one idea in mind, to support life in its many forms. As scientists on Earth are beginning to learn, life is no accident and neither are the many natural laws that govern it; laws that are found in any solar system. On every level of life in the physical universe we have found patterns, order, and cycles which we accept and learn from.

The Cosmic Being has not forgotten man, one of the higher life-forms in the physical universe. Just as the laws of physics and chemistry can be found everywhere, so can the minerals, plants, and animals. In fact, you may be surprised to find out how many plants and animals are really not native to Earth, but which were brought here by the colonists. Every planet has been designed to support life at many levels, and so it was no surprise for us to discover through our travels that most planets do support human life. Man is not a creature of the Earth, but a creature of the Universe who has colonized Earth. The human species has been universally designed and can adapt to exist in many places. If explorers had never found Eskimos living near the Arctic Circle, the common belief today might have been that man could not adapt to those extreme conditions. But over time the human body can and does adapt to very different conditions in different extremes.

Sooner or later the truth of what I am saying will be demonstrated. Man, as a universal form of life, has evolved on other planets, and in some cases to levels that are spiritually, intellectually, and physically inconceivable to men of Earth.

The Venusians and our friends in the Brotherhood are compassionate people. We too had a history very much like yours up to the present day. Venus has had its wars and power struggles, the oppression of the poor and the cruelties. Our concern is that Earth is having trouble growing up. The same mistakes are repeated over and over again. Instead of progressing beyond the age of wars, Earth has been arrested at that level for a frighteningly long time, and the situation is getting worse instead of better. A black cloud hangs over the entire planet.

With good reason our scientists continue to work in giant spaceships high in Earth's atmosphere, while people from all walks of life continue to live here. We are drawn in compassion for the suffering that Earth's people are going through.

A number of us are living on Earth to fulfill our own personal needs for growth, myself included. As the negative planet in our solar system, Earth attracts people who need negative experience as a part of their growth. In the East, people call this need or duty Karma, which fits hand in glove with reincarnation.

Reincarnation is an accepted fact of life among the people of our Brotherhood of Planets. It is very real, as anyone who lives in an advanced culture knows. Scientifically we have broken through the barrier you call death, thanks to ages of spiritual and technical progress. Every person alive today in the physical universe has lived many times before, but Earth's people in the West generally do not know it. Keeping reincarnation in mind, it is not really so tragic for us on Earth to be living on a negative planet.

Negative experiences are only a part of a long period of growth through many lifetimes on many and sometimes different planets. Each personality will be an individual forever, even after he no longer incarnates on Earth or any other place in the worlds of time and space.

Karma is an invisible law which we all obey, whether we like it or not, or even believe in it. It is known as the law of cause and effect because all that a person does, thinks, or feels has an effect on him. Sometimes the effect, or fruit of his actions, comes years or even lifetimes later, but there is no escaping it.

The law of Karma governs every circumstance of life until all the debts are paid or collected. It is not determinism, because every moment we are creating fresh Karma and reaping the old. It is a very exacting law, and no one can escape the suffering or happiness he himself has caused.

One of my reasons for coming to Earth was to balance out some of my Karma. I needed to learn the lesson of compassion, and to tie up some loose ends left behind from my previous lives on Earth. Life on Venus was bliss and I could easily have chosen to stay. But I realized that living out my full life on Venus would only have delayed the inevitable. Eventually I would have been reborn on Earth. As I look back now, I am glad that I made the decision to spend the rest of the days of this life on Earth, despite all the suffering and hardship I have had to live through.

It is not unusual for our people to come here for this same reason of balancing out Karma. Either they need to settle Karmic debts with people living here, with whom they have had relationships in past lives, or they need some kind of negative experience as war or poverty. In our solar system, these experiences are no longer available anywhere else.

My arrival here as a child was unique and different. Becoming absorbed into a new society is not only tricky but dangerous. An adult who lands on Earth arrives here prepared with training and experience, but I had to be planted into an Earth family without their knowing it. With the resources my people had at their fingertips, the plan was a success. I am sure there are families who know of us and who would have offered to raise me, but Karmically I was drawn to this one particular family.

As a youngster I never dared say a word about Venus, not to my family and not to my best friends. Before leaving Venus I was warned over and over how foolish and dangerous that would be. People were not even aware that life existed on Venus. In your movies astronauts always seem to find monsters, evil dictators, and warring empires on other planets, which sounds more like what our ships find on Earth.

A psychiatrist, I'm sure, would have been called in to treat my overripe imagination and "save the poor child from a world of fantasy." Later in life the explanation would have sounded more sophisticated, if I would have made the mistake of talking. "There is no doubt that she is just a mixed-up kid from the backwoods of Tennessee. Her emotionally painful childhood sent her to seek escape in a dream world. Venus is a fantasyland in which to seek comfort, a place to find new meaning in life." Now that I have begun telling my story, I hear this reaction often. It does not offend me because I know it is due to a limited understanding.

In the city of Retz I was first told of a chance to live on Earth, as well as working off some of my Karma. I was at the same time to fulfill a special mission for our people by breaking the secrecy of my presence and telling of our Brotherhood of Planets. I would be contacted later in my life with more of the details.

I was chosen to be in this spotlight because the story of our people should not be given only through phenomena in the sky, or landing spaceships on the surface. These can be attacked, explained away to others, or covered up as they almost always have been in the past. Breaking the news should not be too shocking, such as an occupant stepping from a spacecraft in a public gathering. That denies too many the opportunity for free choice and may result in unacceptable cultural shock. Instead, the real story needs to be told by someone who wouldn't seem like an alien suddenly arriving from space.

I am not endangering any secret mission by admitting that I was born on Venus. I am not a scientist with any secret knowledge about convoys or magnetic power. Today my mission is to write this biography. It is just a sincere effort to share with you our way of life.

Because I have spent so much time here, people will find it easier to accept and understand me as a real human being. I can identify very easily with the people of Earth, and they can identify more easily with me. Many of the pains and ordeals I have gone through are the same as those others have experienced in their own lives.

When I first decided to leave Venus, I looked to my future more as an adventure than anything else. The spiritual Masters in Retz of course warned me not to expect an easy pleasant existence, but the excitement of going to another planet filled my mind. The suffering I had heard about didn't seem very real to me. We are aware of the pain, the poverty, and the wars on earth, but these had not been my personal experiences in life. It was much like being an affluent westerner who is little affected by the starvation in Asia because it isn't his personal experience.

When I stepped down from our ship that night in Nevada I was unsure about myself, uncertain and uneasy about all the things that were to happen. I was fortunate not to have known then how bad Karma can be, or I may have turned around right there and gone back home. Venusians Don't Cry was one of the earlier titles I had in mind for this book, because there is so much joy in our lives that we rarely cry, except of course when we think of Earth or our past lives there. Since being here I have cried and cried, so much that it could well be the story of my life on Earth.

My life here has been full of adventure and intrigue. But on the other hand it was a rare thing for me to be among people who really cared for or loved me. Coming here meant leaving all that I knew and loved, a life of creativity and peace. After my uncle left me behind in Arkansas and returned to go back home, I was alone, "a stranger in a strange land."

In my life here, I have been hurt by others in so many ways and so often, that today I would rather die than to hurt another living being. I know all too well what suffering, pain and misery is like. In the Earth families that raised me my stepfathers were a dire punishment I had to learn to endure. One raped me when I was fourteen and the second at sixteen, while holding a loaded gun to my head. I didn't feel too bold or heroic in trying to resist because he had already shot me in the arm, and I didn't feel it was time to die.

Once I was knifed trying to keep my drunken stepfather from killing my adopted mother, and I don't even remember how often I have been beaten. Until I moved out on my own, life was absolute hell. Since then my life has not been heavenly, and who knows how much harassment I will inherit from writing this all down!

I have learned from experience how very real Karma is. My life here has been a giant heap of Karma compressed into this one lifetime so that I shall be done with it forever. If only people knew how surely all their misdeeds will one day meet them face to face, then who in his right mind could knowingly hurt another person? Do unto others only what you would have them do unto you, because everything you do unto others will be done unto you eventually. That is one big lesson I share with you.

I am not embittered today. The past is behind me and I try to enjoy the happiness of the present moment. The world has treated me just as I once treated it, and everyone grows from his experiences, good or bad. I for one learned the simple lesson of compassion, just as every other individual on any planet learns his lessons. My life on Earth proves that just because I happened to be born on a more advanced planet, does not mean that I escape the lessons of my past.

Less than a few decades ago, people would not have been ready to accept the idea of this autobiography. It would have been useless for any of us to do much talking, and those who did soon regretted it. It is the new level of consciousness, or level of awareness, that has made this book possible now. And depending on the public's reaction to me, there may be more of us making ourselves known.

Above and beyond our individual reasons for being here we are very much concerned with the consciousness of men of Earth. This has to do with his basic understanding of life and the Universe, and his awareness of his own self in it all.

Natural powers such as mental telepathy and precognition all of which we are adept at, weren't too well accepted not too many years ago. Esoteric subjects were mostly studied in small, private groups. Books on the occult subjects were given little attention and often ridiculed by the less informed, and the media were reluctant to treat psychic subjects seriously. The natural powers of man were looked upon as either satanic or nonexistent, really a sad state of affairs indeed.

Our overall concern in this age is to play some part in the spiritual awakening of Earth. Political and social reform is not directly our goal. As the people of Venus understand it, the way of life on Earth is only a reflection of the spiritual unfoldment or consciousness of its people as individuals. The reason for life in the physical universe is nothing more than spiritual awakening, and no part of life is ever separate from this main overall scheme.

Our understanding of spirituality is probably not what you would expect. It does not necessarily mean being a religious devotee or trying to live an apparently saintly life. Our spiritual teaching is a planetary teaching which is really an advanced form of science. At one end of the spectrum it offers a complete understanding of life, death, God, and the hereafter, and all the various subjects which religious and spiritual paths on Earth delve into. We allow each individual to prove to himself via actual experience what life after death is really like, and what that Being you call God really is. At the other end of the spectrum, our teaching includes a thorough understanding of the physical universe and its laws, which reflects in the wonders of our marvelous technology.

We have always been interested in the spiritual paths, religions, and the occult schools that have sprung up on Earth. In past ages we were involved in sending spiritual leaders here, around some of whom religions later developed. Most of the paths are limited today in the freedom, wisdom and love they offer their followers, but we cannot criticize any of them because each attracts followers at a certain level of consciousness, and those levels are not all the same. If a path offers what the individual needs, and satisfies him, then for that one it is a good path.

As a person matures spiritually, he learns that the conventional religions and paths no longer satisfy him, because something vital is missing. I had this same problem when I came to Earth. I was frustrated being in such a young body but having a head full of knowledge beyond many people's understanding. I found it difficult suppressing things very natural for me, such as picking up other people's thoughts. There were times when I had to hold myself back from telling all my friends and even people on the streets that they were walking around in sleep.

Because my spiritual upbringing was so very different from the teachings offered me on Earth, I didn't accept any while I was here. As a child in Tennessee I was raised in a protestant church, which seemed very primitive to me. I became disillusioned and hurt by the limits of the spiritual teachings in religions that I came across in this country.

The Venusians live according to spiritual and natural law, rather than manmade laws, in every area of life. This is a very basic difference between the other planets and Earth. Personal experience is the "vital something" which is missing in conventional Earth religions and paths.

Before leaving Venus I was told of limitations in Earth's spiritual teachings, and that I would not find satisfaction, but I was promised that some day in my life on Earth I would find the universal teachings, which on Venus are called Om-Notia Zedia, The Laws of the Supreme Deity. The name would be different but the teaching is the same, and it would be brought forward when the time was right and the people were ready. It has existed on Earth since the planet was colonized, and has been taught under many different names, at times openly, and at times secretly from person to person. During the time of Lemuria, and of Atlantis too, it was brought into the open, but most of the time camouflage was necessary because of the freedom and awareness this teaching offers. Organized religions and rulers consider it dangerous to their well-being and self preservation. For this reason you usually find it suppressed in some way by those authorities.

Pythagoras was one master of that teaching who taught it secretly under the guise of philosophy. Jesus taught it as the wisdom of love. This most ancient of teachings has been known in Tibet for thousands of years. It has been known here since first colonization. Then, a time came when it was successfully suppressed by powerful religions and had to be brought to Earth once more. Remote places in the Himalayas were chosen to guard the basic works where they still are today. If there is any one factor more responsible for the progress of the people of Tythania, it would have to be this science which we may call Laws of the Supreme Deity. It has allowed us to discover the deepest secrets of the Universe, of time and space, matter and energy. We have discovered some of the deepest and most profound secrets of man himself, of the mind, and the consciousness. All this is reflected in the wonders of life on Venus, wonders rivaling science fiction, and utopia on earth.

We have no wars or poverty, and our people do not know disease. Lifetimes span into hundreds of years. Physical aging ceases at between 20 and 30 years. Our cities are small, simply designed, and free of crime. Long ago, the magnetic and solar power developments revolutionized our lives.

Space holds some of our greatest challenges. We are a people hungry for knowledge. The Universe has been so designed that there is always more to learn. Our ships are not limited by gravity, friction, or the so-called speed of light, and some of them are miles long. Other planets in this solar system are only a few days away. A trip between solar systems is even faster.

As individuals, the Venusians are well aware of the real powers of the mind and consciousness. What you call psychic powers are child's play to us. Mental telepathy is the usual way in which we communicate, and we are also able to look into the future, remember past lives, or move objects by thought. Many of us have learned to move backward or forward in time. Any person trying to use such powers must have the spiritual maturity to be responsible with power. In living on a negative planet it is all too easy to misuse power, and people all over Earth who are unknowingly and unwisely dabbling with such powers will pay for their mistakes for many lifetimes to come. I never use such power except in dire emergency, and then I must be very careful.

We have discovered the existence of other universes beyond the physical, and we have leaned to visit these worlds at will. On Venus this has become a science in and of itself.

Some of your writers on Earth have called them parallel universes. Such worlds of being actually do exist, at different coordinates of time, space, matter and even energy. There are also worlds beyond time, space, matter and energy. In discovering and exploring them we have solved the mystery called death, which happens to be nothing more than a transformation to one of these other worlds and a very natural part of an individual's life. Death remains a mystery here on Earth simply because so few here have discovered and explored these levels of reality and being and returned to tell about them.

So the great challenge for man on Earth lies in unraveling the mysteries of life. I hope this book will unveil for you a greater conception of the world you live in, and a greater conception of yourself, the individual

I am not disturbed if you choose to call my life on Venus imagination. Every creation of man, everything manmade that you see around you, was born in the imagination. Imagination is the most powerful faculty in man and the key enabling man to become superman. With his imagination, man is as much a creator as is God Itself.

Chapter Two
Laws of The Supreme Deity

1. Importance of these Laws
2. How the Teachings helped me
3. What is Soul?
4. Planes beyond the physical
5. Spirit and creation of the lower worlds
6. Man's many bodies
7. Evolution in the physical world
8. Soul's growth as a human being
9. Fatima
10. Soul discovers a teaching
11. Soul travel
12. Becoming a coworker with God
13. Self— and God— realization
14. A universal teaching on every planet
15. The lower world teaching
16. Venus becomes astral

Venus is one of the older, more advanced planets in our solar system. So ancient are our people that my ancestors were able to watch Earth in its development and to explore the green planet when it first became livable. Since then, we have grown spiritually, culturally and technically as a civilization, and as individuals, to a point inconceivable to the people of Earth. So radically different is life on Venus that it would be useless for me to jump right into the story of my life there, even to mention such simple things as my birth, or my home, without these chapters about our culture and history.

When we say that the basic difference between Tythanians and the people of Earth lies in each individual's self-awareness, that is still a world of difference. The growth of a planet over millions of years depends on how spiritually awake and aware the people become.

Whenever the people of Venus speak of their culture, their technology, or any facet of their lives, credit always goes to our planetary science or teaching called the Laws of the Supreme Deity. Only through this advanced form of science, where spirituality and science are two faces of the same thing, have we grown in so many ways.

Only through an awareness of this science can people on earth begin to understand the Venusian life, and my own life. Without Laws of the Supreme Deity, Venus would be as Earth is today.

As a child I was well grounded in the fundamentals of the Laws, as is every child and every adult on Venus, because the teaching had long ago been discovered to be the true way, the true understanding for the entire planet. Only later in life, on Earth, would I realize how very precious the Laws of the Supreme Deity had been, and how fortunate I was to have received a thorough grounding in this teaching.

Knowing of Karma and the purpose of life in the physical world, and being aware of worlds beyond the physical universe, I found it much easier to survive the nightmares of my life on Earth. During my life on Venus I had gained the emotional strength necessary for me to cope with the hardships ahead. I was able to understand and accept life and my own difficulties more maturely.

Yet anyone on Earth who is open to this teaching can rise above the problems of the physical world. I was told about the future of this teaching shortly before I left Venus. One day, Laws of the Supreme Deity will be recognized on Earth for what they really are. The seeds have already been planted. Our people plan to become more and more involved in making this a reality.

An understanding that becomes a living experience for the individual studying the Laws of the Supreme Deity is exactly what it means by I.

Many different ideas can fill your mind when you ask yourself, "Who am I?" On Earth, there will be as many different conceptions as there are people. It is this self-conception that makes such a world of difference in anyone's life, whether he lives on Venus or Earth, or on any other planet in any galaxy. To grow into the full realization as to what and who you really are turns out to be the purpose of life in this physical universe and several other universes. All the experience that an individual can have through countless lifetimes culminates in a full awakening and a total awareness as to who you really are. The Laws of the Supreme Deity is a spiritual teaching, though under many different names, that has always existed, whether secretly or openly, on every planet, for those who are ready to achieve the goal of their many lifetimes of trial and experience.

Every individual on every planet is Soul — nothing more and nothing less. I use this word Soul because the Venusian word for it would be just a word to you. Whereas on Earth, Soul has been used for a long time by religions and spiritual philosophies, and comes close to what we mean. However, through the Laws of the Supreme Deity, we do not stop at saying "I am Soul," or merely believing it. We know it through conscious experience in the Soul body, using our most powerful senses and faculties which reside there.

Soul is so real that no one should have to wait until death to learn about its reality. It can be experienced now. In the physical world, Soul is usually considered to be located at a point just between and behind the eyes of the physical body. However, you as Soul can also learn to detach yourself from the physical body while it is still alive, so that you may be several feet from the body, miles away, or in one of the worlds which the religions call Heaven.

Soul is a unit of awareness. It can know, be and see. Much more can not be said about its basic nature, except that in quality, Soul is a duplicate of the Being called God. If you were to close your eyes and sit very still, away from noises and distractions, you will find one point in the body where you are most awake. Usually it's a spot in the center of the head behind and between the eyes which can be separate from and aware of physical sensations, sounds, sights, thoughts, and feelings. We have an indescribable something which can observe all the things a person may falsely believe he is. This detached observer is Soul, the real You.

If you close your eyes and create the face of a friend on the screen of your mind, it would be Soul that is looking at the picture. The mind is not looking, because it is only the tool used to form and hold the image.

Another way to experience the reality of Soul goes like this. As I speak to a friend, are the words coming from my mouth? Of course not! But if I were to watch carefully as I speak, being fully aware of each word as it comes out, I will begin to notice that something is listening to those words.

It is not a thought but a unit of awareness. Why is it not a thought, or the mind? Because I can think a certain clear thought as "I wonder if there is a difference between the mind and Soul", and be aware of it as the thought passes through my mind. The still, silent something which watches thoughts being produced by the mind, and knows they are thoughts, is the unit of awareness we call Soul. Very often we confuse thoughts with the unit of awareness that can watch than. We can have a thought such as, "I am fully aware of my thoughts," accept it as true, and forget that it too is only a thought. It too can be consciously watched as Soul. The awareness and the mental world of man are two different things.

By far the best way of finding out that you are Soul is to leave the body in Soul form while you are still living. This is called an out-of-body experience and it proves that you are something beyond the physical body.

It is useless to become involved in how old you are as Soul, because Soul Itself exists beyond time and space. Counting the many lifetimes before this one, you are easily many millions of years old. Through all those lifetimes you have remained the individual, and you will continue to be an individual after the last physical incarnation. The physical bodies, personalities, surroundings, and experiences may have changed, but always there was the real awareness, the real you, learning lessons and unfolding spiritually. To learn, grow, and awaken was the reason that Soul came into the physical world in the first place, eons ago.

Soul's journey to the physical world involved many other worlds beyond ours. These are the so-called parallel universes I spoke of, which the Venusians and many other peoples discovered and explored.

To the people of Venus, these planes of existence are the ultimate frontier, containing within them the answers to all of the mysteries of life.

On Earth books have been written about other worlds, and people have wondered about them ever since they were able to wonder, but few have discovered the secrets of consciously visiting these worlds during their physical lifetimes. Even this will change in the near future. To consciously experience them once could prove their reality, but to never experience them at all leaves them vague and unreal to that one.

Each of these worlds or planes of existence has a different rate of vibration or frequency. The matter in the world just beyond the physical is at so high a frequency that a person living there could easily pass through walls, mountains, and even people here. The highest sounds here, beyond detection by Earth scientists, are the lowest sounds in the plane beyond the physical universe. This explains why the existence of these worlds is a religious matter on Earth, rather than a scientific matter of personal experience.

The worlds beyond have very much in common with the physical world, but they are all much more beautiful and heavenly, they too have all kinds of people, cities and villages, animals, plants, mountains, oceans, deserts, and sunsets; but in every imaginable way, these worlds are vastly more beautiful than the most advanced planets here. The colors are out of this world, so radiant and breathtaking that words can not do justice to then. The universe just one step beyond ours is so beautiful that many people who live there after "death" mistakenly believe it is the ultimate Heaven.

I use a familiar analogy to help explain how these worlds are designed. First let us take a centrifuge, which is a scientific instrument that spins liquids at high speeds. If we take a mixture of water, mud, sand, and stones and spin it at high speed in the centrifuge, the heavier materials will collect at the outer edge in the order of their heaviness. As we look toward the center, we will see less and less gross materials, until in the innermost area we find only air.

The outermost layer can be thought of as the physical universe, the densest and most material of all the universes. As we look toward the center, we will find the layers having finer and finer materials. These are like the worlds of time and space, where everything is at the higher frequencies. To a person living there, things are as real and solid as to us in the physical world. This is because the senses used there are at the same higher frequencies. Likewise, our physical senses cannot record objects and people there because physical senses were designed for use in the physical universe only.

The very center of the spinning liquid, where there is only air, can be compared to the pure spiritual worlds beyond time and space. These worlds are the home of Soul and what religions call God, the Ultimate Reality. Soul originates in the pure, positive spiritual worlds beyond time and space, but It was born as an unconscious atom in this cosmic sea.

The Supreme Deity Itself is actually a void. It has no relationship to anything outside of It. This is why nothing can be said about It. But It can be experienced. The best thing to say is, "It just is!"

Issuing forth from the Supreme Deity, sustaining and giving life to all worlds including the physical, is the audible life stream of Spirit. Matter and energy in our physical world are nothing more than this universal *energy* those vibrations have been stepped down. It is within this sea of Spirit that Soul exists. It is a part of Spirit. As an unconscious atom when it was first created, Soul did not know who It was, what the Supreme Deity was, why It existed, and what the power is that It can control. It was asleep in this ocean of Spirit and somehow needed to be awakened to the fact that It even existed.

In order to provide Soul an opportunity to wake up, the Supreme Deity created the worlds of form where the opposite of Spirit exists, which we call the Kal or negative power. There Soul could be tested and purified in polarity until it became aware. There it could acquire the experience necessary to awaken and then be a conscious atom separate from the body of God, and yet a part of it. It will then remain an individual being for all eternity.

Soul exists naturally in the pure, positive spiritual worlds, where there is no matter, energy, space, or time. Not a trace of the negative power exists here. These worlds are very real, but it is almost impossible to describe them with words, because they are beyond the realm of mind and its workings. To know them a person must experience them for himself.

The denser worlds are constructed as a school for Soul through the creation of polarity and the negative power, Kal. Soul remains in these worlds of polarity, positive and negative, only temporarily, until the schooling is accomplished and the Soul graduates. The lower world with the most Spirit is that level Soul first entered on its way down into the physical plane eons ago. This most heavenly plane of the lower worlds is called the etheric plane. In spiritual terminology it is the crossing over line, between the denser planes and the higher Spirit levels.

As Soul came in touch with these denser worlds, It needed to protect Itself with sheaths or bodies. The best protection for Soul in a lower plane happens to be a body made of the same materials as are found naturally on that plane.

The first body you took is more or less a clear sheath or light that surrounds the Soul, On Earth it is known as the subconscious mind, one of Soul's most powerful instruments in the denser worlds. The limitless resources of man's subconscious mind exist on the etheric plane, where many saints and mystics received the cosmic consciousness. As a world of being, it is as real as the physical plane; in many ways more real. The etheric plane has people, cities, beautiful landscapes and sights that can be seen and remembered by those of us on physical planets who have trained ourselves in the art of leaving the body. *

The next lower plane that Soul entered on its way into the physical universe is called the mental plane. It also is a world of glorious sights and sounds, some of which are recorded in the religious literature of Earth. Your St. John is one individual who visited the mental plane during an out-of-body experience and described what he saw there, which included the capital city that was called Kailash. On this plane are the heavens of many of the world religions.

To exist in this rarified density, Soul must protect Itself with a coarser body, called the mental body or mind. Our mind is actually this body, and its energy appears as thought. Each of us has that body, for it is a tool that Soul uses to operate in the lower worlds. It has no life of its own, but depends on the energy Soul allows it to have.

---

* The term "etheric' used here to identify the highest plane next to Deity is at variance with some of the other schools of thought such as that of the Theosophists and the Rosicrucians. One need only keep in mind here that the description is from Deity through intermediate densities to physical reality as we know and experience it.

Just below the mental plane is the causal plane, where Soul picked up the still coarser causal body. It allows Soul to have recall of past lives in the lower worlds. Some teachings on Earth call it the seed body because the karmic seeds of our actions are planted here to be reaped later.

On the causal plane is a region often called the Akashic. Although the true Akashic records really exist beyond the lower worlds, those who visit the causal plane have the chance to learn of our past lives on the planes below the causal. The famous American psychic, Edgar Cayce, did just that. He viewed these records in his investigations of past lives. Any person can in time learn to visit the causal plane and discover facts about his own past lives on Earth and other planets.

Below the causal plane in frequency is the plane which plays the greatest part in people's physical lives — the astral plane. This is where you, as Soul, picked up the astral body and with it the ability to register what you call emotion. For this reason the astral plane is also called the emotional plane. When a person experiences emotion, this is really an energy flowing through the astral body. In any lifetime, your astral body is an exact duplicate of the physical body, only more beautiful to behold.

The astral plane as well as the other worlds of time and space is a very real world. In fact, everything we know in the physical world, such as people, mountains, trees, homes, and cities existed first in the astral world. The physical plane was created with the astral in mind, but in a less colorful and luminous way. People living on the astral plane have more powers, such as telepathy, manifesting things with the mind, and traveling at fantastic speeds without vehicles or devices. The astral body is luminous and does not have physical pain as we know it in the physical, which explains why people sometimes confuse this astral body with Soul.

Having all these bodies, Soul entered the lowest plane to begin the experiences which one day would lead to becoming a conscious coworker with the Supreme Deity. We all know it as the physical universe, where Soul picked up the physical sheath or body which was needed to survive here and begin Its experiences.

In the beginning, then you first entered the physical plane, you were not immediately a human being in form. For Soul to have every possible experience, which everyone must have in order to be perfected, you need to experience every state of consciousness that the physical world has to offer.

The first experiences that you as Soul had, or the first level of consciousness that you lived within, was that of the mineral state. Granted, minerals do not seem to be very aware (as we think of it), but even the seemingly limited experiences possible by living that mineral state are necessary as Soul first begins to wake up and comprehend Its physical existence. In the beginning, most of us were in the mineral state for a long, long time, depending on what experiences we needed. Of course you were never really a mineral or rock, but you as Soul inhabited such bodies on your way up.

Between lives there is a period of time there you are placed on a plane above the physical, according to your level of consciousness. In the very beginning most Souls go to the astral plane, staying for a while before reincarnating again into the physical universe.

After the mineral state and the experience in awareness at that level, Soul begins to have experiences in the plant state. As a plant, Soul can feel the sunshine and the wind and rain, and it serves as food for the higher forms of life. After many lives and deaths as moss, flowers, vegetables, and trees, on Earth and other planets, Soul is ready for the next step. It begins its lives in the animal state of consciousness.

As an individual, Soul will inhabit bodies that suit its own nature or individuality. Soul is the life force in the animal, but always remains a unique individual. It spends a great deal of time in the animal state of awareness, progressing from one species to another, from insects to reptiles, to birds, to mammals. These lives are not always on Earth, but on many different planets.

The last stage of physical unfoldment, and the highest state that Soul can reach in the physical world, is the human being. This is the divine apex of evolution in the physical universe, and is the form Soul uses to have Its final experiences here. As a human being, Soul must go through every possible experience. One lifetime is only a speck of time in evolution, much too brief a moment in the physical world to do all the learning and growing needed. Man on Earth does not even manage to complete one full cycle of 144 years in an incarnation.

Soul reincarnates as a human being over and over through millions of years in order to have all the experiences it needs. History is not the story of our ancestors; it is the story of our own lives, for we are our ancestors. Each of us has lived as many different characters, male and female, in many different races, on a number of planets, and in an almost uncountable number of circumstances and situations. Each time that we return, we arrive with a new body and a new mind.

New Souls are constantly being created, however, so that the lower worlds will continue to live. The Supreme Deity uses this plan of ever-constant life in order to live through Its creations and to never perish.

It is for our own benefit that the memories of our own past lives are hidden. If a person were deluged with so many memories, he could very easily end up in an institution. These memories are a part of Soul knowledge, of which we are not very aware until we become mature enough to handle it.

Anyone who is fortunate enough to remember experiencing the worlds beyond time and space knows that these lower worlds leave much to be desired. Why then, do we as Soul remain bound to the lower worlds for such a long time? In order for us to be purified and perfected, the negative power was established to bind us here as long as possible. Its instrument is the law of Karma, which, like the law of gravity, holds us here long before we become aware that it even exists. No one would dispute that the law of Karma is invisible, but the longer a person is unaware of how real it is, the longer will he be bound to the physical world.

Christ referred to the law of Karma when he said, "As you sow, so shall you reap." Spiritual leaders of almost every religion or path on Earth at one time taught this universal law, and even today most people of Earth know of Karma, especially in the East.

It has been said that mind can be a useful servant, but a terrible master. Soul should always be in control of the denser bodies, but all too often it is not. Instead of Spirit controlling the mind, the Kal power can take over so that person will sink into the five passions of the mind — anger, vanity, lust, greed, and attachment to material things. As long as this is happening, Soul will be bound to the lower worlds through the creation of Karmic debts; for as long as you have a debt to pay, you must be reborn.

Throughout the many incarnations as a human being, Soul is entangled in webs of Karma. You have been poor and rich, powerful and weak, famous and unknown, healthy and crippled, intellectually keen and slow-witted; but there comes a time that Soul approaches a state of balance in the physical world. As the individual is winding up his lives here, he begins to seek earnestly for answers to why he exists, why he is here, where he is going, and what the greatest power is that exists beyond the Physical world. He finds that the conventional paths no longer satisfy him. At this point a person begins to become more aware of the person within himself — his feelings, thoughts, and intuitions. He may soon begin to consciously explore the planes beyond the physical in his search for truth.

No longer is Soul comfortable with the religions of the day, because there is not enough truth in them, not enough answers. As Soul, you are ready to seek something beyond the physical world.

This is when you discover a spiritual teaching that tells you about Soul, and about your existence before you were ever in the physical world. You find that by having this teaching consciously, you are able to learn Soul Travel. Through this art and science, you leave the physical body temporarily to visit and explore any or all of the worlds beyond the physical universe, in the Soul body. It is like teaching what religions call heaven before death; only this experience can prove life after death to each individual.

Soul travel is the main feature of the Laws of the Supreme Deity, which sets it apart from other teachings. The whole system is based on personal experience within the planes beyond this one. Instead of hoping and trying to believe in life after death, the individual can experience life apart from the physical body and visit the places he will eventually inhabit, after the death of the physical body. He will learn the simple difference between death and Soul travel. In Soul travel, he returns to his living, inhabitable body. In death, he can not return because the physical body is for some reason no longer operable. Instead of believing in reincarnation, he will know that it is real after visiting higher planes and having recall of his own past lives.

With this conscious knowledge, there is opportunity to balance out the Karma from past lives. When one learns that the physical body is just a vehicle in which to learn lessons, then he is reaching a point where it will not be necessary to incarnate in the denser worlds any more. You have a choice to become a conscious worker with the Creator, even before physical death.

The physical world is not the only place where Soul must balance out Its Karma. There are also the astral, causal, and mental planes Soul has lived and created debts. In Its upward journey, Soul cleans up all of its unfinished business in the lower worlds first. It is freed of the bonds of Karma and reincarnation when It is firmly established in the first of the spiritual worlds, called the Soul plane, beyond time and space.

Here you have self-realization, the first full realization that you are Soul. Several worlds above the Soul plane is that higher spiritual world where the God-consciousness is reached. Here Soul realizes that It and the Supreme Deity are the same. Soul has total awareness here, a state that can be reached while you are still physically alive. Even here its growth is not completed. Beyond are many more planes. Throughout eternity there is always one more step to go.

The Laws of the Supreme Deity is our name for a teaching that exists on every planet and every plane. Venus does not have any monopoly on it, but we do recognize it openly as our planetary spiritual teaching. Each planet has this teaching which originates beyond the denser worlds, to help those Souls who are ready to advance.

There are a mind-staggering number of denser world teachings whose purpose is to suit the consciousness of Souls who must stay in the denser worlds for additional experience. These were established to bind the Soul to the denser levels until it is strong enough and aware enough to escape. They have a limited truth and serve their purpose well, and they are varied to suit the many levels of consciousness that exist in the denser worlds.

Each individual must be careful not to be trapped by a teaching which does not satisfy his inner need for his truth. The seeker must also be wary that he does not mistake a lower plane, within the realm of Karma, for the true spiritual worlds. The astral plane is today peopled by many who believe it is the ultimate heaven, so much more beautiful than the physical world is this plane.

Any planet whose people live in close accord with spiritual laws will have conditions that seem almost heavenly to people of Earth. Venus is the way it is because of the consciousness of the people living there. The same is true of Earth. Souls who have much negative Karma will be attracted together on one planet, to maize negative experience possible.

I am not saying that Earth is a completely negative planet. It too is balanced by a positive side to life. Any planet or plane in the denser worlds, on which you exist, can be negative or positive for you depending on your own attitudes, for these create your personal world with the power of thought. It all depends on your level of consciousness awareness.

As I mentioned, Venus too was once a very negative planet, as Earth is today. Over several million years, the people of Venus grew to a point in their unfoldment that is not unique, but seems unique to the people of Earth because they are not aware of such things. Our spiritual and technical growth became so positive that our entire civilization no longer needed to exist on the physical plane. While the physical planet Venus did remain alive, the entire culture and its people achieved transition to the astral level.

Chapter Three
Tythania Canes of Age

1. Origin of life in the physical universe
2. Cosmic cycles
3. Every planet is at one time negative
4. Why this history of Venus is vital
5. The golden age on Venus
6. Times deteriorate
7. Living underground
8. The work of Zaedrian
9. Decrepit cities and wars
10. The Beginning
11. Growth as a new people
12. Laws of the Supreme Deity
13. Translation to the astral
14. Physical Karma of the Venusian people
15. Physical body can be manifested
16. Physical planet Venus continues
17. My life on the astral plane

Trying to learn where life itself came from is not so easy here in the physical universe. It is very ancient history. Before Earth was colonized there were advanced, well-established civilizations on other planets in our own solar system. And before this solar system came into being, there were other solar systems in this Galaxy having planets supporting ancient civilizations. Earth is like a baby, just beginning to become aware of the vast world in which it lives.

Earth scientists today work devotedly trying to find out where life itself comes from. For thousands and millions *of* years, scientists on planets much older than Earth have done the same thing, but they learned that their efforts were in vain.

Life cannot be created here in the physical universe. However, when conditions are right, it can enter this world from the worlds beyond. Only when a person has the God-consciousness can he know the where and why of life itself.

As the people of Tythania studied and analyzed their own past, as well as the history of other planets, they found that all is not as chaotic as it seems. Life on the planets follows natural law just as surely as anything else in nature. Growth of a planet and its people goes through natural cycles and ages just as the growth of an individual passes through stages. The order of the ages gives an idea of the kind of life a planet goes through. First is the Golden Age, which on Earth related to the mythical time of Adam and Eve and the Garden of Paradise. Of all the ages, this is the most beautiful. It corresponds to the people's inner consciousness of beauty and innocence. Life during this age is peaceful, with the land bringing forth all that is needed for the comfort and well-being of life. Manmade laws do not exist, because the individual is led by an inner sense of spiritual justice. Neither do wars and petty conflicts play a part in people's lives at this time.

The Golden Age of Man leads right into the Silver Age, when a more negative way of life spreads across the face of the planet. Here the elements turn against man and good protection begins to make a difference between survival and death. Divisions between men and petty conflicts gather momentum in breaking up the stable way of life of the Golden Age, and as the planet proceeds into the next age, life becomes even more negative. This Silver Age is several hundred thousand years shorter (on Earth) than the Golden Age. Each new age is shorter than the one before (the foreshortening of the days perceived by the prophets in your Bible).

Next is the Copper Age, where the positive and the negative are equal for the first time. The five passions grow, and any group or clan of people faring better than another is subject to attack. As manmade laws seep into every area of life, rulers take for themselves the right and privileges belonging naturally to each individual. In less than one million Earth years the Copper Age also comes to an end.

The fourth and most negative of all the ages takes up the next several hundred thousand Earth years. It is well named the Iron Age or Kali Yuga (negative age). Darkness and decay are widespread during this age, and crime floods the streets. People are slaughtered by the millions and cities are entirely wiped out in senseless and brutal wars that embroil the entire planet. Soon this can shift to interplanetary wars and vast destruction through nuclear warfare and the rampage of black magic. A planet in this stage is justifiably quarantined because it is a danger to all others.

Fortunately, this ends one entire cycle, which on your Earth lasts four and one-half million years. As this negative age comes to a close, the planet enters a dormant state until it is readjusted for further life. A new Golden Age then unfolds, and life begins anew in yet another cycle of ages.

The Venusian people learned from their study of the Venus past that it indeed had gone through countless cycles of ages. But the pattern was the same — from Golden Age to Iron Age, a rest and then return to yet another Golden Age. When we first met the people of Mars and Saturn in this cycle, we found that both of these planets had evolved through similar cycles. Earth as well as numberless planets visited by the space travelers of the Brotherhood also obeys the cosmic cycles of ages.

All planets are not within the same age at the same time. Earth recently entered its Iron Age, while Venus is entering another Golden Age. It is at the beginning *of* Venus' previous Golden Age that this story of our past will begin. Actually, recorded history on Venus takes in several cycles before that Golden Age, but my own memory takes me back only so far.

The history of Venus is colorful and exciting, but so is the history of any planet, including Earth. The real value of including this story probably lies in the fact that our past is so strikingly similar to your own. We at one time had the same problems that are plaguing Earth today. We had the wars, the decrepit cities, crime in the streets, moral decay, exploitation, and a meaninglessness in the everyday lives of our citizens. How we conquered these mountainous problems and the periods of hopelessness and questioning perhaps will inspire those of us on Earth in the years and decades ahead. The story of our past will also explain how Venus came to occupy the unique place it holds in your physical universe today, and the how and why of my birth there.

Venus' last Golden Age was much like any Golden Age, a very peaceful and balanced time. The people were by no means primitive or savage. Much time was spent in outdoor gardens, and most of their needs were satisfied by the rich, natural surroundings. Vegetables and fruits grew abundantly in the tropical climate.

A critical period came near the end of that Golden Age when over a number of years the vapor envelope was reduced and frequent dry spells and disastrous droughts spread across the land. The sun was especially hot during these times, before a heavier cloud cover developed. In some areas a strange disease began to catch hold, a disease that was attributed to some mysterious rays of the sun.

All of this frightened the people to no end, until in mass hysteria villages were abandoned across the planet and colonies were established underground. For almost a century no one dared to venture forth into what was sure death under the hostile rays of the harsh sun.

Venus in this era was technically advanced enough to make life comfortable under the surface. The colonies were mostly horizontal and small enough so that walking was the only way to get around. Power was provided by small generators hooked up to underground streams and crude solar devices left on the surface. It was used sparingly for lighting and ventilation, for growing food, and for preserving and cooking food. The people did not have televisions, radios, and appliances because energy was in such short supply. Life underground was primitive but comfortable, with the people feeling fortunate that at least they were alive.

Although this kind of life lasted less than a century, it was nevertheless a long time for any group of people to live underground. Several generations were involved. There were many families whose parents and grandparents had been born and lived all their life underground. The younger families were the ones who eventually took part in the journey back to the surface. The fear of the sun had not been their own experience, but that of the older people. Now it seemed to the young people that perhaps it could only have been a superstitious belief of the old ones that had driven the people of Venus underground in the first place.

Even with the suspicion that fear of the sun was foolish and primitive, no one at first dared to venture out to see if it was true. And then, someone was born with the mission to lead the people out. His name was Zadrien, which later became well-known. He must have been a spiritually advanced individual to stand so firm in his beliefs that living underground was foolish and quite unnecessary. To prove that venturing out into the sun did not mean certain death, Zadrien shocked his family and friends by moving out of his own colony, living on the surface so long that everyone thought he surely had died and then returning one day. To the people's amazement, the rebel Zadrien was very much alive and obviously in good health. His skin had developed a more beautiful and radiant tint, much less pale than before. Zadrien also brought back vegetables grown in the sun to show how much more nutritious natural food was.

Communication between the colonies did not exist in those days, so Zadrien began to travel a great deal with his more courageous disciples, to prove to the people of Venus how good the sun really was. In many ways he was like Christ. All kinds of romantic stories, tales, and songs were created in his honor after the people had realized the truth in what he was saying and had moved back to the surface to live.

Zadrien was one of Venus' first spiritual leaders in this great age. As the people were led back to the surface, Zadrien took on the role of spiritual master in the people's lives. Much of the knowledge he gave them about the Creator and the universe formed the beginning of their Laws of the Supreme Deity. This was Zadrien's own personal knowledge taught to him by his parents, who were against going underground in the first place but were compelled to go along with the rest of that civilization.

Zadrien taught the people that they did not need manmade laws, but rather the laws of the Creator. I know of three principles which Zadrien taught. One was always to replenish the earth with whatever was taken from it. Another was to look at each individual as Soul rather than as a personality in a body. The third was not to condemn any man until you yourself have undergone his experience.

As they passed through their cycles within the Ages, civilizations rose and fell and sciences advanced and collapsed or were destroyed with the civilizations. As scientific knowledge grew, adherence to Spiritual Law became weaker and weaker and life became more and more negative. Wars and divisions between the people developed, whose terror the people of Earth have not yet seen in modern times. Exploitation of the lower classes became so complete that these people had no choice but to plan a revolution of planetary proportions.

Venus had one race of light-skinned people, and so the prejudices and conflicts never revolved around racial differences or nationalities either for that matter. In fact, nations did not then develop on Venus. Each major city

was the center of a region, and wars were most often fought between individual cities or allied cities. And a planetary government was not successfully formed, although several attempts were made to establish one over thousands of years. Too often, dissension among these city-states broke up any attempts at a unified system of government.

The wars which did plague the Venusians were sparked by the people's differing attitudes, and of course greed, much like on Earth. Since there were no nations, any war was more localized than on Earth. The power groups of a city were never quite satisfied with ruling their own city and region, so they always managed to create a justifiable conflict with the well-to-do neighboring city-state as a pretext for going to war.

Venus was quick to develop most advanced forms of power and technology. Magnetic and solar rower had been discovered not too long after the people moved to the surface. Zadrien himself played a strong role in motivating his people to seek contact with neighboring planets, and it wasn't long thereafter that Venus was traveling space. Nuclear power and nuclear bombs were a part of the planet's growth. In desperation, cities had used these weapons against each other, destroying vast regions of their beautiful lands.

Venus came to be ruled by a small group of wealthy people. Exactly the same situation exists on Earth today. Life was a game for this small, elite group, and the winner was he who could control the most money and the most people for the longest time. The pawns were of course the vast majority of the people within the lower classes.

A look at a Venusian city of the past will give a better picture of those sad times. On the whole the cities were beautifully developed, but the streets, buildings, parks, everything was to be found on a number of different levels. The poor, uneducated working class lived at the lowest levels, which compared to the worst slums of Earth cities because they were so dark and dreary. Sunlight very seldom was able to filter down to the lowest levels. As time went by, life deteriorated in all ways for the unfortunate masses. Petty revolutions had been attempted for ages, but none succeeded, for the people unwittingly continued to play the game set up for them by the ruling classes.

A silent revolt of the working class in every city of the planet simultaneously was finally realized as the only way. The people were tired of their lot and vowed that not even they had any right to rule others, should they succeed with their secret plan. But their plans would involve many years of hard work and sacrifices for the greater cause. A planetary movement just did not develop overnight.

The working class began earnestly to infiltrate the governments with those who were loyal to their cause and who could be trusted. Their hopes were to elect their own hand-picked political leaders into the highest offices, individuals who would turn from power and lead the people freely. It took a great deal of time to groom the right candidates and support them in many different campaigns on the way up into the highest offices.

At last came the day when enough key men had been elected, the day that all had been anxiously waiting for which in history is simply called The Beginning. On this most unforgettable day of all, Venus' most respected and honored leaders abolished the government and military forces, while people in the cities threw all their money into the streets and garbage cans or burned it with joy. On that first glorious day, people everywhere marched from the cities in droves, taking along only their clothes, food, and seeds for planting. They left forever the decrepit cities, their possessions, homes, cars, and everything that stood for the old way of life. Their intentions were simple — to move into the country where each individual would work for himself to support his family. It was just remarkable to see these people's determination, and their courage and faith in leaving the security of home for an uncertain new life. Many people were of course reluctant to leave because they had become attached to their everyday conveniences. At the same time they realized that they would rather not be left behind in the deserted cities.

The wealthy and powerful were in bad shape. Instead of retaining some kind of social structure and seeking a redistribution of the wealth and power, the underclass had turned their backs completely on the old way of life with no intention of return. They created their own new game the powerful could not play, and would not want to play. Overnight, the upper classes of Venus had lost everything.

In all of Venusian history, no one day has changed the face of the planet so completely and so dramatically. The Beginning launched Venus on the road to becoming an astral civilization as well as an important capital to your physical universe. Up to that time, wars, revolutions, and coups had only shifted the power around. One group of power-seekers replaced another, leaving the overall way of life unchanged, and the political and economic systems as before. But now all was different.

The consciousness of the people had itself changed, had been raised over a long period of time. By turning their backs to material comforts and the secure established way, the people of Venus demonstrated a transformation in their basic attitude and understanding. Greed and attachment to form diminished.

The upper classes were left alone. Without obedient masses and with depleted organs of government, they were out of business. Without factories and services the powerful were as poor as anyone else. Without employees and broad-based markets businesses failed. Everything changed drastically as the bulk of the people moved to the simpler self-supporting life taking their accumulated technological knowledge and production crafts with then. The cities were almost completely abandoned. Although some dissidents attempted to establish their own colonies, they were far too few and even these were abandoned. The remaining upper class, including the defeated leaders, had no trouble deciding what had to be done. These people made a choice to leave the planet.

The plan was to colonize a more suitable planet, and of course they enjoyed the knowledge that Earth was such a lush green place, and not too far away. As such, Earth became the most likely candidate for welcoming the departing Venusians. Under the circumstances, much of the talk about it being an unbalanced planet was ignored. Spacecraft soon began delivering the first of the Venusian aristocrats, people who could no longer live in the transformed Venusian society.

Events of similar nature sooner or later provided the impetus for humans on other planets also migrating to Earth, some from within this solar system and some from beyond.

For the Venusian people whose vision of a better life took them into the countryside, hardships lay ahead. In many ways they were like the pioneers who settled America, facing great hardship but gaining the way of life they sought. What these people were going through was little different from a normal cycle of growth common to other planets as well. During the more primitive beginning, people lived simply on the land, growing the food required and seeing to their own needs. Then a form of industrialization specialization took place, making life more complex and more negative again. Finally, as the new technology became more advanced, the people moved back to the land without becoming primitive in the process. The more natural technology and the natural way of life resulted in a more advanced, individualized, technical creativity than the complex, artificial technology such as Earth has now.

During the Beginning, the people of Venus were escaping a life of little or no freedom. Devoting all their hours to an employer was nothing but a form of slavery, they realized, and neither was it meaningful or fulfilling. The economy was so specialized that few people could achieve a sense of satisfaction in their jobs. And there wasn't much of a choice in the kind of job a person could get. It depended on the standards society had set up for the kind of formal education he needed. Most of the poorer classes either could not achieve the standard, or they were never afforded an opportunity to work in their fields of talent. So many manmade laws had been created that spiritual law became as well known as on Earth today. Life seemed to be an ocean of do's and don'ts, and the people were like driftwood tossed by the waves.

In the new life, each family strived first for itself, settling a parcel of land just large enough to provide its own food needs. At first some goods were exchanged back and forth, as some people inevitably knew how to do some things better than others. Yet they had every intention to keep specialization to a minimum and to strive for self-sufficiency. Classes were set up to teach everyone the basic skills, so that after a while each family was able to satisfy most of its own needs. Within a decade, self-sufficient villages were spread across the face of the planet.

Managing to grow enough food was probably the greatest hardship. Every family was deeply involved in this project of learning to cultivate the land productively with no artificial fertilizers or chemical sprays. Crops did not always turn out well in those first years, and even Venusian technology could not alleviate hunger pains.

To handle larger projects in a village, the men joined together to build community workshops. Here were tools and facilities for building small flying craft and other devices where they needed to pool their knowledge and effort. Production lines and specialization were never again allowed to develop. Even the spacecraft were built individually by one or a few people. Eventually computerized machines built the spacecraft automatically. Physical labor in the new way of life was not looked down upon because being personally involved in creative work gave each person a sense of fulfillment. Each family had built its own home, as well as a workshop where whatever was needed was made. On every level of life the individual was most important, much more important than the modern conveniences the people had given up to escape the slavery to it. Never was a single way of doing things decided upon, because it always seemed to lead to conflict, and it didn't promote personal individuality.

The new life on Venus was so different from what it had been before, that it would easily take an entire book to explain it well. The most important idea to remember is that this new way of life only reflected the higher consciousness of the people. It cannot be forced or imposed on the people who are not ready for it.

No one owned land or paid taxes in the new Venusian community. If a family wanted to move, they would leave the home and land behind for another family. A central government was never again established because it would only provide a fertile environment for power-hungry men and manmade laws. Neither were laws passed, or police departments needed or money printed. To this day no form of currency exists on Venus.

I do not know whether such a way of life ever existed on Earth. Perhaps experimental communes at one time or other tried. I know that much of the success of the new life on Venus came from their understanding and living the universal Laws of the Supreme Deity. There was less greed, anger, vanity, and attachment to material things than ever before. Each individual's understanding that he was Soul, and therefore immortal, living many lifetimes, helped to make life run smoothly. Knowing that their stay in the physical world was temporary, fighting over possessions or more land seemed simply absurd. Instead, if one family found that they were blessed with more material things than another, they would gladly share. Personal attitudes about these things had been changing long before the Beginning, but the traditional structures and systems of society had been holding them back.

Life in the Venusian villages after the Beginning was never primitive, only simple and natural. The most advanced technologies already existed and only needed to be refined and adapted, such as the use of solar and magnetic power for all energy needs. Disc-shaped flying craft, with all their magnificent capabilities, were used in the exploration of space. Conversation machines existed that gathered data from remote areas, and even translated foreign languages into our planetary language. Mining was accomplished by using devices that magnetically drew the element to the surface. This is only a sample of the technology that was available to all. Our technical growth did not come to a standstill, but rather became more servant than master.

The greatest single challenge became the exploration of space, to learn ever more about this great universe; but space travel, in our case, was not limited to a few scientists and astronauts. The neutralizing of gravity by Venusian spaceships made space travel possible for the common man. Communications developed between the planets, and friendships or brotherhoods developed to help all to conquer the mysteries of the Universe. Space travel tremendously expanded our people's horizons on the physical plane, and was responsible for much of our growth in the centuries before the planet's life became astral.

Observing the Laws of the Supreme Deity, individual spiritual unfoldment became greater than it ever had been before. More and more, individuals learned to visit planes above the physical at will, which makes a great difference in anyone s life. They became more aware of their identity as Soul, and of the minor place the physical plane holds in the Soul's life. This high state of consciousness of the Venusian people led to a very positive way of life as the planet entered its most recent Iron Age. Instead of becoming very negative, the life-wave on Venus became so positive as to lift it up to another level. When this happened, Venus became a very special planet. Our capital city, Retz, is still the capital of our new universe.

The people of Venus did not suddenly wake up one day on the astral plane. The transition was very gradual and subtle, taking place over a number of years. I must remind you that all of what I have said about Venus' past took place over millions of years, making this a very condensed history.

As the people grew in spiritually, they lived less and less for the physical world and its physical pleasures. Communication became more and more mental, and their consciousness reached closer and closer to the astral level. Spiritually and technically, the people of Venus arrived at an understanding where they felt the control of life and death in their own hands. As their consciousness became more suited to astral levels, no longer did they feel the same attachment to their physical body and that density. Eventually most of the Tythanians had decided to translate, dropping the physical body and continuing their life on the astral plane of density.

In this process of moving their civilization up one dimension, the people of Venus remained the people of Venus. The race did not end, and people had the same form and appearance after the Great Transition as before. Remember that the astral body is an exact duplicate of the physical in form, but less dense and of a more durable nature. The culture remained the same as before. People carried over their habits, customs, way of thinking, dress styles, architecture, and language. Cities and landscapes were the same as what was left behind at the physical level but brighter and wore beautifully maintained. My own city of Teutonia existed in counterpart or astral reality, as did all the others. Our friendship and interaction with the other physical planets continued, and our interest in Earth also continued with little change. We learned to control our density.

Though it seemed as if the people of Venus had disappeared by leaving the physical plane, they merely continued their Venusian lives on the astral plane by choice. Even they have karmic debts in the physical world and must some day leave the astral to be reborn to the Physical to balance the accounts.

The move to finer density is only temporary for the civilization, as a way of positively living through the last years of the dense negative Iron Age. Today Venus is reentering a new Golden Age, and the physical planet will be colonized by people leaving the astral plane.

Many of those who gave up their bodies and made the move to the astral plate during the Great Transition are alive there today, on account of their long life-spans. These people can no longer return to the physical plane unless they die on the astral and are reborn into physical. Their children and grandchildren who are born on the astral plane however, need not die there in order to come into the physical world. They only need to manifest their physical body. Once in the physical world, there is no returning to the astral to live until the physical body dies, because once manifested, they are responsible for maintaining it.

In this lifetime for me, I was born and raised on the astral Venus, at a time when most of the people and life were astral. As a young child I lowered my vibrations to manifest my physical body, which is of course a duplicate of my astral body. With my uncle and a companion I left the physical planet Venus in order to live on your Earth. The story of my early years on Venus describes our astral culture, and it was during those years that I also learned about the cultures on the physical planets.

If I had been born on physical Venus and left at the same early age, I may not have written this book. How many people can remember their earliest childhood well enough to write about it in detail? The story of my life is unusual because of my vivid recall of those earliest years. Being born and living on the astral plane gave me an almost photographic memory. The astral plane, remember, corresponds to a higher level of consciousness than what usually is possible on the physical plane, and the people who live there have greater powers in every area of life. So it was no great feat for me to be able to remember clearly what has happened. In fact I can well remember my days in the womb!

Chapter Four
In The Womb

1. In the womb
2. Karma with my new parents
3. Birth
4. My mother dies
5. First surroundings
6. My aunt and uncle take me home
7. My new home and the first day
8. Playing
9. The garden
10. Temples of learning
11. Temple of arts
12. Childhood games
13. Uncle Odin
14. Spiritual life
15. A surprise birthday party

In the womb there was at first an abundance of room. I was nothing but a seedling, and darkness and warmth filled my world. As Soul, I myself was the only source of light, and although I could not actually see or hear, I was aware of the new world I had entered. I remember well my first days and weeks on Venus in the womb of Shawik-Echo Lei, my mother.

It is a wonderful and peaceful feeling, this security of being a part of another being and yet completely separate. I was aware how very much

I depended upon my loving mother to supply the energy I would need to build my strength to be born.

To be so knowledgeable and yet so helpless is a strange experience. As Soul, each of us has limitless knowledge and power. But when we are born into a new life and even before we are born, once we have chosen a family and a body in which to live, we become helpless. Because the new body has new limbs, new senses, and a new brain to be trained, we must spend a great deal of our attention and energy in growing accustomed to them. While learning to control the vocal cords to communicate in the language of our new environment and while learning to use the new senses and brain, our knowledge as Soul is usually buried in the subconscious mind.

In rare cases of genius the subconscious and conscious minds are not separated, so that young children sometimes have knowledge from many lifetimes. Each individual has access to this knowledge later in life, but initially it is submerged. On the astral plane I was one step closer to Soul awareness, so my memory of those early moments has remained with me.

As my new body developed I had much time to contemplate all the things I knew. As Soul, I remembered the beginning, when I was first sent down into the denser worlds, and the countless lives as minerals, plants, and animals. Then there were the almost numberless lives as a human being, of both sexes and in every situation imaginable, on many different planets. Between those millions of physical lifetimes were many others beyond the physical plane.

I could go on without end about what I remember as Soul, but mostly I contemplated about my new family. I had chosen both my mother and my father because I had been with them before, and I was destined to be with them again to fulfill my spiritual and emotional needs.

We three had lived together before on Venus, but now I would become their first and only child, Omnec Onec. In that past lifetime my new mother and I were sisters, and Venus was a younger planet striving to end wars. Disease and plagues haunted the people in those turbulent years; and she was one of those stricken with a terrible illness that could not be cured.

In willing her to live and healing her psychically with my own energy, I took the Karma of her illness upon myself and died instead of her. My father in this new life (on Venus), who was my lover and a doctor then, resented my sister because she lived and I died. In grief over my passing he starved himself to death. My sister (and now mother in this new life) loved him even then. In the end she lost both of the people so dear to her.

In this lifetime on Venus he and she loved one another as man and wife, giving him a chance to make up for his resentment of long ago. She was also able to share part of her life with him this time, as she so longed to do in that past life.

Now I am to be born to her. To make up for my giving up my life then, she will give life to me now and translate (die) when I am born. It is her choice and fate to balance this debt generated in the past. In this life he will lose the one he resented living then and have the one he so loved and lost then. Being an emotional person he will long for my loving mother and turn away from me to his work. All of these things I knew as Soul.

I thought about my new mother often as I grew inside her womb. I felt the warm love she had for me, and as I began to move about I was aware of their interest and delight. My father's warm love also radiated toward me. I heard their muffled voices and I could sense their hands feeling around as I kicked and turned.

I lost myself in the indescribable joy of being one with the universe. The rhythm of the universe flowed through me, that life-stream of light and sound flowing from the Supreme Deity to support all life and form. Being in the womb is a special time of life, for Soul is able to travel freely into the planes beyond.

Time passed and I grew. Every day I could feel myself becoming more human in appearance. The space around me was so close that I found it harder to move about. Just stretching was almost impossible. Sounds from the outside were muffled, but my mother's heartbeat and breathing were very close to me.

As my time to emerge grew near, there were mixed feelings of joy and sorrow. A feeling of gladness washed over me, and fear too of a new experience about to begin but the choice had been made and the time had come.

Suddenly came the confusion of emerging into lights and sounds, the shock of being new, separate, and having an identity. Strange, smiling faces greeted me, yet I recognized and loved this new family immediately. I had arrived, crying because I couldn't communicate all I felt and knew, and because I was so small and helpless. I was held and nursed by my mother, feeling warm, wanted and loved.

As I rested there in her arms well understood that she would not be with me for long. Her silence and her loving gaze said many things. "I love you dearly, but I am going to leave you. I will not be with you to share the joys and sorrows of life. The choice is being made so that you may live and I may balance my Karma."

Feeling warm, wanted and loved, I fell into a peaceful resting sleep. When I again opened my eyes I was alone in a bed. Dimly I was aware of my father pacing around the room at a distance. He did not come near me. Mother was nowhere to be seen. Her last words just before I fell asleep flashed through my mind. "Take good care of my baby," she said to my father. I didn't realize fully until later that my mother had already translated, but as Soul I was fully aware of all this.

My memories as a tiny baby are mostly blurred, then there are bits and pieces that are very clear. Only by putting together the bits and pieces am I able to have a picture in my mind of these earliest days.

Near my bed stood a stranger, a neighbor who was to nurse me and take care of me. She was the only one who greeted me into my new home in Teutonia on Venus.

All around me in the room I felt the heavy air of disharmony. Reaching high above me in the shape of a dome was the ceiling. In the very center was a sculptured flower, like a lotus blossom, and all sorts of delicate but intricate designs reached down from the petals surrounding the dome and extending down the walls of my round bedroom. My bed, shaped like a bowl, hung from the ceiling on a golden rope encircled by flowers. Nearby was an open window with a view to the garden and its sweet fragrance. A gentle breeze swayed and slowly turned the bed.

I enjoyed all the new sights. Birds sang in a golden cage near my bed. One of my mother's last requests was to have live birds in my room.

Above me, automatic toys flew around or sat motionless in the air making delightful musical sounds.

Every day the nurse came to take care of me. The feeling I sensed was one of duty instead of love. I guess she was detached because I did not belong to her. As a baby I was aware of this coolness, and I am sure that babies in the physical world have this same awareness of the mother's true feelings.

Often I could hear my father's voice in the distance, but never did I catch a glimpse of his face. I had seen him only once, shortly after I was born, but after that first day of grief and loss he never came near me again. I had the sure feeling that I was the main cause of the disharmony that I sensed. At times, when I was taken out into the garden, I could hear the machinery from my father's laboratory, but I would never see him.

On a sunny morning the nurse took me outside and laid me on a soft blanket in the garden so that I could enjoy the butterflies and the birds, and the beautiful flowers there. But I was much more interested in a very familiar sound——my father's voice.

He and two other voices were discussing what was going to happen to me. As a newborn baby I didn't realize that these were my aunt and uncle, but I did recognize my own name being mentioned ever so often. It wasn't until later in my life that I learned what was happening.

My mother's sister Arena and her husband Odin were visiting Father, and discussing what was to be done with me. Being grieved over my mother's death, he held me responsible for everything. He explained to Arena and Odin that he did not want to become emotionally attached to me or to have any kind of emotional feelings for me. It was difficult enough that he had lost my mother, but if he became attached to me it would be the same story all over again.

My father could not bear the emotion of watching his child grow up looking too much like his lost love. And since he had been so emotionally attached to her, he was not agreeable with my mother's choice, selfless as it was. Of course that was being selfish on his part and he admitted that. I was only a child, not a companion. That is the way he looked at it.

He explained to my aunt and uncle that he had no time to devote himself to raising a child, for a child needed much love and care. He was a scientist and had his work to do, and to care for me would be too much.

Since I did not have a mother, he felt it would be best if they took me home and raised me as their own child. My aunt and uncle were of course overjoyed to have me since they themselves did not have children.

I was sound asleep when Arena came into the garden to bring me inside. Dimly I remember being carried in her arms and gently being laid down among the covers of my bed as she prepared to gather my things.

Opening my eyes I saw a smiling face above my bed as Arena stood over me with her reddish-golden hair falling to her shoulders in soft curls. I felt as if I was her own child, seeing her friendly loving face and gazing into her green, smiling eyes. My aunt was a very beautiful woman, much like my mother in appearance.

With his widow's peak of silvery-blond hair falling to his shoulders and his sparkly, almost turquoise eyes, my uncle Odin was a most pleasant looking man. He was tall and stately with a wonderful cheery look about him, more masculine, but much resembling Arena.

Arena picked me up ever so lovingly and held me close. It was the first feeling of warmth and love I had felt since that first day my mother had nursed me. I missed her now and I knew she was gone, but I did not understand all the changes that were taking place.

All of my playthings, clothes, and even my bed were being packed up. I realized that I was leaving the house, and I was leaving my father whom I loved so very much. I remember being carried out the front door and seeing for the last time my familiar surroundings. As we approached my aunt and uncle's bubble car, I heard my father saying goodbye from the distance. My nurse kissed me goodbye on the cheek and that was all.

The three of us entered the spaceship and took off. Ships are actually not needed for traveling on the astral plane. There we travel by thought, by putting our attention on the destination and appearing there. When a number of people travel, individuals sometimes get separated and appear in the wrong place or at a different point in time. Therefore, people in groups prefer to travel in the same ship and arrive at the same place and time together. Enjoying the scenery is also a more aesthetic experience together than just appearing somewhere else.

Our bubble car was an amazingly simple craft, looking like a clear glass bubble with seats inside. Because my uncle could propel and direct the ship by thought-power alone, there were no engines or controls; only a simple, gleaming bubble.

As our ship rose above the multicolored trees, I caught the last glimpse of my father's estate. In the center of our house was an elegant white dome, slightly pointed, under which I had slept and played during those weeks of my life. Together with the wings on each side, it reminds me now of the capitol building in America, although the dome seemed to be more Turkish in design. The spacious grounds had a gorgeous abundance of colorful trees and flowers expertly arranged. Off to the left was the laboratory where my father worked. It looked like an iridescent glass bubble sitting among the bushes and trees of the garden.

I fell in love with my aunt and uncle's house the moment I saw it, looking so much like a moon rising above the horizon or like a circle rising from the ground. It couldn't have been much simpler in design. The shallow, milky, blue-white dome surrounded by elaborate gardens of exotic trees, colorful flowers, statues and fountains of flowing water.

At the end of a stone footpath was the main entrance, a graceful-looking arch joined by two smaller arches on each side. These smaller doorways led directly to the bedrooms. Just inside the main door, curving off to the left and right, stood shoulder-high white wrought iron fences decorated with green leafy vines and purple and white flowers. These separated the sleeping area from the living room. The fences were themselves intricately designed with leaves and flowers.

Ahead in the very center of the room was a round fireplace sunken into the purple, blue and white fine marble floor. The curved couches which surrounded it, I would learn, were a different color from day to day depending on my aunt's moods and likes. In other parts of the room floated brightly-colored sofas made of furs and pleasant soft materials.

The musical waterfall and pool of our indoor garden was toward the back of the room. Here exotic trees shaded the fish, and cute little birds hopped among the branches singing merrily. Our house looked as if nature had been brought indoors. The plants, flowers, and birds my aunt Arena had befriended were everywhere to be seen.

Only the living room and the bedrooms to each side were on the main floor. Looking up we could see their round, floating marble floor of the dining roan above. To the left of our indoor garden, a marbled jade staircase led to the railed balcony that encircled the inside of our house, and between it and the second floor was a space the length of a man all around. Oriental footbridges made of a deep, earthy red wood arched over at selected intervals.

All around the edge of this floor rose a waist-high wall of the same deep red glistening wood. Plants, figurines, and pottery tastefully decorated the broad top of the wall. With the five table and chair settings of carved and inlaid woods, the furnishings were complete. My aunt was one who loved simplicity and elegance.

Our ceiling, round and domed and reaching down to become the curved walls below, was a spectacular sight. Looking out from the inside, the walls and ceiling of the house were clear as glass, offering a permanent view of our gardens, the colorful clouds, and the nearby mountains. Directly above our arrangement of tables and the chairs, in the very center of our domed ceiling, was a rectangular mosaic of stained glass. Looking down, the second floor itself was also clear as glass, but from the living room below only a ceiling of purple and blue and white marble was visible.

Every piece of furniture in our house was a work of art, exquisite and unique, not to mention the works of art themselves. The whole place was a feast for the senses with so much beauty and harmony that words will not do it justice.

My aunt and uncle's conversations about me that first day were sympathetic. They could not understand my father's feelings, but they recognized he was a separate individual and they had no way of really knowing how he felt, unless they too went through the same experiences. They accepted his decision, and they accepted me with a gladness in their hearts that they would have a child to raise.

The fact that I belonged to Arena's sister made a very great difference, and although my aunt and uncle were very happy to have me, they also felt sorrowful because I had lost both my father and mother. At the same time they well realized that it was all a matter of Karma, and that they would do their very best in taking care of me and offering me a good life.

My new bedroom was close to the waterfall, and hanging from the smoky-colored ceiling on a golden hook and chain was my bowl-shaped bed. It was like pink woven wicker, and a chain of blue and yellow flowers with green leaves zigzagged from top to bottom all around. Aunt

Arena had made a new coverlet for me which felt like downy feathers and was soft as a cloud. Embroidered all over were little animals and flowers that changed color. Before putting me down she fed me a delicious fruit juice, and I remember falling into a peaceful sleep listening to the heavenly melodies she played for me on her golden harp.

Nursing or feeding children here is really not necessary, although it does give them a feeling of security and pleasure. People who live on the astral plane absorb all the energy they need to stay alive directly from the ether, usually during rest. It works this way because the astral body is made of a much lighter frequency of energy than the physical. We do set tables and eat elaborate meals on special occasions. As a people we have carried over our likes from the physical plane, which includes enjoying the tastes and sensations of eating good food.

Most of a Venusian child's first five years, beneath all the fun and games, have to do with learning the basics of life. (What I mean by five years is the amount of time it takes for a child to look the same age as a five year old child on Earth.) It is a duty of the parents to teach these basics at home before the child begins to visit the Temples of Learning. Aunt Arena devoted a part of every day to help me with lessons about our culture and about the Laws of the Supreme Deity. At a very early age I learned our alphabet and language, the number system, and simple crafts as well.

At first I played learning games, as most children do. I enjoyed drawing, cutting out things from paper, and playing with letters. What my aunt would do was help me put together words out of the different letters, and count the numbers. In this way I learned very quickly.

My playthings included all the basic geometric shapes made of many different materials and colors, as well as many different shapes of building blocks that I could use to build miniature cities. The blocks were a variety of beautiful woods, metals and crystals. My uncle Odin thought of me often and brought home many interesting things like magnets or learning toys where I could turn knobs, push buttons, and turn cranks to make all kinds of noises and to have different things happen.

As I reached the ages of two and three I became more involved in creative pastimes and crafts. At first my aunt guided me along, such as drawing pictures for me to color. But soon I was painting my own and doing wood carvings with tools that couldn't hurt me. I also enjoyed playing with two puppets that represented the positive and negative forces in our world.

Before long I began playing the harp as well as a piano-like instrument, and ever since then music has been a vital part of my life. Because I loved to dance more than anything else, I always looked forward to when my aunt played music during her own lessons, because then I could practice all the new movements I had in mind. It was easy to see that dancing was my favorite pastime. During the day I would dance for hours in front of our musical paintings, or to the music that I myself would create.

Our music system looked like a loudspeaker built into the ceiling of the living room, but it was far from being a simple device. By thinking of a certain symphony or piece or music it would begin to play, bathing the whole house in sound. It was completely thought-controlled and operated by mind.

Surrounding our house in a giant circle was one of my favorite worlds — the garden. Here in one place my aunt and uncle had collected trees, bushes, and flowers from many parts of Venus and our neighboring planets. They were in all sorts of shapes, sizes, and colors. The variety of living things was absolutely wonderful.

I especially enjoyed a certain tree that looked like an oriental fan, with its four trunks spreading up and out from one root. The trunks were alternately bright green and bright blue, and the leaves were bright yellow color in their natural state. Together with the flowering vines hanging down from the branches the whole plant looked like a big fan. I played under it almost every day. I loved it very much and sometimes I climbed in it pretending I was a bird.

Strange-looking trees were a common sight in our garden. Some of them looked like huge flowers and others had trunk, branches, and leaves all of the same color such as bright yellow, blue, or red. Some of the flowers looked as odd as the trees, resembling feathers and giving off delicious scents as they swayed in the breeze. Sunflowers, roses, tulips, and many other flower types familiar to Earth's people also had a place in our garden.

I spent much of my time going out to the birds and the animals, feeding and taking good care of them. I always found new birds and insects as pets. They grew to love me and I grew to love them.

Fruits and vegetables grew freely among the shrubs, flowers, and trees. This is a carryover from the physical era when every family grew its own food. My favorite fruit, which I remember eating all the time, was the delicious yunya. It tasted like a cross between a pear and a cherry, only much juicier than either.

I loved to sit near and watch the gurgling and splashing waters of the fountain in our backyard, which during day and night was brightly illuminated from within. It looked much like four glowing mushrooms on top of each other, each with scalloped edges, and the upper smaller than the one below. Clear water shot up out of a sculptured lotus blossom at the very top, turning yellow at the next lower level and purple below. At the lowest level the water was bright orange. Enchanting!

In a grassy clearing was the special swing that my uncle had created for me. It didn't hang from anything. Whenever the wind blew, this floating swing gently swayed back and forth. In a way it seemed like a hammock, with its pretty white lacy design. My friends and I enjoyed many hours of playing in that special gift from my uncle Odin.

My first friend was a girl named Zemura, who was about the same level of consciousness as I. Every day Zemura's parents brought her over to play with me. More important than age on Venus is this level of consciousness which can be sensed but not seen. Playmates or friends spend time together and enjoy each other's company when they share the same inner qualities.

The games we played together were like those most children play, but much more elaborate. In the garden we could manifest entire cities in miniature, complete with tiny people and cars. With our thoughts we would have them move around, have the people talk to each other, and even dress themselves. The buildings we erected were elaborately detailed so that the whole city was a duplicate of some real city on Venus or the other planets. Nothing was forgotten. There were gardens, rivers, boats and bridges, animals, and anything else that a real city might have.

Being on the astral plane, Zemura and I could easily make ourselves invisible or change our body form into flowers or trees or play hide and seek. And by making ourselves tiny we pretended to be elves and created stories of ourselves as miniature people. The new experiences ahead of us in life were almost unlimited. I remember creating a giant butterfly and climbing on its back to fly around the neighborhood, just to see what it was like.

As we grew older my girlfriends and I became more interested in copying our parents. We played house and we dressed up, and gave parties where everyone would dance and sing just as our parents did. Because each one of us was creative and talented in some way, we all took part in the entertaining.

Whenever we played we always tried to learn something new or develop our talents. In our acting games one of us would come up with an idea and another person would act it out, or dance, or recite a poem to express it. Using the books my uncle would bring home about the histories of different planets, we dressed up in the various costumes and hairstyles to act out those eras. The clothes we created were replicas of what really existed in the past.

Our power of mind over matter makes games like these quite possible. Matter is at such a high frequency on the astral plane that our thoughts can move it, change it, or manifest it directly from energy. Whenever we played house we actually manifested a real home, and in dressing up we created the clothes exactly as we visualized them in our minds.

Children used to be taught this ability to create just as surely as children on the physical planets must be taught to walk and read and write. I was very young, about two or three years old, when my aunt began teaching me the discipline of creating. I was to have an exact image in mind with all the correct dimensions, colors, and textures, and I was to limit myself in how many things I manifested.

I cannot say that we on the astral plane create things out of nothing. We use our thoughts to convert free energy into whatever we wish to have, and it only seems like magic because the things we manifest appear as if out of thin air. The same power of thought over matter exists in the physical world but does not seem magical because it is a much slower process of creation and requires raw materials and labor effort.

I was taught those many great responsibilities that go along with powers like this. Because all of my actions create good or bad karma unless properly done in the name of the Supreme Deity, I was careful that my creations did not interfere in anyone else's life.

Lying on my hanging bed and listening to the waterfall of our indoor garden was one of my favorite experiences. It made an entrancingly beautiful musical sound, as if water was being poured over a harp. I never grew tired of listening to the ever-changing melodies or of gazing into the ever-present rainbow appearing in the mist it produced.

Through the transparent wall of my room I could see the purple Kumli Mountains in the distance and our lush, colorful garden just outside. This was more than just a simple bedroom to me. It was a world of my own where I could be alone to entertain my thoughts and feelings. Most of the furnishings I had designed and manifested myself, at a time when I was about four years old. Covering the purple, blue and white marble floor of my room was a rug that looked and felt like grass spotted with little yellow and blue flowers. As a special gift my uncle Odin had hand-carved a small natural wooden table in the shape of a small tree. Intricately carved and handpainted green leaves edged the circular top, and the solid base was carved to look like a tree trunk.

Each of our bedrooms had its own bathtub, and of course I have been allowed to design my own. It was a round sunken tub lined with sea shells. In the very center on the bottom was a starfish. The spigots were in the shape of golden sculptured fish that spouted water. A star-shaped spigot in the ceiling was for showers.

Strangest of all was the live tree which grew in a corner of my room. When it was yet in the garden I loved it so much that I moved it inside, and it grew very well there. Just as our people do not need to eat, trees do not need to be rooted in soil, for they too absorb the energy they need directly. It looked almost like a twisted oak tree with dark green leaves and purple blossoms whose scent was heavenly. I enjoyed many hours on the small white swing that hung from the branches. Trees are a symbol of life to the Venusian people, for if a tree grows somewhere, then a human being can live there also.

Learning has always been an invaluable part of my own life. In Venusian society it is something that happens every moment of every day in the life of each person, no matter what his age may be. We have no school systems like those on Earth, which are more like the production and assembly lines of a factory than anything else, and which pour out finished products. Learning as we know it is an unending experience in an individual's growth as Soul. Venusian children find education to be a joy and a satisfaction instead of a burdensome chore. Because we are freed from the burden of making a living here on the astral plane, our lives center around creativity and imagination in the arts and sciences, and our educational system reflects our way of life.

Central Teutonia is a cultural center for the people living in our area, not a commercial center. Commerce has no place in the astral life. Most of the city is devoted to Temples of Learning, each structure being a work of art in its own right, dedicated to furthering one of the arts or sciences. At each Temple, children as well as adults are guided by masters of the field they have chosen to study. And there is always a progression from student to Master for those who are dedicated to a field. Advanced students are always invited to participate in guiding the newer students.

Every child is given the freedom as to when he will begin studying at the temples. No one but the child has the right to make that decision and enforce it, not even the parents. There is a complete freedom of choice about which subjects a child learns and when, and there is no such thing as a curriculum, graduation, or degrees granted. Learning at the Temples is a personal matter.

Of all the Temples of Learning, my favorite was the Temple of Arts. I was close to five years old when I began to study there, and I could almost always be found on the floor that was devoted to the art of dancing. Dancing has been a part of my life ever since one of my most valuable incarnations as a court dancer in ancient Egypt, in the palace of Moses. Of course there were many different Temples that I visited, but I enjoyed none as thoroughly as this huge, dome-shaped Temple of Arts with its marble columns and steps all around.

Every morning before going into the city I began my day by getting up from resting. Sleeping or resting on the astral plane is more or less a resting of the mind because there is no physical body that gets tired. We simply focus our attention on one thing, a word or a thought or object, until the conscious mind becomes blank. Upon awakening, my first job was always to decide what kind of a person I was going to be that day. Every day we try to be something different, for to have the same personality all the time would be a limited and boring way of living.

Some days I liked to be a very bubbly, happy person, and on other days I preferred to be quiet and reserved. Or else I chose to be a princess and pretend I was royal and everyone would accept me that way because this was not just a child's game. All of the people try to change their personality from day to day to make life more interesting and to not limit themselves in those experiences. I would choose a dress each day to go along with my new identity, and I always liked very feminine, light and soft dresses. Only my imagination limited me in the designs, materials and styles. I could wear the sun, a dress that looked like sunshine, or a dress that looked like starlight, or like the waters of a brook running over beautiful rocks. It was only a matter of manifesting what was in my mind.

I rarely bothered to eat before leaving for the Temple of Arts. Usually I simply appeared there in front of the marble steps, although on some mornings, whenever I was in the mood for a change, I would walk through our village and over the bridge at the ravine into the city, enjoying the sights and sounds along the way.

Inside the temple were many levels, each devoted to one of the many arts so that the vibrations would always be established on one floor for a particular subject. A huge, circular hall on each floor could seat several hundred people. This was the main learning area, while surrounding the hall were small study rooms where individuals work or think on their own.

On the first, level we could learn basic art or manifesting on paper our feelings, ideas, and images. I am not saying here that we sit down and just learn how to manifest a sketch by using our power of thought. At the

Temple of Arts we learn to be creative by using our hand and other faculties just as artists on the physical planets do. On the next floor was the main hail where we could learn painting in the different mediums. Also there were entire floors devoted to sculpting, collage, paper cutting and folding, woodcarving, and all manifest mediums of art. Higher up was the floor for dancing.

Every Temple was designed in a way that the different rooms and floors always were used for the same art or science, for the same reason of setting the vibrations.

After school each day I went home to play with my good friends as children do on Earth, but without the dispute and arguing. One of the pastimes we enjoyed most of all was to make long, long chains of colorful and fragrant flowers, and then run through our neighborhood draping the trees and houses. Our neighbors enjoyed them as much as we did. In a few days they would vanish and we could start all over again.

Parades were especially popular among the children, and of course we didn't wait for special occasions to have them. Every day seemed like a special occasion to us children anyway. All the children then dressed up in outlandish costumes and brought along their favorite musical instruments to have a grand time marching around the neighborhood making lots of harmonious noise. Afterwards we would collapse and roll over in the grass, in great delight.

Most of the children were very much in tune with what was happening in the physical world. We loved to play at make believe in historical periods which we could create at will in great detail.

At home I continued to develop myself in singing, dancing and playing the harp. Dancing is like any other art in that the more a person becomes involved in it, the more he realizes how much more there is to be learned. It is also a unique form of art because dancing can express spiritual experiences in a way that no other art can. And because

Venusian dancing does not follow rigid steps and rules, being more like interpretive dancing, there were an endless variety of combinations and movements I could master.

I have always considered the art of designing clothes to be one of the most challenging. The finished work can be enjoyed every moment of the day. I was very interested in creating clothes that would be a balance for a person rather than detract from him. Everyone cannot wear the same style and look good in it, which inspired me to experiment with different styles and designs to see how they suited different kinds of people.

Ingrained into our consciousness is an attitude of selflessness instead of selfishness, which naturally affects every area of our lives. In education it means that as a child masters an art or a skill, he will be allowed to guide other children who are beginners. I had guided many of my friends in learning to dance, while I in turn improved my talents in playing the harp with the help of a friend.

Once a week I joined my aunt in going to idea class. As a way of being creative and at the same tine helping people in the more limited environments of the physical plane, the women in our neighborhood would meet each week to share and evaluate creative solutions to problems. The projects were always a challenge, such as developing a new clothing fashion for an entire era on a physical planet. Everyone would take into consideration all the factors of that life - the climate, transportation, moral values, and many more. Then the various ideas and solutions would be shared at the next class, and the best, or combinations, are sent to the Astral Museum, where all new inventions for future use in the physical plane are stored. Inventors from Earth and even other physical planes visit the Museum either consciously or in the dream state while out of their body to obtain solutions to their problems.

My uncle Odin was one who had devoted his entire life to science. This was his love and contribution to mankind, to make life easier for all on the more difficult physical plane. There are many like him everywhere at astral levels, helping to make the physical world more conducive to spiritual unfoldment. The truth is that all inventions in your physical universe originate from the great Astral Museums. The initial inventing is first done by scientists like my uncle who live on the astral plane, bringing the idea down from above and perfecting it for this plane from which it may then be adapted for the physical. (Each change in density requires adaptation to the properties and laws of that density.) Creativity in the denser worlds is nothing but a receptivity of what already exists in finer planes of reality. The underlying spiritual law is "as above, so below."

When my uncle was home, hardly a day went by that I did not see him tinkering with some new gadget. Much of the time he was away, meeting with scientists on Venus and equivalent planes on other planets who could contribute ideas about his projects, or who were also working along similar lines.

It was always fun to have him home because he had a habit of using us as guinea pigs for his latest inventions. That is, he always tested them at home before he sent them to the Astral Museum. Among his projects were advanced ways of using solar energy, using a harmless penetrating ray to cook food, controlling the indoor climate without electricity, and many more geared to making the homemaker's life easier.

My uncle's greatest and most significant undertaking was a project that Earth's science fiction writers have given a great deal of attention, and that the advanced civilizations of our solar system have not yet perfected. Both he and my father have dedicated their greatest effort to this. It is a physical teleportation system which can safely transmit a live person from one location to another in the physical world, by temporarily raising his vibrations to an astral level and then lowering them again without using a receiving apparatus.

Nobody on the astral plane needs an invention such as this because of our natural ability to travel with the power of thought. However, on the physical plane it may revolutionize transportation, going so far as to make our convoys and mother-ships obsolete.

Odin and my father developed the system as far as it could be taken on the astral plane, until a point came where they needed to continue the work under physical laws in the physical world. This is why my uncle chose to lower his vibrations and live on the physical planet Venus at the same time that I left for Earth. At last notice he is still working to perfect the system. It is a much more difficult project than he at first imagined, partly because being creative is easier on the astral plane than on the physical.

I always looked forward to when my uncle would bring home his latest invention, and of course the neighborhood kids would be over in no time whenever they heard there was a new invention in the house.

Odin had an air of quietness about him. He was reserved but carried himself well, being so magnetic and stately that if you saw him on Earth you would think him a king. His presence alone attracts other people's attention wherever he may be.

His eyes always had a twinkling sort of look, as if he was about to burst into laughter at any moment. His personal sense of humor was great. He was forever pulling amusing jokes or doing something funny, but being very quiet about it. No one would know it was him. Quietly he would stand off in a corner watching all the confusion he had caused and everybody getting excited, acting as if he knew nothing about it.

My uncle was a big hearted person who was always more concerned with other people than with himself. And he was probably one of the most detached people I ever had known. He never lost his patience when something was broken. Either he would forget it or do it again, because he realized that he had all the time in the world.

My aunt was just the opposite, very emotional and attached to different things. Thanks to her sense of organization, everything had to be right, otherwise she would be upset. My uncle was of the opinion that if something was not right we could do something else, but if it was her project, then they would make it work somehow. This was a rule in our house to maintain harmony.

In the evenings all of us sat down together, usually around the fireplace, to practice the spiritual exercise of the Laws of the Supreme Deity. Study time as we often called it, was a time of devotion to spiritual studies, and our day was never complete without it. The spiritual exercises are really the whole foundation to the whole works, because they allow Soul to experience the higher planes while the lower bodies are left behind.

The spiritual travelers or true spiritual Masters are those who are adept at Soul travel and guide beginners out of the body. They can be found on every planet and plane, and are especially active on Earth at this time, where they are badly needed. A true Master is one who can lead Soul beyond the lower worlds, and who himself lives on the plane where he is active. If he assists a person in leaving the physical body, then he should be a Master who lives on the physical plane.

As a child, my experiences were often with playmates on the planes above the astral; but those experiences in the worlds beyond time and space are almost impossible to explain in words. They must be experienced by each individual in his own way.

After our spiritual exercises, which often involved keeping our attention on the master until he appeared in the inner vision, we shared with each other what we had learned and any thoughts that came to mind. Being the child, I asked most of the questions and in that way learned a great deal about our spiritual teachings.

Reincarnation and Karma, Creator realization, the Kal force, love, detachment, balance, and noninterference were some of the topics we talked about, although each one of them could be a lifetime of study. To share viewpoints can be very uplifting because every individual is unique and can offer a new way of looking at something.

One of the special days of my life began not with joy but in sorrow. I had been playing with another of my uncle's intriguing gadgets, a little black box that could levitate things, which was destined to be sent to the Astral Museum for eventual use in the physical world. Somehow it broke. My punishment, Uncle Odin told me, was to sit alone in the swing all day without playing until I was called back into the house. My feelings were terribly hurt. It was one of the few times I was disciplined. But out of respect and love for him, I was sorry for what I had done and realized my punishment was due.

Sitting in the swing and not playing meant that I must not think about anything, because then I would be creating. It was dreadful! For hours I sat there almost motionless, concentrating on what I had done and on being immobile and miserable, Oh, I was relieved when they finally called me into the house, but for some strange reason my uncle asked me to close my eyes. He led me by the hand into the center of our living room where I opened my eyes again. Surprise! All my friends were in there, laughing and wishing me a happy birthday. What a wonderful sight to behold — what a delightful surprise! I had completely forgotten my birthday, and I was so overjoyed and excited to see all these colorful, beaming friends that I was speechless.

Glancing around, I saw that the whole house had been transformed inside to look like a medieval castle. Setting a sparkling crown on my head and pointing to the throne, my uncle declared that I was the queen of the land, and all present were my subjects. I was to preside over the royal festivity from my jeweled throne.

In all my life on Venus, I never once experienced a plain simple party. When it comes to celebrating, our people go all out to imagine and create an extravaganza, and this birthday party was no exception. As the queen, I had no trouble deciding that my uncle would be the court jester. My aunt was to be the maid-in-waiting, mostly because she was the one who usually asked me to do things and perform errands.

The first gala event was our royal banquet, featuring a steaming roast stuffed pig resting on a table that stretched from one end of the room to the other. We never did eat it, but I always imagined a roast pig with an apple in its mouth as part of a royal banquet. Together with all the spectacular-looking foods and the golden goblets for wine, the whole setting seemed as if it were taken from a fairy tale, which indeed it was.

The special music I requested arrived from town and the entertainment began. Our dance and song games and all that the queen desired carried the gaiety well into the evening. I chose six of my friends to put on an acrobatic show before the throne, and another group of eight to do a cultural dance. All the performances were splendid.

Afterward we hunted in the garden for my present. Hidden around the stem of a tiny yellow flower, down among the leaves, was a ring my mother had worn until the day of my birth. Kneeling in the grass with the precious gift in my hands, I felt a wave of sadness rolling in like the tide and out again as I realized that the past was forever gone. It was an unusual but charming ring; strips of enamel and chips of titanium bordered an oblong dark reddish-brown carnelian on a band of silver. Because my fingers were much too small, I wore it close to my heart on a silver chain that Uncle Odin placed around my neck. He explained that my mother also had received it when she was a child, and it had been a gift from her mother. From that day until the time came for me to leave

Teutonia and Venus, I wore it always.

As I was lying in bed that night, my mind was brimming with all the wonderful memories of this unusual day. I sent thoughts of love to my aunt and uncle for bringing such joy into my life, and then I realized that my punishment was nothing but a way to keep me outside while the preparations were being made. Then it dawned on me that I had learned a great lesson — you can only appreciate joy if you have experienced sorrow.

That was my last birthday on Venus.

Chapter Five
The Venus Plane

1. Planes compared
2. The astral body, astral travel
3. Not the ultimate
4. Physical death, astral life
5. Landscapes and sub-planes
6. Lower astral
7. Psychic powers of man
8. Lower planes are limited

The astral plane is an immense universe, even greater and more vast than the physical plane with all its solar systems and galaxies. Venus is a mere speck in that one of many other realities, and is a speck in our limited reality also at its dense physical level. But the astral plane is only one of many planes of lesser density in being.

Many individuals who have experienced these worlds in out-of-body travels have called them heavens. Conditions are so much more beautiful and peaceful there that their vocabulary failed them. What they were able to write down in the past is today called religious, mystical or spiritual literature.

The astral plane existed long before the physical, and will endure beyond. The most common things known and recognized here in the physical world first existed there. Naturally there is much on the astral plane which does not exist here, but all that exists here does have its counterpart there, and more.

The differences between the astral and the physical planes take some explaining. Just as x-rays are at a higher frequency than solid rock, the entire astral plane is at a much higher frequency than the physical and this is one reason why scientists on Earth have not yet proven its existence. None of their scientific instruments can detect such very high vibrations.

Because matter on the astral level is so high in frequency, those of us who live there can have complete control over it by thought power alone. On Earth, few people have developed the power to directly control matter with the mind. On Venus, mind over matter is a way of life.

Any form or thing that a person on the astral can imagine, he can manifest by the power of thought alone. It is a law of nature there, just as gravity is a basic law of nature on the physical planets. What really happens is that people convert the energy around them into the form of matter desired. The created object then appears wherever the person puts his attention. Homes, clothes, furniture, plants, food, jewelry, and anything imaginable is created by a special mental process that has to be mastered at a young age.

There are limits. This same power will not destroy things or reconvert them to energy. Things disappear only if the person who created them leaves the astral plane, unless they were originally created with the definite intention that they be temporary, and how long, such as our castles and ranches and elaborate play creations. If I had created a toy that soon bored me, I may change its shape into another kind of toy, but I could not point my finger at it and have it disappear in a flash, forever gone. If my aunt Arena no longer liked a certain chair, her only choice would be to reform that chair. She could not remold it into a table or anything other than a chair.

On the other hand, when we create things, they do seem to appear out of thin air. For people on the astral plane this is as common and accepted as driving a car here on Earth.

Because we respect each Soul's individuality, people do not interfere with another's creations. If I did not like the bright blue tree in front of another's house, I would not think of changing it. That would be interference, which creates karmic responsibility.

Just because our thoughts precipitate matter, the common every-day things on the astral are no less real. A marble floor looks and feels like marble, skin feels like skin, water feels like water, flowers smell like flowers, honey tastes like honey, and so on.

Moving things is of course very easy, just a matter of choosing and thinking. If I wanted, I could have a glass of water rise up from the table and float, just by mentally commanding it. No more effort is involved in moving a huge sofa up into the air than in swinging the bed as I am resting on it.

Traveling from place to place is just as easy. People who like to walk do so. We can also levitate and float in the air or glide instead of walking, by willing it to be so. For longer trips we travel at the speed of our thought directly to our destination, which usually seems just a matter of appearing there. Whenever I decided to visit the Temple of Arts in downtown Teutonia, I would place my attention on exactly where I wanted to be. One moment I would be standing in the bedroom; the next instant the surroundings would change and I would be standing in front of the Temple. It is very simple. I do not know the mechanics of how it works — it just works. (People on Earth say the same thing about electricity.)

The speed of thought is much faster than the so-called speed of light known to physical scientists. In the astral body we can travel so very fast because it is made up of condensed energy, as completely under the control of thought as everything else on that plane of being.

The astral body has the same form as the physical, except that it is much more beautiful. It is not just a blob of light, but unlike the physical body, it is luminous and stays alive by absorbing energy directly from the surroundings. Although there are no actual internal organs, people here do eat out of habit and for the simple pleasure of it. Food conveniently turns back into energy as soon as it is swallowed.

Using the power of thought, we can easily change our outer appearance or make ourselves completely invisible. There is no physical pain or fatigue as on the physical planets, which is one good reason why newcomers to the astral call it heaven.

The colors in our everyday lives are indescribable. Compared to the glowing, vibrant colors of the astral plane, colors in the physical are pale or dark and muddy at best. The dullest red of the astral world is the brightest in the physical. Also very many colors which we take for granted don't even exist the physical plane.

Our surroundings at home had such an assortment of magnificent colors that I can't even begin to describe. Just as wonderful is the fact that everything glows. Matter on the astral plane is luminous, like stained glass being lit by the morning sunlight. The sky and clouds are a sea of cheerful colors.

The astral body and the astral plane are not completely unknown on Earth. Each person living in the physical world has an astral body as well as several others, as taught in the Laws of the Supreme Deity. Quite a few people have written books about their experiences with astral projection, which is a limited form of out-of-body travel in the astral body. The safer way of visiting the higher planes is by using the Soul body, which is not limited to any one place as the astral is. But of course not everyone who does astral projection is aware of Soul travel.

Each person living in the physical world experiences the astral body every day, although he may never in this lifetime see the actual cities or people there. The physical body is not capable of having emotions. The physical senses like sight and smell are there, but then these are not quite the same as feelings — love, anger, joy, hurt, etc. All of us may agree that our emotions are very real in our lives, but where are they, and what are they?

The astral plane has been called the emotional plane, and the astral body the emotional body for a very good reason. Whenever we experience an emotion, we are really feeling it through the astral body. Emotions are nothing more than different kinds of energy flowing through this body and influencing thoughts and actions. The astral plane, then, is a place where emotions are a great force and Soul must deal most fully with emotional problems. It is true that every physical person actually lives partly on the astral plane, but it is not normally fully conscious of life there.

All of this is also true for thought. Thought is not a vague something, but a very real thing at a higher frequency than physical matter and energy, or astral matter and energy. Remember that the mind is really a body also, called the mental body, which operates on the mental plane, still another whole universe of being beyond the astral. The mental body is a bluish sheath of light surrounding Soul. Whenever we think, this body generates thought forms that can be seen by the higher senses.

Thought is nothing more than energies flowing through and outward from our mental body much like radio waves. In having the mental body, every person also lives partly on the mental plane, although everyone has not consciously seen the cities, people, and landscapes there.

If you were to visit the astral or mental planes consciously via Soul travel, you would see not only your own emotions and thoughts in full radiant color, and your astral and mental bodies, but you would also be able to meet beings who once lived on Earth. Many of Earth's religions have their heavenly abode in existence on the astral or mental planes.

More and more can be said about the astral plane, and about the ability of each to travel there consciously before physical death. Remember that all of us had lifetimes there and we know that plane well as Soul. The astral is really still one of the lower planes, although it seems to be the ultimate heaven to many people who are living there. Above the astral plane are several others which also seem like ultimate heaven to planes below, but they are not. Everything below the Soul plane is a part of the lower worlds. Our goal is to reach up to and beyond the Soul plane, possible even in this life if we are willing to make the effort. The choice is up to each one of us.

Perceptions of the future usually take place on either the Soul plane or the causal plane above that. Soul may zoom above the time track to view the future or the past as it may choose. This experience seems much more real than ordinary dreaming, although a person might not recognize that he was looking into the future until that future came to pass. Those who are psychically aware will know. On Venus we are able to see about 40 days ahead into the future with good accuracy. Our ability to foresee future events helped in preparing for my trip to your Earth.

The astral plane has many levels or sub-planes to suit different people's consciousness. These are more like distinct regions with different levels of consciousness, rather than levels stacked on top of each other. Venus life is normally somewhere in the middle between lower and higher astral, because most of the people are still attached to physical habits and customs, and of course their whole culture. Certain regions of the astral are set aside as religious paradises for the people who die having a definite idea of heaven.

After a person's physical body dies, he is met by a friend or relative who has passed on before. He will then be taken to where his body lies and is made to realize that he is no longer living on the physical plane. Usually the individual is then allowed to sleep a resting period on the astral plane. Upon awakening, he is taken to the particular plane he has spiritually earned, one that his consciousness is suited to. All of this is determined by an astral being in charge of administering Karma. In some cases a person may be immediately returned to the physical world after death, even if it means being reborn into another body, especially if it was a sudden death as in war or some suicides. Sucides are reborn again to face the same or similar problems as that which they tried to escape.

If he is to continue on the astral plane for a time, a person will wake up in a home and familiar environment. Friends and loved ones will be found living nearby. He will also find the spiritual path or religion that he belonged to in the physical. The reason for all this is that when most people lose their physical body, they still have a great emotional attachment to the physical plane. The astral plane is designed so that people can be comfortable and adjust gradually by having recreated their old home with the power of thought. This is very important.

People who do not realize that they are Soul will be so attached to the physical world that they fear the unknown planes beyond.

Eventually, because of the beauty and harmony there, the individual will come to believe that he has reached the ultimate heaven. People can easily become attached to astral life because they can have anything they want, and they scarcely consider venturing beyond. This continues until it finally dawns on them that there is more to life than their astral heaven.

Religious literature on Earth has accounts of cities on the astral because the authors have had out-of-body experiences taking them there. A few days before I left Venus and the astral plane, my uncle took our family on a tour of a place called Sahasra-dal-Kanwal and other parts of the astral plane. Now I can easily understand why so many people believe it is Paradise. There one can find any landscape imaginable. Some are much like those of Earth. People who have similar natures and the same likes all live in the same areas. Then there are beautiful landscapes that can be seen on other physical planets in our system. The lower astral planes attract Souls with negatively developed states of consciousness. One might say this is where evil people go after death and between lifetimes. Those who expect to find hell with fire and brimstone can find it there,* although it is only temporary. The lower astral plane is also the home of the hideous monsters and devilish creatures created by the lesser evolved levels of consciousness.

Almost any aspect of the physical sciences now so popular on Earth can be quite simply explained in terms of the astral plane. Most psychic powers have their origin there.

Telepathy, which is sending and receiving thoughts from mind to mind, is the most popular form of communication on astral Venus as well as the more advanced physical planets, and it works because thoughts behave like radio waves. Each person has an invisible barrier which keeps secret thoughts hidden, and those who are able to read minds are subject to a spiritual law against trying to penetrate this barrier.

Astral projection is the separation of the astral body from the physical for temporary displacement of the astral part to another location. It is a dangerous practice if continued over a long period of time. It is best to progress from astral projection to Soul travel as soon as possible.

Levitation, or moving objects with the mind, is of course a power we use every day on the astral plane. It can be learned on the physical plane also, but it takes much more effort and discipline.

Visualization is another power of mind over matter; as on the astral plane it creates each individual's world. Everything begins with

* We may see here that the lowest astral vibrates beyond the highest physical and recapitulates the equivalent physical in finer and greater degree, except one octave different. As the delights are more delightful and the pains more painful, so also are the properties of the realm exaggerated. Observing how Venus' lowest astral borders nearest the highest physical, we would not expect to see much beyond the lowest with our highest physical perception. What do we in fact see with our physical senses and their most profoundly instrumented extensions? What we observe is quite similar to the dark dense hells of mythology; high temperature, high pressures, dark sulfurous skies, no water, no vegetation, and for anyone there, utter physical misery. Is this simply coincidence, or is there another basis to our world religions?

visualization before it is created, the only difference being that here in the physical world it requires physical effort and physical time.

Extrasensory perception is the use of our extra senses in the astral, causal, mental, etheric, and Soul bodies. The Soul body's senses are the most powerful of all and they are limited to no one plane as some of the others are. Miracles are actually a matter of the psychic and spiritual powers being used in this physical world.

Physically densified transport vehicles definitely look metallic, and take on a physical shape, like the Venusian convoys that have been photographed by the American, George Adamski. *

Please keep in mind, however, that physical, astral, causal and mental planes are all limited worlds.

* The controversial figure, George Adamski, is casually mentioned here in connection with his having photographed a Venusian spacecraft back in 1953, only two years before Omnec's arrival. Omnec's description of the convoy (Venusian name for this ship) that brought her to Earth is very similar to the one that Adamski photographed through his telescope. Gabriel Green of AFSCA once told me that a movie special effects laboratory studied that photograph extensively, using every analysis procedure and every trick of the trade known at the time, but were unable to duplicate the photograph because they could not accurately achieve the distance-greying effect of the atmosphere between the lens and the object some considerable distance away. Nobody has duplicated that photograph since.

Chapter Six
Teutonia

1. Downtown Teutonia
2. Jewelry from mother
3. Aunt Arena
4. Tythanian clothes
5. Dance of the Universe
6. Pilgrimage to Tetz
7. The Temple of Wisdom
8. A special meeting

My aunt was always one for keeping special experiences in reserve, for holding them from me so that I would always have something new to look forward to in life. Our visit to the public ballroom was one such special occasion planned by Aunt Arena. It would give me a taste of our culture when it was yet physical, when the people could not yet levitate on their own.

It was going to be my first trip to the city of Teutonia, for this was a time in my life shortly before I began visiting the Temples of Learning. Although our village is nearby, I as a child allowed my aunt and uncle to guide me in the experiences I would have, and so I had never ventured on my own to see the beauty which I knew existed there.

No one actually lives in the city, and as I mentioned once before, neither Teutonia nor any other Venusian city on the astral plane has commerce or industry. Our cities are centers of culture, as enchanting as those you read about in fairy tales.

Without a clear picture in my mind of what Teutonia would be like, I was filled with a great sense of anticipation as we all prepared for the occasion. This evening also turned out to be my first adventure in formally dressing up. Aunt Arena brought to my room a beautiful sky blue jersey-like dress with long, flowing sleeves and fleecy white clouds printed all over. In the center of my chest was the bright sun, sending beams of light and warmth in every direction. I loved it!

Our walk through the village onward to the city was a treat in itself. We could very well have manifested ourselves in front of the ballroom, but then the whole experience would hardly have been as enjoyable. Above, the sky was deep orange in color with a shimmer of pink.

Several of my friends joined us in appreciating the fantasyland beauty of our neighboring homes, each of unique design and surrounded by fantastic arrangements of trees, shrubs, and flowers. We paused often to smell the fragrances of our favorite flowers and listen to the merrily singing birds. Together with the familiar distant rush of the sea we were treated to one of nature's finest symphonies. After crossing the meadows and a small wooded area, we came to a large oriental-looking arched bridge that spanned the canyon between our village and the city. Below, waters rushed madly to the sea.

How can I describe the enchanting beauty I saw in my first glimpse of Teutonia? Our cities need to be seen to be experienced, not just read about. Seeing all the temples of learning and museums in this white and pastel colored city was my first experience with buildings that were more than two levels high. My excitement mounted as we approached closer and closer through the flowering gardens everywhere.

Teutonia a cluster of exotic-looking structures, with such a splendid variety of designs that my senses were overwhelmed. Towers, domes, bubbles, and pyramids were used liberally; and although most of the temples were pastel-colored, some were made of mother-of-pearl inlaid with jewels of gold. Others were made of various gleaming metals or crystal. Every one was exquisite and unique.

The ballroom resembled a giant lavender bubble set onto a golden crown. We followed a narrow, spiraling stairway to the entrance and went in to be greeted by our friends and neighbors who had gathered in the hallway. There we received a jeweled clip to help fasten our long flowing dresses so they would not fly up over our heads. The men's dancing trousers were fitted at the ankles and were a ballooning style.

Stepping into the ballroom was like stepping into air and instantly floating away. It took away my breath. I felt as if I were dancing deep in space, for the walls of this gigantic sphere were made to look like the dark blue starry sky, with shooting stars as a special effect.

Around the edge of the ballroom was a balcony where Teutonia's musicians played the most heavenly music I had ever heard. Also on the balcony were romantic settings of candlelit tables where couples sat to enjoy the sights and sounds.

Being a lover of dancing, I hoped the evening would never end. It was one of the most thrilling experiences of my life, because dancing without gravity adds a wonderful dimension to the art. Many of the adults acted just like I did, as if this was their first visit to the ballroom. It was good to see that everyone was doing something different without being self-conscious. Some of the couples were simply holding on to each other and turning over sideways and upside-down. Others were involved in performing elaborate cultural dances. The children had fun doing all sorts of acrobatics and linking up into giant circles.

I was told by Uncle Odin that the ballroom was very popular when our civilization was physical, before The Great Transition, which was very easy to understand. It had never entered my mind, however, to try floating away on my own dancing in the air. By this I mean that we do not on the astral plane readily try new experiences until they are introduced to us, or a special day arrives such as this evening at the ballroom.

Living in an unlimited environment, we must be careful not to have every experience at once; otherwise we would find ourselves bored halfway through life, which on the astral plane can last thousands of years. (My uncle was well over one thousand years old.) We were always encouraged to use the available facilities and in this way enjoy life together with other people.

During the evening I joined my aunt and uncle and a small group of children in going downstairs into the crown of the building. Here was Teutonia's instrument shop, which displayed the various musical instruments people had created throughout history. Some of them were very unusual, very old-looking, but nevertheless, I could see how the instruments of the day had evolved.

On our way home my aunt and uncle stopped to visit the museum where inventions dating back to the physical era were on display. I stayed outside to admire the luminous Temples all around. There are no streets in Teutonia. Beautiful walkways weave around the buildings. I also waited outside while Arena and Odin visited the library. This is where the literature created by Teutonia's people over the centuries is kept. Anyone living in our area was welcome to add a book of his own.

I was very tired and I felt that by waiting outside and not filling my mind with too many new sights and sounds it would be easier to save my experiences in the ballroom. But my interest in the city was sparked and afterwards I visited there quite often, especially the Temple of Arts.

After the dance that night I was in sheer ecstasy and when I told my aunt how happy I was, she mentioned how very much my mother also had loved dancing. In fact, it had been one of her favorite pastimes. This was now the first time, I realized, that Aunt Arena had said anything to me about my mother. Perhaps she had been afraid of bringing sorrowful memories back into my life.

I learned from Arena that I had many qualities like my mother - the shape of my body, the way I moved, and the shape of my hands. She was said to be a beautiful woman. Her natural grace and the way she carried herself always attracted attention. My mother had some quality, a certain expression of her dark, moss green eyes that intrigued people. And she had the same sharing nature as my Uncle Odin, always being concerned for others more than herself. The dress I was wearing, my aunt said with a warm smile, was one that Mother had also worn as a child and it thrilled me to be compared with this wonderful woman who gave birth to me.

That night I was already in bed sitting up against a pillow when Arena came to the door asking if she could enter. "Yes, of course," I said. She came in and sat by my side showing me a little wooden box as she said with **a** laugh that she had forgotten a special present for me, until having gone into her bedroom and seeing it there.

Inside was a necklace with matching bracelet and earrings that had belonged to my mother. They had been very special and dear to her, being one of the first gifts from my father.

I was overjoyed that my aunt wanted me to have the precious jewelry which my mother had worn for so many years. And I was even more happy to learn that my father had sent the jewelry for me to keep. It meant a great deal to me because it was a gesture of love.

Occasionally my father would ask Arena and Odin how I was doing and if I was well. On my birthdays he would send a gift, but I never saw or heard from him personally. For him to send something of my mother's was a great honor to me. He found it very difficult to let go of anything that belonged to her.

What a wonderful day this had been, so full of joy and new experiences! I remember going to sleep and having dreams of my mother and of my first and only day with her.

Venusians wear little jewelry, realizing long ago that at a certain point jewelry begins to detract from the beauty of the wearer. The few pieces that we do wear need to be very special and exquisite. Each piece is created with feeling, which in turn is transmitted to the user. Jewelry is also made to reflect the inner light and beauty of a person. Metals and stones that are among the most precious and valuable on Earth are commonly used because these too can be manifested on the astral plane.

Tythanians enjoy very intricate designs as well as the very simple ones. Not being limited in supplies, each individual may go to special effort to create the most elegant, balanced pieces imaginable. There are no jewelry factories because every person, being unique and creative simply manifests his own jewelry just as he also creates his own clothes. Jewelry is usually passed from one person to another as a token of love, and is created in the first place in such a way as to make it virtually indestructible.

When we were yet a physical civilization, space explorers would travel to distant planets to find precious and rare jewels and stones. It was always a thrilling experience for a woman when her husband returned from a trip with a rare, unheard of stone or metal.

For special occasions we wear headdresses made of natural things like flowers, leaves, feathers, and beads. I suppose it was from us that the American Indians received their ideas about headdress. I do know that space travelers from Venus were those who introduced the early aborigines to corn and sunflowers brought from our home planet.

We are actually a very sentimental and romantic people, which is especially true because we live on the plane of emotions. Happiness in our lives is found mostly in the small things of life, the everyday joys, such as this splendid gift from my father.

Aunt Arena was always a happy person, always could see the good in everything, especially people. And she had a wonderful way of soothing those who were upset, and relaxing people who were nervous and high-strung. In whatever had to be done, she took her time and did it well. I learned my keen sense of organization from her. Everything had its place in our home.

Arena loved the simple and natural surroundings of our home. Entranced by the beauty of nature, she could not be without her indoor garden and the hundreds of plants that decorated the rooms of our house. She loved to spend a part of every day outside, caring for the flowers and blossoming trees. She enjoyed working with her hands.

My aunt and uncle enjoyed a variety of creative interests, as does almost every individual in Venusian society. In addition to the scientific work which took up most of his day, Uncle Odin was a fine sculptor, woodcarver, and musician, to mention just a few talents. Aunt Arena was also talented in sculpting. Many of the statues and fountains in our garden were projects undertaken by both of them. Two of our four bedrooms were set aside as their individual work areas, one for each. A third was the bedroom they shared.

While playing the harp and flute were among her personal joys, designing and creating learning toys was one of her contributions to the world. She was dedicated to developing new toys that would teach as well as entertain a child. I benefited a great deal from this because she too tested her inventions at home before sending them off to the Astral Museum.

Arena was also known in Teutonia for the clothes she designed. Although everyone designed and manifested his own clothing, quite a few people, becoming bored with their own ideas, turned to her because she was good at putting together new designs and materials. My aunt's main concern, always, was to suit the nature of the personality of each individual.

Venusian clothes are usually loose-fitting and flowing in style, and quite often sheer, made of materials that are always pleasant to the touch and very comfortable. To a certain extent our people are sensualists, but not so much as to hold back spiritual development.

Because each person is so individualistic in experimenting with different styles of dresses, pants, robes and gowns, there is never a fashion trend. And because everything imaginable can be created by each individual, every dress is unique. For ladies, full-length dresses are common in our culture. For men, ballooning pants and robes are popular. This is not a fashion trend but comes about because individuals are drawn together by their levels of consciousness unfoldment.

If you were to visit a Venusian village, you would notice that many people have one thing in common in their dress. Everyone wears sandals, which are very comfortable and beautiful footwear, because the natural shape of the foot is visible and decorated instead of hidden. This is a carryover from our physical era. The soles of our sandals are paper thin, allowing us to feel the grass and the springy ground of our natural surroundings yet they are created of an impenetrable fabric that protects the feet. The tops are what makes each pair of sandals unique. Depending on personal taste, the straps can be any color, width and design. Aunt Arena and I liked delicate straps with simple designs and colors that would enhance the beauty of our dress.

Being such an admirer of the beauty in nature, my aunt designed dresses for both of us that represented the elements. For example, the sun dress sparkled and was as orange as our sun. On the back was embroidered a flaming sun radiating warmth and light in all directions. The water dress had the print of a waterfall with bubbly, cascading waters; while the cloud dress was fluffy, fleecy and white. The moon dress was especially beautiful with its bluish-white glow. It was a full dress with long, ballooning sleeves, and fell to the floor from under the bust. One of my favorites was the butterfly dress, which felt like velvet and was gifted with the same design as nature uses to decorate real butterflies. I wore it on many of my outdoor excursions near Teutonia as

I grew older, as well as a chiffon-like dress that looked like the colorful leaves of an autumn tree.

As I reached age six, my friends and I enjoyed entire days exploring the Kumli Mountains, which rise between Teutonia and the sea. Camping out and making new friends from our neighboring villages gave me a lasting love for the outdoors. But it was the golden beach that I grew to love best. I was content just to be sitting there day after day facing the sea and burying my feet in the gold sand crystals. I would often be there early in the morning to soak up the sun and marvel at the dazzling glow of the beach stretching almost to the horizon to each side of me as I faced the sea. I would stare into the waves breaking along the shore, and the dark blue and purple waters beyond. The musical sounds of the sea and the shells were simply enchanting. Yes, even the pretty shells gave out a music of their own as they lay here and there along the beach. The beauty of the purple, red and blue mountains captured my attention as well. Those heavenly colors and sounds were all over.

The sky above was a sea of ever-changing bright colors and against an orange-pink background was the bright orange sun and the clouds. The sky itself responded to the thoughts of the people living below. If a person preferred a lavender sky above his home, it would be so.

Behind the beach was a dense growth of jungle with all sorts of exotic trees and flowers. Just beyond were the beginnings of the Kumli Mountains and a downgrade into a valley where many people of Teutonia had created homes.

I always enjoyed the birds and animals that kept me company on the beach, and I imagine they enjoyed my company too. And I loved to daydream as I stared out to sea. Mostly I wondered about my father and mother, and recreated in my mind what they looked like. Father had asked Arena and Odin not to speak to me about him and they respected his wish. Often I reflected on my childhood and wondered about my future.

Ever so often I would see a little glass bubble-boat skim by across the waters, and my eyes would follow it until it was no longer visible. Its only colors were those of the people sitting inside. Sailboats were popular too because of their graceful pretty shape.

Sitting there on the beach I often sang songs about how I felt, or played the harp for my friends, who in turn played their favorite instruments for me. My best friends, Zemura and Neyma joined me in doing dances like the dance of the universe. It was one of my favorites but also one of the most difficult to master.

A momentous event that took place again and again in our lives was the annual journey to the city of Retz to see and hear a master of wisdom speak. Actually seeing him was very special to us, even though one does have an inner communication more powerful than telepathy. This time of year was approaching, and soon our journey on foot to the Temple of Wisdom would begin.

At one seminar I recall that the Master spoke of the difference between truth and an individual who gives out truth. "In the physical worlds and on many planets, as well as spiritual worlds, there are spiritual teachers. They have much truth to give. But when the teacher is worshipped and held more important than the Word, the truth is often lost. People must learn that truth is more important than he who is a channel for truth."

Under the Laws of the Supreme Deity, each person strives to attain mastership himself. This is the Master's goal for all of us and our goal also. The teachings that really encourage and guide students to become Masters of wisdom are few in number, especially on Earth where so many teachings give out only a certain amount of truth or none at all. Overloaded with rituals and superstition the people are led to worship the spiritual leader and follow manmade laws.

For the upcoming seminar my friends and I were planning to do a dance about the balance of Soul. It would depict Soul coming into the lower worlds and being separate polarities, male and female, giver and receiver. A Soul-mate is not another individual somewhere out there in the world waiting for you. It is the other part of one Soul after polarization. Soul incarnates at any time as either male or female and learns to deal with either male qualities or female qualities in any incarnation.

There are times when Soul teaches a neutral state in which male and female qualities of an incarnation are close to balancing each other. Until Soul becomes spiritually aware, this is a temporary state. The balance holds forever when the Soul-mates join and the individual realizes his identity as unpolarized Soul. This is a self-realization which takes place on the Soul plane.

Our dance depicted this original separation and final balance by having a girl and a boy represent the two Soul-mates. It began with us sitting together back-to-back on the floor, bound together, as the different colors of the planes moved upward behind us to represent Soul's journey down into the lower worlds. First was purple for the Etheric Plane,* then blue for the Mental and Ochre for the Causal. Finally there was pink for the Astral arid green for the Physical Planes. Then we stood up as we separated and went off in different directions individually expressing our thoughts and feelings. Once in a while we came together to touch hands or touch fingers, or sometimes to completely embrace each other, but only for a moment. At the end of the dance the Master came out and held his hands and arms up in the air as the two Soul-mates seated themselves together in a balance at the Master's feet. We practiced this dance often in anticipation of the soon to come journey to Retz.

It was on the beach shortly before the seminar that I met my new friend Rimj. Every day he would be there at about the same time as I, in his familiar balloon trousers and purple robe with its rope-like belt of gold. At first we did not talk. We just sat together on the golden sand and stared out at the purple and blue waters or at one another.

I remember well his dark blue flashing eyes and curly dark blond hair, and his long straight nose. Most of all I liked his charming crooked smile. Rimj and I grew to love each other very much, even at our young age. We included each other in everything we did, and my aunt and

---

* It should be noted here that Etheric is used a little differently from the popular Theosophical and Rosicrucian understanding of this. These concepts rank the ever finer levels of being as: Physical (including the finer non-tangible grades of matter called by the above Etheric, i.e. Solids, Liquids, Gasses, 4th Etheric, 3rd Etheric, a 2nd Etheric and 1st Etheric or assimilation level), Astral, Spiritual, Mental, Causal, Monadic and Divine. Omnec understands the same 7-fold natural division of the vibrational realms of being, each finer level interpenetrating the preceding coarser level and in turn being interpenetrated by the following finer one, except that Omnec calls the 5th finer grade of matter Etheric. Omnec considers all of the 7 minor levels within the Physical realm simply physical, because in her view they are all no different than the minor divisions of any of the other major groupings. This may help to clear up an apparent conflict of terms for some already familiar with those other philosophies.

uncle and girlfriends enjoyed him as well. We often climbed the Kumli Mountains together and sat up on the very highest peak, listening to the wind rushing through the valley and echoing off the cliffs. Then on our way home we would pick flowers for each other as a reminder of the joys we had shared.

Rimj and I spoke often about our lives and our futures and of course our performances at the upcoming seminar. Rimj was preparing to sing a song of spiritual love that he himself had written.

The day of our great journey to Retz arrived and I was more excited than ever before. As a younger child I had always looked upon this yearly event as a routine part of our lives, being too young to appreciate the beauty of everything. Now I had the strange but welcome feeling that this was to be a very special time of my life and that it was important for me to soak up the beauty of Retz and the thrill of seeing Rami Nuri (the Master).

On foot the trip to Retz lasts several days, so we always packed plenty of clothes. Especially for the seminar everyone had designed an entire wardrobe around a theme that was individually his own. This yearly journey was a tradition in our culture, dating back to a time when our civilization was physical, and although we very easily could have manifested in Retz this would not have been as much adventure and a less complete experience.

The people of Teutonia and the villages in many parts of Venus left at their own time and walked at their own pace. I had asked that Rimj and Zemura travel with us. As soon as their parents and Arena and Odin had gathered we were on our way.

Retz lies in the opposite direction from the Temples of Teutonia, beyond the Kumli Mountains that Rimj and I so often climbed. We traveled through the cavern, a natural passage through the mountains that had been discovered before the Great Transition. Here were underground pools and waterfalls, fantastic rock formations, and weird-looking animals. Overall it was very quiet and echoey, and we could create the most beautiful sounds whenever we chanted or sang. Crossing the chasms on narrow woven rope bridges was a special adventure for us children.

A day later we emerged from the Kumli Mountains to see ahead of us a vast plain of flowers, all varieties and colors of gorgeous flowers. Thousands of people joined us. The roads were now crowded with beautiful travelers all gaily dressed and carrying their colorful loads. My own dress was a gown of white with golden threads and a golden rope-like belt.

Next we came upon a dense and silent forest having a vast variety of tall trees from many different planets. There were redwoods, pines, fir, maples and others not found on Earth. We had a precious habit whenever walking through a forest not to talk and make undue noise, but just listen to the sounds of the birds and animals, the crunching of our feet in the moist soil, and the peaceful silence. The damp earthy and mossy smells were unforgettable, along with the pungent trees and flowers.

Deep in the forest we arrived at a small village where several families had created huge, sprawling homes with lavish gardens. It was one of the many Venusian villages which do not go by a name.

As it was getting dark, we decided to stay overnight in the village. People's attitudes there toward strangers is such that if anyone arrives having a need, then it is fulfilled without question. Every person trusts everyone else and offers them the same hospitality that someone in the family would receive.

At dawn we had "breakfast" together before moving on, though it was not food that we ate. We call it breakfast because consciously absorbing energy together is much like a meal. Sitting in a circle and closing our eyes, we took a deep breath and visualized energy being drawn in through every pore. It was a very stimulating breakfast indeed!

Beyond the forest was yet another range of mountains much too high for us to cross. Skirting them, we crossed a desert and encountered another group of mountains wherein lies an eerie plateau. Climbing up a steep grade we reached the Plain of Water, an almost completely barren flat surface of blue, purple and green marble. Rocks were strewn here and there. In some parts of the plain the ground had the appearance of being pushed, and other parts were quite rough, with faults and crevices.

The Plain of Water was strange because everything looked so parched and dry, yet an uncomfortable dampness filled the air. Looking down into the cracks and crevices we could see water rushing along, and there were places where the plain had sunken several inches and was filled with pools of water. In the cliffs surrounding the plain were several waterfalls. The plain itself was raised and water rushed down in many places.

Many of the spectacular sights here would on Earth be called natural wonders, but the people of Venus accepted them as a part of the beauty of The Creator's works. They did not seem so spectacular there because when beauty surrounds one every day it does not mean as much. Great wonders are taken for granted because they are everywhere.

Beyond this plateau the landscape turned into mountainous green hills and grassy rolling meadows. Whenever we reached this point we knew that soon we would see the lush green valley in which lies Retz. Below us in the distance would be the enchanting walled capital of our planet. Retz is a round city, a simple circle of fantastic-looking Temples, flowering gardens, fountains and beautiful statues. Viewing the city from above we could see how the buildings and walkways seemed to take the shape of a double cross.

Retz is encircled by towering white luminous walls of marble with tints of luminous pale blue. Together with the spired towers to each side of the mammoth carved wooden doors, the main arched gate resembles the face of a mighty cathedral of the style that can be found in England here on Earth. As our group approached the city we could see the tops of a number of the taller Temples beyond. The city emanated vibrations that held us spellbound in awe. No matter how often we had been here before, its beauty overwhelmed us every year.

Retz is completely unlike any city to be found anywhere on Earth, but much like a place you would read about in stories of fantasy here. It is a fantastic display of the most harmonious and balanced architecture imaginable. As the capital of Venus, Retz is a spiritual city of Temples of learning devoted to spiritual teachings as well as the arts and sciences.

Unlike most Venusian cities, which are centers only for culture and learning, Retz has many inhabitants. Among them are Masters of knowledge.

Temples which exist on Earth are actually poor copies of Temples in Spiritual cities on the higher planes. We must keep in mind the truth about creativity, that it is nothing more than a receptivity to what already exists on higher planes of being. However, the most beautiful buildings on the physical planets can never compare to the beauty of those in the worlds beyond.

Each Temple on Retz is unique, has its own character, which reflects in the design. Most commonly used decorative materials are the precious and rare jewels and metals such as gold, silver, diamonds, rubies, emeralds, jade and pearl. These are abundantly inlaid within and without, around windows and doorways, on stairs and ceilings and floors, or the entire building may be made of precious materials, as what is desired is simply manifested as needed. When Earth's religious writers use the words "streets of gold" in describing their experiences, they are referring to astral cities such as Retz.

As in Teutonia, most of the basic shapes were liberally used in creating Retz. There are spheres, cubes, pyramids, domes, cylinders, cones, and more. There were styles similar to some of Earth's finest architecture, and there were other styles found only on other physical planets, unknown to Earth. There was a temple built in the shape of a pyramid. It was covered with bright silver and rather small. I did not have a chance to see what was inside. One of the buildings that I did explore was a museum of rare sea animals from different planets in the physical universe. It was a huge, pale blue luminous sphere without windows or doorways, and transparent from the inside. A temple I have sketched was a sphere of dark blue crystal resting atop four towering supports of silvery metal. A number of windows ran up each of the base supports, which altogether looked like the side of a concave lens in a side view. This Temple's beauty is difficult to describe in your words.

Another Temple that I enjoyed looking at was a cube made completely of unpolished amethyst with edges of silver. The arched mahogany door was a work of art. Each panel had an elaborate carving of fruit and was very colorful. The several arched windows of this building were made of purple, yellow, and white pearl-like glass in an abstract pattern. In the rear was a spiraling staircase leading to the second floor entrance. Vines were hanging over the edges of the roof.

This is very common in Retz where they often have trees arid gardens growing on flat roofs.

One of the main structures here, the Temple of Golden Wisdom, exists simultaneously both in the physical city of Retz (equivalent to Earth upper physical in density) and here on the astral plane. It is a circular building made mostly of gold and marble. The base is of sky blue marble streaked with white and purple. A number of steps all around lead to the main level. Sixty golden pillars in the shape of spiritual beings support the flat marble roof with their outstretched hands. These statues have unusually slender waists, and they depict the balance between male and female polarities. Here there are indoor gardens and pools surrounded by comfortable benches.

To just capture the spiritual experience of the seminar in words is useless. Our seminar was a sharing experience in which each individual participated. A number or talks were given on spiritual subjects, and although a number of them overlapped, there was no repetition because each speaker, being unique, gave us a fresh insight. There were musical presentations and poetry, art shows and plays, and there were many dances and songs.

Our dance was a great success like every other performance because our hearts, minds, and soul were dedicated to it. Everything was appreciated and enjoyed for what it was.

One of the seminar's highlights in my mind was one particular talk that many of us did not fully understand until later, after we had contemplated a while on it... There will always be a question, as long as there is man as to why the world is as it is. Here on Earth you believe that everything is made of atoms, which are nothing more than a number of positive and negative changes of energy. But what makes the variety of things and what holds them all together?

The answer lies in mind. Man creates his own world in the physical plane through the power of thought. The world is created to reflect man's collective thought. Mental images of what trees look like are handed down from generation to generation and these thought expectations keep trees from changing. When his mental images of them change they can also change.

When a person says "This is not possible," he is speaking from a limited way of thinking. Everything is possible, but man limits himself out of ignorance. Then he has a limited world which further limits his thoughts and further limits the world. Man's world can never be changed unless he changes his thoughts. When you enter a family or join with a mate to create a family unit, the stronger one will create for that family what is to be, depending on whatever the stronger one desires. And if that person is confused then you have a confused family, confused children and a confused way of life.

We should not blame others for limiting their worlds. If they have security and an organized mind and way of life, this could be because they have experienced the opposite in other lifetimes and are reacting in fear against something. When looking at the overall picture of Soul's growth through experience, there is no room for blame or judgment, only understanding.

The speaker was referring to Earth in this talk, and of course how life once was on Venus. All this was said while remembering that a limited world is only a step toward an unlimited world and unlimited being.

Between functions we gathered in groups according to our interests, which is very easy to do with our ability to pick up thoughts. At night we slept wherever we wanted to, whether at one of the Temples in the city or outside in one of the many flower gardens. We were so involved in the seminar itself and all that was happening that it was difficult to break away and tour the city.

It is true that most people, including Venusians, take much of the beauty in life for granted until it is no longer with them. After having seen Retz for that last tine I regretted not soaking in more of the beauty. Then it was just a normal part of my life. Now I miss it so much it is difficult to bear.

The Master spoke to us about the Supreme Deity, how It had created all Souls equal, and how inequality began in man's mind. Man on the physical plane has yet to learn to live with and accept other individuals.

On many planets people were having problems accepting one another because they knew nothing of Deity or Soul, or of living more than one lifetime. He explained that much of man's struggle arises from a belief in only one life. Upon dying he is so fearful that he is drawn into rebirth soon and grows very little spiritually. And it takes many lifetimes to grow to reach an understanding that all of us on Venus and a few on Earth are fortunate to have.

In not criticizing others for their level of consciousness, but understanding and accepting them as they are, we help them to grow. In sharing our love and knowledge with others willingly rather than using it as a tool for more power, we in turn receive the same from the Supreme Deity.

The Master concluded his talk by answering a questioner who wondered why absolute power did not corrupt the Supreme Deity. The answer was that Supreme Deity never claims absolute power. It is shared by all Soul and is distributed equally in all things. I would reflect on these things, and all the things I would like to know. As time passed the physical Universe became more and more intriguing. Our people often sent blessings to the physical plane, and to Earth, because of the great suffering going on there. To think of Earth brought sadness to our lives of joy and peace. I remembered that I had spent many past lives on Earth, and I realized how much more pleasant this life on Venus was. Nevertheless I had some strange attraction to Earth and the physical plane, but at the moment I was not aware of what that meant.

Later, back in Teutonia, Arena and Odin broke the news to me one evening at Study Time, about a conversation they had had with the Master at the seminar. There was a good possibility that I would soon be making an important choice about my life. I would have an opportunity to leave Venus and live with a family in the physical universe. It was apparent from my Records that there was a considerable Karma in the physical world for me to meet. At some future time I would again need to live in the physical universe. But I was fortunate. If I were to go in this lifetime I would be better able to withstand the trials that I faced. If I waited to be reborn there then my time in the physical worlds could well extend into thousands of years.

My uncle said that we would soon make a special trip to Retz, to see if it were indeed possible to leave the astral as a child to go directly to the physical world, and whether it would break any spiritual laws. I was excited of course because the Master did not make a habit of speaking directly to private people.

Sitting on the beach a few days later I thought back to one special person I had seen in Retz. In a way he was familiar to me, and yet he was unfamiliar. I sensed that he did not live on the astral plane but was projecting from the physical. He was a short, nice looking young man, maybe in his late twenties, with pretty blue eyes. I had seen him several times, and also a dark-bearded fellow. He glanced at me once, staring at me for a few moments. That was all. But there was something in that glance that left many things unsaid, and I had no idea what it was. I wondered, would I ever see him again and why was it important that I see him anyway? I did not know.

Arena made a special point of telling me to clear my thoughts and be very adult-like. This was of utmost importance. They both said that I did not have to make a choice just to do what others thought best, or to have an adventure, because I was welcome to stay at home for the rest of my life if I so chose. They loved me very much and had made me aware of this choice for my own good only, because such opportunities were not always available.

Chapter Seven
The Creative Life

1. Venus like a fantasy land
2. How life changed as we became astral
3. Manifesting instead of manufacturing
4. The creative life
5. Homes and gardens on Venus
6. How we manifest things
7. We master arts and handicrafts
8. Everyone an artist
9. Science
10. Beyond the astral

Compared to life as we know it on Earth, some physical planets are like fantasylands. Life on Venus probably seems even more fantastic and unbelievable because there is the added dimension of being on the astral plane of reality and being.

If you can imagine how difficult it would be to understand life on Earth from reading one book, then you will realize how difficult it is to understand life on Venus and the Astral Plane in reading only this autobiography.

One way of looking at our transition to the astral is to think of it as our good karma. Because we learned to live in harmony rather than conflict and war during our negative Iron Age, we were raised to enjoy our culture on a more beautiful level until the beginning of the next Golden Age at our physical level.

Venus (astral) has exactly the same cities and landscapes as the physical planet had at the time of the Great Transition. The Temples of Teutonia had been designed and built while the city was physical, by the Masters of each subject, and were recreated on the astral plane. Our homes of course changed over the years with the changing tastes of the people.

As our culture entered the astral dimension or plane, we found that colors were more radiant and more abundant in every respect. Our sky was iridescent, a sea of ever-changing colors, and everything was luminous. Mountains, fields, trees, grass, buildings, clothes, furniture, and even our bodies gave off a warm, colorful glow of their own nature.

Now the weather was controlled by the collective thoughts of the people. Never again was it too cold or too hot, too dry or too rainy. People who desired a change discovered that their thoughts could manifest a snowstorm enveloping their own homes and no others. People learned to control the color of the sky above their estate as well, and allowed other families their own free will in accordance with the spiritual law of noninterference.

What a wonderful freedom it was not to need food in order to stay alive! And because the astral body travels at such tremendous speeds, physical transportation became obsolete. Anyone had the choice to simply appear at his destination or to enjoy vehicles powered by his own thoughts. Around the house and neighborhood, walking (or gliding along just above the ground) remained the easiest way of going from place to place.

In being able to manifest things directly from energy, we no longer needed to physically build anything piece by piece, unless we just wanted to enjoy the craftmanship, which most of us desired to learn.

As one unfolds spiritually, he becomes more of an individual than ever before. This truth shows up in the spiritual growth of a planet. Earth, in its spiritual infancy, is a planet where the masses of people are controlled and where conformity is widespread. As Venus was growing up, its people left the cities and mass-produced conveniences to lead a more natural life in independent villages. Each person learned to supply most of his own needs in order to learn to become more individual and creative.

The spiritually advanced planets naturally are populated by individuals, who express their individuality creatively. Before the Great Transition, the people of Venus were very much involved in the arts, and nothing was more important than creativity in every area of life. Expressing oneself in the creation of harmony and beauty was considered to be the very purpose of one's existence.

And because our flowering culture had already evolved to an astral level, translating to the astral plane did not change it so drastically. Our people had much more time to devote to the creative joys in life rather than what was necessary for survival; but the family and the home continued to be the center of life and creative expression.

After the Great Transition, each family had much more freedom in creating its own home. Unlimited by physical materials and physical laws, anything imaginable could be manifested by thought alone. Building our own dome house together with the floating second floor was not a feat of engineering but one of creative designing.

Most of the architecture on Venus is based on circles, ovals, and graceful curving lines. In our neighborhood were homes that looked like several bubbles sitting atop each other or arranged in clusters along the ground. Domes were very popular. Many others were a combination of different geometric shapes. A few were elaborate and extensively detailed structures, like palaces and castles, but every single home was unique and enchantingly beautiful. An architect from Earth would probably call Venus a paradise where fantastic ideas have come true.

A house of solid gold studded with diamonds, rubies, emeralds and pearls is manifested as easily as a house of colored bricks. It would be almost impossible to create a home sculptured from a single giant diamond or ruby on the physical planets, but on Venus (astral) it is a matter of designing it in your mind and instantly manifesting it. Knowing of the unlimited possibilities, our people nevertheless create homes that suit their individual sense of beauty. It is the beauty that counts, not the amount of precious gems and metals. One can have all those he cares to manifest.

I cannot remember seeing a house in Teutonia that was not surrounded by lush, flowering gardens. Now that our creations are only limited by our imaginations, the flowers, trees, and bushes are much more exotic and colorful. If my aunt had wanted three-foot tall red mushrooms with white dots, these could easily be created. These would have been real mushrooms, smelling, tasting, and feeling as mushrooms do on the physical planets.

Weaving throughout our elaborately designed gardens were walkways of stone and brick, or perhaps gold, depending on one's tastes. And a garden would not be complete without fountains, statuary, ponds and waterfalls. There would also be marble, wrought metal or exotic wood benches. Our statues represented all kinds of beings — spiritual masters, angels, mythological figures, and rulers of the elements. A person whose love was sculpturing would create each piece by hand. If his interests were elsewhere he would probably design each statue in mind and simply manifest it.

The Tythanians love lots of room and open space in their homes and grounds. Rooms are never cluttered or over-furnished, and everything that is created to adorn the house serves some useful purpose. Our furniture is of course created for practical reasons, but it always has about it a quality of exquisiteness, of beauty, of individuality. A table can not be just a table, or a chair just a chair; it must be something that others exclaim over when they come in. Each and every piece is a work of art.

A chair may look like a very beautiful, gracefully carved wooden chair with cushions, but the feel of it may be completely different. If the person who created the chair liked the feeling of sitting on feathers, then sitting in it would seem like being comforted by soft downy feathers. Or if he liked the feeling of clouds or floating, then a chair or couch may feel that way.

Plush carpets may feel like marble; or the floors may look like marble and yet when you walk on them they may feel like grass, or water, or feathers, or some soft material. Anything can be created to look one way and feel another way, depending on the individual tastes.

Every room is a reflection of the family's individuality, personality, and interests, so there are bound to be an almost infinite number of variations.

Some families devote their entire home to one of the senses, such as sound or smell. Or the different rooms of a house may be devoted to sound, sight, smell, touch, and taste. In going from room to room a person would experience various sensations in each sense.

In a room devoted to sound, everything responds to sound or emits a sound of its own. Walking on the carpet may create a certain sound, while lying on it may cause a variation of the same sound. Sitting on the cushions, or just moving around the room may set up whole vibration patterns that cause the furnishings to emit harmoniously blended sounds. Everything there would contribute to a heavenly combination of melodies. A number of musical instruments may also be in the room for visitors to play.

A person who has devoted his life to music may do the same with his house. Each room would be devoted to a different kind of musical instrument and its particular sounds. Fountains in the garden would emit musical sound as the water falls, and all of the trees, flowers, and shrubs would together create enchanting natural symphonies. The garden would not be complete without a windharp which is a harp that catches the wind to produce ever-changing beautiful melodies.

In a room devoted to smell, everything has its own peculiar aroma. Stepping on the rug would cause a certain fragrance, perhaps that of a rose, to rise up. Touching a plant or a small cushion would cause it to emit whatever scent the creator had in mind in manifesting it. A painting of the countryside could very well emit the fresh natural smells of country air, a cold mountain stream, or the lilies of the fields.

Just entering a room devoted to touch could bathe a person with a soothing vibration. In addition, there may be wall hangings of fur and textures that feel wonderful to the touch. The floors could feel like wet grass, and a painting of a waterfall could very well feel wet to the touch.

Another room may be devoted to color. Here, a couch or a coffee table would constantly change colors from red to purple to green to blue to yellow and red again, or the change could be random. The walls may change colors, or the floors, or the lighting in the room. This can be combined with sound so that by singing different notes the colors of the furniture will change. Everything depends on the imagination of the creator and of course the limits of what the senses can handle. Too much change overwhelms the senses.

It is the woman of the household who usually experiments with new furniture designs, colors, and the whole field of interior decorating. However, each member of a family usually has one or more rooms of his own where he does the decorating. Where we on Earth spend the day cleaning house, the homemaker on Venus may create an entirely new set of furniture in an afternoon. Rapid change is a way of life.

Life is not quite so easy as it may seem. A great deal of training and responsibility must go with the manifesting of things. The laws of balance and harmony must be obeyed, just as they are on the physical plane. In creating something, we cannot have simply a vague image in mind and get results. If a person thinks of a picture of a chair instead of a full chair, he will get something like a flat cut-out. And it is not possible to command a chair to appear by saying, "chair."

In the beginning of astral life, creating things is not easy. Even though children are given much freedom at home, they need to learn to properly use a thought form. They do not have the same attention level as adults. In their curiosity they tend to jump from one thing to another. So it is not at a very early age that they begin manifesting all sorts of things. Their first toys and clothes are created for them by their parents.

At first they are underdeveloped on the astral. Children need to get used to life there, and they need to go through adjustments just as children on the physical planets do. Children on Venus are trained by their parents to control their vivid imaginations with the power of concentrated attention.

In being able to manifest things from energy we have eliminated only the manufacturing step of creation. Designing is the main challenge for any individual, especially for a child who is learning the techniques of individual manifesting.

At first the designs are incomplete and unbalanced, or are not harmonious with their surroundings. A child must learn to visualize in the mind a complete picture in all the dimensions with exact measurements, textures, colors and design to the finest detail. If one leg of a chair is missing in the mental image, the real chair will be manifested with one leg missing. If the measurements are off in the visualization, then the real chair will be distorted and unbalanced in the same way.

The colors, materials, and shape will have to balance out and agree with the theme of the room. Careless creating results in a pile of junk.

Venus (astral plane) is not a chaotic place as of the power of thought. Everything is solid and stays as it is until the individual changes it. Had my aunt and uncle left Teutonia for a few years, the house would have remained as it was. No one interferes with another's creations. And matter, once created, cannot be easily dissolved. It can be redesigned, so the people are careful not to manifest a pile of junk. Once a certain room is created, it will stay as it is until someone changes it. Sitting on the orange sofa will always give off the scent of roses until its creator decides to change it.

Eventually, after a great deal of experimenting, a family will settle with a home and furnishings that are pleasing, a style or mood that is just right for them. Once my aunt and uncle had found what they really wanted our house did not change from day to day.

People live securely within their lives of continuous change because they are accustomed to it and are in complete control.

On Venus, each learns a variety of crafts and creative activities. People take great pains to do things by craft instead of simply materializing results, because it is more fulfilling, meaningful and personal to do so.

With life-spans that stretch into thousands of years there is plenty of time to learn and master a number of arts and crafts. We realize that life could become mundane and boring if we just snapped our fingers to fulfill all our desires. There would be less to look forward to in the way of challenge and achievement.

On the astral it is possible to master talents such as playing a flute simply by willing it, but on Venus this is looked upon as laziness and shunned. We strive to develop our talents through effort and practice as people on the physical plane must do. With the exception of constructing homes, we try to do as much by hand as possible. One having little talent or interest in building furniture from basic materials would probably manifest it. Someone unskilled in the art of painting and not interested in learning that art at that time may at first manifest paintings to decorate his home. Everyone develops his talents in many areas, but only those of his own choice.

Art is so much a part of people's lives that each home is filled with art forms that stimulate arid inspire, and reflect that family's individuality, tastes and loves.

A woodcarver's home would be decorated with handmade carvings. A weaver's home may have textiles of his own creation decorating walls, furniture, etc.

Not only are talents in the various arts developed and refined over many years, but they are carried over from lifetime to lifetime. Being born with a strong talent and then devoting an entire lifetime to it usually means that in previous lifetimes, Soul had already been involved in that art. My own interests in dancing did not begin in this life, rather many centuries ago when I was a dancer in ancient Egypt.

Sculpting is another popular art. A few of the homes in our neighborhood had entire rooms that were sculptured. These were an adventure because the tables, chairs and even shelves on the wall were all molded of the same piece of material as the walls and ceiling.

Music is one of the most beautiful ways of expressing your creative nature. Most Venusians learn to compose their own music and play musical instruments because of the sense of personal fulfillment and joy. We can sing or create a piece of music that expresses our feelings more beautifully and completely that by speaking and by writing. The feeling element in our music is most important. Simple beautiful sounds convey much feeling.

I know of nobody in Teutonia who did not play at least one musical instrument. Most studied and mastered a number of different instruments.

Many of our musical instruments are much like the ones here on Earth. The reason being that all instruments now used in the physical universe were first created on the astral plane and stored in the Astral Museum for searching minds to discover. Flutes, violins, and harps are among the most popular on Venus, as well as our version of keyboard instruments. We also have various instruments that copy the sounds of nature, such as wind, running water, the rush of the sea, etc.

Percussion instruments are rarely used in our music, although once in a while there is a drumbeat or a clash of the cymbal. Harsh sounding brass instruments are not popular either. The dense vibrations of these and the percussion instruments are more suited to the denser physical plane or the lower astral.

Our music is flowing and inspiring, very unlike your popular rock and roll on Earth. Our higher form of music may seem foreign to Earth ears, but more beautiful than he has ever heard. The heavy beat of Earth's modern music (in the western world) gives spiritual indigestion and stirs the lower centers of man instead of the higher but this does not mean it is to be condemned, because many different kinds of music are needed in the world to accommodate the different levels of individuals. It all serves its purpose.

Most of our music is a personal experience enjoyed at home. However we do have a few orchestras assembled by artists who have devoted their lives to music. We have an orchestra for which Venus is famous, the Chelli Orchestra in the City of Retz.

Dancing (and singing) is ingrained into our culture as much as our planetary language. Everyone in a Venusian family learns to dance and throughout life enjoys expressing feelings in a way no other art form can.

Venusian dancing can best be compared to what on Earth is called interpretive dancing. Remember that the astral plane is the plane of emotions, which suggests that we are very much involved in expressing our feelings. Our dancing gives us this creative release.

On Earth, acting may seem to be just another form of art, but on Venus it is much more. Each one realizes that every day he acts out the drama of life in the lower worlds. This is true on every planet, although without the viewpoint of Soul the act is confused with reality. Most of Earth's people are so involved in their daily lives that they never have a chance to stand back and view everything objectively, as Soul.

Acting is what children do most of the day, using the imagination to be something different or to make up stories. It is a very important part of childhood and also of life itself because acting develops imagination and creativity. A person who cannot act cannot really live. We as human beings are constantly entertaining others or doing things to attract attention, all of which is acting.

As a child I played the acting game of looking into the mirror every morning and deciding what kind of a person I would be that day. What kind of a personality I would have. Then during the day I would be that kind of person. Adults play at this game too because boredom is a very real threat for people on the astral plane. Having all the material possessions imaginable does not guarantee happiness. By pretending to be something we have always wanted to be, we can actually have that experience. Many Venusians play games to make life more interesting.

It is not easy to understand life on Venus as a whole by looking at the parts. Our people do not lead fragmented lives. Each person is an individual and, depending on his personality, tastes, and past lives will be attracted to various creative pursuits. His whole life may be devoted to painting, and designing new musical instruments, though he may also be adept at writing, sculpting, and woodworking. Another person may be fascinated with physics and sciences, as well as playing the flute.

No matter how interested in his favorite art or science one may be, there is no end to what can be learned. He could spend a whole lifetime studying plants and never reach a point of knowing all there is to know.

As an example, for years and decades people of Earth have studied plants, yet they are just now discovering that plants have feelings and respond to emotions. This is a great discovery here, though it has been known on other planets for a long time, because we recognize that a Soul inhabits these plant bodies as we once did.

No matter what planet or plane you live on, there is always something new to be learned. Throughout eternity, even though you may live in the physical world again, there is work to be done and there are problems to be solved. Even the highest Being, in the highest state of consciousness, is still learning. Just because the afterlife is a mystery to many people on Earth does not mean that death is the end of everything. It is a shift of scenery, a new beginning on another level. The Supreme Deity itself has new experiences every day through all forms of life.

The sciences are as much a part of our life as are the arts. We continuously study the Universe, nature, how it works, and how we can work with it. Every day we try to work more with nature instead of against it to keep from depleting any part of it and thus creating an imbalance. It may be difficult to live this way, and take much effort and time, especially for people on physical planets, but we know that if we love nature it will love us in return.

Helping people of the physical world is a goal that many of us share. Not only do we personally work out karma in this way but we also have the satisfaction of helping people in need, especially those of planets like Earth.

Scientists who die on Earth and other physical planets often continue their work on a higher plane to benefit all mankind. It is not unusual for their talents and knowledge to carry over through many lifetimes.

Those of us who plan to lower our vibrations into the physical world and live on Earth, often learn useful occupations. Quite a few of the Venusians living on your Earth today have come from the astral plane, where they acquired vast knowledge. Astral scientists frequently have no other choice but to continue their work in the physical plane. They must work with physical laws under physical conditions after a certain point, as my uncle discovered. A device that works well under the power of thought must be designed to function physically once it becomes physical, and this involves experiments in the physical world.*

Fortunately we have kept our culture intact in every way. It would have been easy to rely on the astral powers of creating everything by thought instead of developing our physical talents. Then our culture might suffer for we know that one day, at the end of our Iron Age, our life would return to the physical density. By preserving our faculties intact we may be able to continue our life in physical density without succumbing to the elements.

Venusians are very gregarious and they gather for many occasions. Music, dancing, and singing are so important to every party. The entertaining is shared by everyone, because everyone is talented in some way. Guests bring their own instruments and share a new musical creation, or they may act out a past life, or read new poetry that they have written. Here the rich culture of the Venusians is brought out in a festival of creativity and sharing, through which a real community, a real understanding among people, real relationships develop quite naturally.

---

* Odin accepted densification to physical to work, from physical density, along with Omnec's father at astral density, on a project to learn to teleport physical beings from place to place without using sending and receiving stations and equipment.

Among party games enjoyed was one that only people who live on planes above the physical can play. In a way it is like a masquerade, but instead of the guests just wearing costumes and masks, they actually change their body form and appearance. We use the power of thought to change the astral body but keep the same personality, mind, and Soul — the same inner qualities and identity. The host and hostess would then have the delightful job of guessing who the guests really were as they came to the party. The challenge in keeping their identity secret was not so much in manifesting an unusual body form as in disguising the vibrations. Every individual has a certain expression, a certain look in the eyes that is always the same from lifetime to lifetime, no matter what the body looks like. Then there are the peculiar personal movements — the way one sits, or holds his head or uses his hands, or smiles. All of these are clues to successful identification, and one's success was a matter of being aware of the inner qualities of his friends, beyond outer appearances.

Along with the colorful costumes familiar-looking animals showed up at parties too. Perhaps a bright pink cat or a shaggy purple hound, or an orange pony with a blue tail. These were not really animals of course, but those of us who had chosen such a disguise. As a child and an admirer of butterflies, I often flew to parties as one.

The experience of having a plant or animal body yet being a human taught me that our human bodies are the more perfect vehicles for Soul living in the human state of consciousness. Having a butterfly body was fine for a while but it had too many limitations.

Although less restricted than the physical, Venus is far from being a utopia or the best world that Soul can imagine. Our study of the Laws of The Supreme Deity is so very important because we too are growing just as any other Souls in any of the denser worlds. We too have problems to solve and lessons to learn, and we too are striving for higher awareness.

Because we can have all the material things we desire, our lessons and problems are different on the astral plane. In the Physical, emotions are mixed in with the material problems like earning a living, being ill, and living up to all the physical responsibilities. Here physical problems for the most part override purely emotional problems, while in the astral we are released to experience and deal with our emotions more fully.

Venusians must put a great deal of effort into keeping an emotional balance. An unbalanced emotional state can be damaging to Soul. We find that emotional problems have a tendency to be much more overpowering here.

Attachment is very dangerous on any plane for it keeps Soul from having freedom. We need to be careful because it is very easy to become attached to family, to others, to ritual and a way of life.

A good discipline is to try to like the things we dislike, because every dislike has a reason, usually emotional. As Soul we try to be aware of things that are not Soul, such as attitudes and assumptions. We also try to discipline ourselves not to do everything at once, to not be in a hurry, and to live life to its fullest in a balanced way. We are thankful for what we have and what we are at every moment. Because we live such a very long tine, it is important to pace all of life's possible experiences. It is very easy to get carried away because a person can have everything he wants just by using the power of thought. Often we must put our desires behind us because if all our experiences come in a few years we might well be bored for centuries.

One of our people's greatest problems is love attachments. My father was one who never recovered from his grief over my mother's passing. It is one problem that can seriously unbalance a Venusian and stall his spiritual growth. Emotional feelings can avalanche on him before he is aware of what is happening. Emotional balance is crucial. A Soul can create karma on the astral plane just as well as on the physical or any other of the denser worlds.

For many, the astral plane is heaven when the physical body dies. Life as it is on Venus should give you some insight into life in your astral after leaving your physical. It can be very beautiful, but like life on any of the lower planes it is limited.

Chapter Eight
Earthward Bound

1. Another trip to Retz
2. My choice
3. Vonic trains me
4. My last day on Venus
5. Lowering the vibrations
6. A different Retz
7. Denser body limitations
8. On to the mother-ship
9. On the mother-ship
10. Our trip to Earth

Our trip to Retz was faster this time because we had been summoned by the Master. My uncle and I stepped into the bubble-car and seated ourselves. Within moments we appeared just outside the gates of Retz. Briskly we walked to the Temple of Golden Wisdom, and bearing our gifts, entered to greet the Master, Kanjuri.

Kanjuri was an older, beardless man with remarkably white, almost silver-white long, flowing hair. As he stood before us I sensed how ancient and yet how young Kanjuri was. It is a paradox I cannot explain. His deep green, flashing eyes spoke of endless wisdom and compassion. Like any true Master, Kanjuri was a beautiful Soul surrounded by an air of serene silence

We presented our gifts, a plant for the Temple and fruit for the Master. Together we seated ourselves on cushions and chanted aloud the word amaul, the Tythanian word for love. The room suddenly glowed with a warm pink light and Kanjuri began to speak.

"I've called you here for Omnec to be able to make a choice." he said. Omnec Onec is my Venusian name, using English letters to spell the Venusian sounds. The name means "Spiritual Rebound." Kanjuri went on to say that a little girl was living on Earth with whom I had formerly shared a past life during the time of the French Revolution. We were sisters during those turbulent years, very close to each other.

I had been involved in acts of treason and my life was in danger, when my sister stepped forward to take the blame. Out of her love for me, and because she felt it important that I continue my work. She was beheaded in my place. Kanjuri explained that she was now a little girl living in the United States and suffering a great deal within her family. Her mother was taking care of her as best she could, but both she and her husband were caught up in drinking and fighting.

At the age of seven, this little girl, Sheila, was to be sent to her grandmother in Chattanooga, Tennessee as a protection from the trouble and fighting at home. Now looking into the future, the Master had seen Sheila being killed in a bus accident enroute, on the outskirts of Little Rock, Arkansas.

Since I was an older Soul and at this time had less ties on Venus, I had a special choice. I could lower my vibrations into the physical and go to Earth to balance out my Karma in this lifetime. After the accident had occurred, her body could be taken care of and I could go on in her place. Then I would live in her family as Sheila instead of Omnec Onec, and, in doing this, work off some of my own karma and hers, therefore balancing cause and effect relations a number of different ways.

Instead of being reborn on Earth I was being offered the unusual opportunity of having my Venusian body densified to the Earth physical plane. I would retain my consciousness awareness and memory as a strong background to help me through the trials I would face. My Karma would be difficult for me to understand or cope with if I were just born on Earth without knowing the truth of the higher planes.

By going to Earth now, the Master explained, the conditions were such that I could work off my Karma with less anguish, and may never have to come into the physical plane of Earth again. In addition, I was destined to a spiritual work on Earth, and a plan. It had to do with opening the people's minds about the Brotherhood of the Planets. The details would be revealed during my life on Earth.

This was a great shock to me, and of course frightening. I had not realized that I would be leaving so soon and I had never heard of any of our people leaving as children. Adults who have physical Karma often do lower their vibrations to leave the astral and live on Earth. This had been mentioned by Masters during the Seminars in Retz.

At the same time it was all very exciting. I did not know much about Earth in this lifetime. I had only heard about it as many people in America hear about Asia or some remote part of the world. The suffering other people go through does not reach you and does not mean as much as it should if you are removed from it. Being a child and filled with the spirit of adventure, I felt that my living on Earth would be exciting. So I said to Kanjuri that I would make up my mind and let him know.

Kanjuri assured me that if I decided to leave Venus I would be given all the necessary knowledge, and all the preparations would be made. I would learn about the girl's family and be taught the American English, the language they used. And before I left I would be briefed on the people of Earth, their consciousness, their culture and technology, especially what I could expect to experience in the southern United States.

On strategic occasions I was promised the help, the mental guidance of my people through Odin or someone close to me. With that final word of encouragement Kanjuri concluded, adding that I had several days to consider the prospect.

Without hesitation I said that my decision had already been made. I would leave Venus to spend the rest of my days on planet Earth. Kanjuri remained silent for a moment as my aunt began to speak. She reminded me that I was not compelled to go if I did not feel that it was right. I understood that, I told her, but I felt the decision was one of Karma, that I was destined to leave Venus rather than having a choice about it.

I understood that in the physical world I was to be a child of seven years. My astral body when I would leave Venus would look like a seven-year-old girl, and yet my consciousness upon becoming physical would be more advanced because I had been born on the astral plane and inherited the culture and teachings of Venus.

My first inner vision of Sheila was very revealing. I favored her a great deal partly because of our Karmic ties. Physically we looked very much alike, which gave me all the more reason to believe it was all planned, that it was Karma. I accepted this as my karma and I had a strong desire to work it off and be finished with these obligations.

I also felt it was necessary for Sheila to be released from the physical world. She had suffered enough. My decision to leave was more of an intuition than anything else, and the inner prompting I felt makes me realize now that my choice to come to Earth was itself Karmically determined.

Kanjuni repeated his promise that the training program would begin. Someone would call on me within a few days. We thanked the Master, and he told me I had made a very wise decision. In my life on Earth I might not find the spiritual teachings of Venus until much later, and I was not to talk about these teachings because people would not understand. When the time was right they would be openly revealed in America, but I was not to seek them. They would come to me. And I will find a surprise with these teachings. With a smile the Master fell silent. We said goodbye and left.

At home I wanted to be by myself thinking about the consequences of my decision. I reconsidered more than once, yet I felt ever more strongly that it wasn't mine to be made, that it was destiny. I was thinking about my upcoming journey in a childish way, as being an adventure with many unknowns.

True to Kanjuri's word, several days later a Master appeared at our door, a very unusual person for people on Venus. With his dark brown eyes and long black hair falling to his shoulders, he was striking in our society where most people are blond.

Vonic was his name. He said that he had come to teach me about Sheila, her family, about English, and how people's attitudes differed on Earth. We sat down for the first of many long conversations.

Vonic had been chosen as my teacher because of his patience. Throughout my life and many lifetimes, I was known to be impulsive, to jump into things abruptly without thinking. I was given to interruptions with completely unrelated thoughts that just happened to pop into my mind. This discouraged a lot of people, but not Vonic, who was very nice about it. He was very quiet, only told me the facts, listened to what I had to say, and did not give any point of view or criticism.

In those next few weeks Vonic covered just about everything I needed to know. Never before had I done so much memorizing at once, but it was necessary for me to learn quickly. Fortunately I was gifted with a good memory and was not encumbered with a physical mind.

Vonic briefed me on Sheila's personal history and her family's, so that I would be familiar with their personalities and their way of life. I learned as much about Sheila's grandmother and mother as a seven-year-old child would be expected to know. I needed to learn the description of each relative so that I would be able to recognize them and speak with them in the right way when I met them.

Vonic also familiarized me with the southern people's customs and consciousness. We went into some detail on the living conditions as well, the kind of poverty I would be exposed to. "In the physical world," Vonic said, "people are often deprived of basic physical needs, unlike the astral plane where our thoughts instantly create whatever we desire."

All of this training took a great deal of time, day after day of getting together, going over these facts, and me pretending I was Sheila. Vonic and I worked wherever the mood of the occasion took us — around the sunken fireplace, in my room, upstairs, in the garden, or on the golden beach. I practiced talking and acting like Sheila, and Vonic would ask questions about her family that I had to answer properly. It was very important, he said, to think of myself as being Sheila rather than just acting the part.

This went on until I learned about her mother's childhood, her real father, the marriage situations that produced all her cousins, and the kind of person her stepfather was. I memorized the illnesses Sheila had had, the many places she had lived, and the hardships she was going through up to the time of the bus accident. Most of Sheila's own experiences, what her mother had told her, and what she had learned on her own were covered in my talks with Vonic.

I never asked Vonic how he learned all of the very personal information about Sheila's family, but I am sure that one of our people living on Earth had become friends with them.

Vonic made a special point of mentioning what would be expected of me, and what I could not do, such as using the psychic and spiritual powers I had developed. People generally would not understand, and they might became frightened enough to accuse me of Satanism or black magic. I was certainly not to tell anyone of my true origin until the time was right, which would not be until I was older.

Vonic taught me about the different religions of Earth, how most of them were merely social gatherings instead of true spiritual teachings. I learned about the many different concepts of God, and the concept of the negative power as a mythical being called Satan.

I was not to expect the freedom allowed in Venusian society, or be very disappointed by limitations in every area of my life. The schools I would be attending, Vonic explained, would not be as advanced in their teaching methods or in what they taught, so I had to be careful not to show that I knew so much. I was to pretend that I was learning and not be discouraged. The educators on Earth, Vonic said, did the best according to what they knew and according to the limitations of the conditions on Earth.

I had to remember that there was no turning back once I had arrived. It would cause a great deal of trouble for everyone. I would not be paying my Karmic debt and I would be creating more Karma on top of that. In times of great anguish I was not to try escaping by saying, "I'm not really Sheila and I won't put up with this!"

I was paying back a debt that Sheila had suffered for me long ago, and I was suffering for her in return. Often I was reminded by Vonic that there were many hardships ahead, but he never went into greater detail. The only promise made to me was that they would keep in mental contact with me but that they could not change any of the future events.

As I look back now, I realize that Vonic did a thorough job of preparing me for life on Earth. That is, I had more than enough knowledge to comfortably become a part of an Earth family. Vonic and I became very good friends.

During my training period the anniversary of my birth arrived. Unknown to me, Arena and Odin had made a plan for a special experience for me, a journey into other levels of the astral plane. They had mentioned only that there would be a party to celebrate my birth.

In the morning on that special day my aunt and I visited friends who lived not far from our house. When we came home Rimj and all of my best friends as well as Vonic and my uncle were waiting to help celebrate my birthday. All of the rooms were decorated with flowers and butterflies, the things of nature I most loved to draw. There were paintings and wall hangings, murals and cut-outs, even mobiles and butterflies. Zemura presented me with a dress having the print of a butterfly, to go along with the theme of my party.

After dinner we sang songs and danced and played music and games, but the best was yet to come.

Aunt Arena took me aside to spring the great news. That evening our family and friends would go on a journey through the astral plane! In order for us to keep the same level of consciousness, and somebody not get misplaced or hung-up somewhere, we would all be under the supervision of the pilot, Uncle Odin.*

A joyous feeling of anticipation filled the air as we climbed aboard the bubble car. I knew that one of the most memorable experiences of my life was ahead. It would be my first adventure beyond the surface of Venus and my first journey through the vast world which is known to many of Earth's people as Heaven.

As our ship took off and the city of Teutonia became smaller and smaller below us, I saw the first of many breathtaking spectacles. Teutonia is shaped much like a giant angelic star with one longer tapering point reaching between the two mountains toward the sea. All around us as we left Venus swirled beautiful color forms of unmanifested

* Although spirits in the astral can travel entirely by thought and need no vehicle to carry them, when a group is traveling some can get misplaced in time or location by a simple variation of thought. For this reason they usually travel together in a thought-form vehicle to arrive together at the same place and time. These vehicles can be elaborate or a very simple transparent bubble, as they choose. For certain reasons or particular requirements, a special form or adaptation may be used, such as what they call the Convoys that carry them on travel to physical densities. These are thought constructed vehicles but have a dense form.

thoughts and emotions. Some were like fireworks, magnificent shooting colors never seen in the physical world.

These were the regions of the astral that had not yet been manifested or created into form — delightful seas of heavenly energy. All of outer space looks like this on the astral plane.

Our first destination was the lower astral plane, the land of nightmares and ugly passions. I do not mean to say that the astral plane has a number of layers through which we traveled up and down. We call the various regions lower, middle, and higher to indicate the inhabitants' level of consciousness awareness, which reflects in the body forms, colors, landscapes, and overall feeling of the area.

A feeling of fearfulness overcame me as we entered the lower astral plane. It was an eerie region with distorted landscapes, twisted trees, giant spider webs, smoking forests, and grotesque creatures. If you can imagine what a haunted forest would look like, then you are probably picking up mentally what already exists somewhere on the lower astral plane.

The Souls who live here are so attached to the passions — anger, greed, lust — that they take on horrible-looking subhuman forms. Some of them are intriguing to see but most are as frightening as the dark murky colors surrounding them.

Here too are homes and communities, but instead of devoting themselves to creativity and the arts, these people spend their days indulging in their favorite passions. A glutton could be seen day in and day out surrounding himself with tasty foods to delight his senses, and spending little time away from the dining table. Likewise a miser would manifest jewels and gold and precious things until his home left little room for him to live.

The lower astral is where evil Souls spend time between physical lives, temporarily, until they became somewhat detached from their passions. Many of the orthodox religions have in fact created hell regions on the lower astral plane for themselves, which unfortunately have become traps for Souls who believe their stay there is eternal. Hell is as real as the people who want it believe it is.

Returning to the middle astral we flew over many very beautiful civilized areas where different religious groups had established their

Heavenly communities. The people here lived in peace, learning creative talents as we did at our level on Venus, and being very much aware of their return someday to the physical worlds. Many of them had recreated the homes and surroundings of their physical planet. The landscapes and villages we now saw were much more radiant and colorful than their physical counterparts on Mars, Venus, Jupiter, Earth and other planets.

There seemed to be an endless variety of landscapes —painted mountains, craggy mountains, soft rolling hills valleys, meadows, lakes, deserts, and forests. As on Venus, nature was a luminous festival of color. The sights were truly heavenly

As we continued on, my uncle explained as best he could whatever attracted my attention. The higher astral is a much more spiritual region where more highly evolved Souls live. Anyone who has experienced it will agree that it is not easy to describe in physical terms as the colors are more refined and inspiring, and there is a greater feeling of peace, joy, serenity and the spiritual high.

Within Sahasra-dal Kanwal, the capital of this place, was one of the most beautiful regions I had ever seen. It was called Zreph. I can understand why so many religions have their heavenly abodes here. The flowering gardens of Zreph cannot be described in words. They exist for the inhabitants to enjoy. When people arrive here after their physical demise they believe this is the highest achievement in the afterlife, yet it is only the first step on a long and arduous journey.

We did not have time to stop here, or to explore many of the intriguing regions of the astral. Such a tour could very well last several lifetimes in Earth standards of time.

One of the most spectacular sights was below us as Odin told of the Seres race, ancestors of the inhabitants of Sahasra-dal Kanwal. Near the center of this heavenly white city stands a colossal statue, so huge that our bubble-car seemed like a speck in the sky next to it. Seeing it from the air is a breathtaking sight. Looking up from the ground, a person would strain his eyes to see the top.

This giant statue represents the Seres race, which, my uncle explained, were the space people who first colonized planets of this physical plane. Among the giants who settled in what became Atlantis were members of the Seres race. I was hypnotized not only by its beauty but also by its dimensions. The feet of this colossal statue stand far enough apart that on foot it would take days to walk around it. Since this city is as big as Earth's continents, many of its attractions are very spectacular in their sheer size.

A luminous white wall easily as high as the tallest skyscrapers on Earth surrounds the city. In the very center stands the majestic Mountain of Light, powerhouse of this plane. Out of the peak of the Mountain of Light stream thousands of colored lights, and each of these is made of smaller lights. Each light is alive.

It was an utterly breathtaking sight. The sound of the roaring sea filled the air. The lights flowed into the sky and onward to support the physical plane and its many forms of life.

The Mountain of Light is higher than any in the physical universe. As our ship passed directly over it I had to shut my eyes for a moment. Even for the astral eyes the light was so intense as to be painful. Odin explained that this was a very important city to the people of the more advanced planets. It is a cross-over city between the astral and the physical planes and would be very important for me in the future. Here is a place which enables an astral being to manifest a physical body. The people here were beautiful, with faces that spoke of much wisdom. With their flowing tunics and sandals they resembled the ancient Greeks of Earth mythology. Among the inhabitants of this city were stately coworkers of the Creator which we call angels. Like our culture on Venus, every moment of life was spent in creative expression.

My uncle stopped the ship for a last look around, and my last chance to soak up the beauty which I have never forgotten. How can one forget a city that is pure white and glowing, with tints of blue here and there and structures so spectacular you are speechless?

A number of the villages we flew over were enveloped in indescribable melodies, the sounds of each village itself. Zreph was like this also. The music seemed like the tunes of a Xylophone and harp, and occasionally violins.

All through the astral plane was a feeling of spiritual high, of freedom, of peace, and beauty. Imagine worlds where the people live completely confident and at ease with themselves, not seeing each other with eyes of anger and vanity, jealousy and envy. They see each other as Soul, each equally beautiful and competent as sparks of Deity.

I suppose this is why it hurts me at times to look back at my past. It is not easy to talk about my life on Venus because to have a taste of paradise and then live here is very painful. And yet I know the kind of life that awaits me when this short life comes to an end. All the sufferings in the many lives on Earth will seem like a bad dream.

We took a faster route home. All of us were tired. We were not fatigued in any physical sense, but congested with so many beautiful memories. At home I lay back and closed my eyes, letting it all soak deep down into my mind so when a time comes that I am feeling low, I can pull these memories out again.

Having seen the wonders of the astral plane, I began to anticipate my trip to Earth more and more. I thought of it too as an adventure, but at times it seemed very frightening. I had been told that parts of Earth were much like the lower astral plane.

I thought, how wonderful it was that I could go to Earth prepared in this way, prepared to take on whatever Karma I had accumulated, to be able to understand how everything that happened was part of my lessons and experiences, to not get caught up in them and let them overpower me, to realize that there is something greater than the restricted physical life, because I had consciously seen it and experienced it in my own lifetime. To know that these beautiful worlds exist for all and not just for a few, and that someday I would live to tell this story to others and give them hope.

Next morning I thanked my aunt and uncle for one of the most wonderful experiences of my life. I would be leaving in about two days and once again see that great white city with the towering walls, only this time we would lower our vibrations and appear on the physical Venus.

From Aunt Arena I received permission to take along the ring and the gift of jewelry. My uncle's gift to me was from the physical level of Venus and would be given later. Jewelry I could easily hide or explain away, but not something as unusual as a Venusian dress, or sandals, or anything reflecting our culture. In not taking along unusual things I would not need to become untruthful to protect myself. I had to be careful to be truthful, they told me, because if I was known as an untruthful child then my story later would not be taken for real.

Most of my preparation for leaving was an inner preparation of getting my thoughts in order. My aunt helped by giving pep talks once in a while. She loved me very much and was sad to see me go, she said, and if I wished to change my mind I could.

Again I was reminded of the bitter times ahead and how I would need strength to hold up and not think I had been abandoned. They could not interfere in my own Karma, however, no matter how much it hurt them to see me suffer. They would watch at all times via the inner sense, and send advice, then when the right time came the Laws of the Supreme Deity (laws of nature) would be taught openly on Earth. I would meet someone that I knew, and I might have an opportunity to tell my story to the world. Until then I would have to be secretive because of the nature of Earth people's attitudes.

They explained that those attitudes were based on the limited surroundings or environment, and the practice of teaching children to be duplicates of the adults rather than individuals.

I would fall into a lot of traps and be taken to different religious paths, but I was not to become too involved.

I remember well my last day on Venus. In the morning my aunt brought to my room the dress I would be wearing on Earth, the same dress little Sheila would be wearing on the day of the bus accident. Arena had manifested it for me, keeping in mind the directions the Master had given her. I put it on and tucked away a duplicate of the note of explanation Sheila's mother had written and Sheila would be taking along to her grandmother in Tennessee. I also wore white socks and black patent leather shoes with buckles. These were very strange. I had never before had my foot completely enclosed.

As I remember, Aunt Arena asked if I wanted to join her to tell my friends that I would be leaving shortly. I would rather stay behind and be alone for awhile, I told her. She nodded and left. I stood in the arched doorway watching her graceful body as she walked away down the softly sloping front path.

Going off to the left and right were many little footpaths of stone winding among the flowering bushes and trees. Two blue trees with blue trunk and leaves formed the front gate. They resembled Earth pines.

Turning around, I found myself facing our shoulder-high wrought metal fence looking so much like white lacy walls. I plucked one of the white flowers and I sniffed it, enjoying its sweet smell and the shiny green leaves.

I walked toward the center of our living room, toward the fireplace where we had so often shared our experiences together during Study Time. It was a huge room. Here and there were floating sofas of various sorts and colors. I looked at the crystal clear walls curving up toward the ceiling. I had always taken for granted the beauty of these walls being transparent, showing us the colorful surroundings and the garden.

I stopped in front of my favorite painting, a very large painting hanging on the wall by no visible means of support. It was made of constantly swirling colors, each color having its own sound and each sound changing as the colors did, as they swirled around. I never grew tired of watching and listening to this painting. It was never inharmonious in any way, always creating a new intriguing melody. Such works of art were popular on Venus.

As I listened to the sweet music of our indoor waterfall, I envisioned my father's face as I had done so many times throughout my childhood. I remembered his face as I had seen it shortly after I was born, his beautiful face which I stamped into my memory knowing inwardly I would never see him again. I always did this when I closed my eyes, burning his image deeper into my mind as if it would bring him to me.

I remember now his broad square jaw, high cheekbones, and very intense almost navy blue eyes with whitish blond arched brows. Father's nose was long and straight with flaring nostrils. His wide full-lipped mouth was a deep red, and his golden blond hair parted on the side and combed to the left rather than being parted in the middle as most men wore their hair. It was shoulder length and fell gently in a wave at his left eye. I remember his smile so gentle and sweet. On the day I was born I saw in his brief gaze the love he had for me. Yes, I remember well my father's face, the deep cleft in his chin, and the dimple when he smiled.

I opened my eyes and slowly got up. I walked around the fireplace and passed the couch, feeling its softness with my fingers as I passed by.

At the waterfall I sat down on a tiny retaining wall surrounding the pool. The top was inlaid with small tiles of mother-of-pearl bordered in gold. Several gold and blue various colored fish flitted around in the water. As I held my fingers out to catch some of the falling water, I noted that it changed the tunes that the waterfall made. I closed my eyes to listen. It always sounded like a harp with water pouring through, if you can imagine such a sound.

All this time I had felt something welling up inside, some emotion I was unused to, some strange feeling that I had almost felt the day I thought I was being punished. I did not know what this feeling was; this sadness was beginning to choke me.

I looked to the left and saw my aunt's great circular herb garden with its hundreds of different interesting herbs. She had explained them all to me, all of their medicinal uses and the mystical folklore surrounding them through the centuries. As I stood there I relived these moments with her.

Ahead at a distance I saw the beautiful fan tree that I loved so much, that I pretended to be a bird in and climbed and played under.. this beautiful tree with its trunk spreading out and vines hanging down making it look so much like an oriental fan.

I listened to the birds singing, and I glanced at my swing swaying to the breeze in mid-air. Its lacy design made interesting shadows on the grassy ground. I walked over and flung myself face down in the swing to watch the little insects crawling around, insects that I myself had created. There really are not any pests or insects on the astral plane, except those which the people manifest. Some of them I thought were cute, and whenever I had enough information I would manifest them for our garden.

I glanced up at the pinkish-orange sky and its colorful clouds. Then I took the footpath back to the house and stood in the doorway. Facing the garden once again and shutting my eyes I tried to burn it into my memory forever.

I turned and walked slowly back into the house, stopping at the door to my room. Going in I sat on my bed, on the covers that looked like flowers and leaves woven together. My baby coverlet, the one that my aunt had made with the animals that changed color, I had made into a pillow. It was one of many colorful pillows, most of which I had designed and created.

As I sat on my bed, I looked around at this familiar place, up at the ceiling, at the golden ropes encircled by flowers, at the tree with its delicate swing, at the wall of vines and flowers. I walked over to the sunken tub I had made from sea shells and starfish, and ran some water out of the golden fish spigots. There I sat sloshing my feet for a few moments.

Then I looked over at the little wooden table that my uncle had carved and colored to look like a tiny tree. I remembered how much I loved it from the moment he gave it to me. As I glanced again around my room, my room that I had created, that I felt was as much a part of me as my Soul, akin to my Soul, I could feel a warm liquid running from my eyes down my cheeks. This emotional feeling that I had never experienced before was welling up inside me.

I was crying for the first time in my life, since the day of my birth. I realized that this pent-up feeling was being released as the tears fell. There was a great feeling of satisfaction, of releasing myself of these emotions. I sat quietly and sobbed, watching the tears as they ran down my face and dripped on to my hands. *

I got up, splashed some water on my face, looked again around my room and sighed deeply. "I'll never forget this," I said to myself.

I followed the curved divider back into the living room. The last place for me to see was the dining room above. Slowly I went up the curving marbled jade stair, watching as I went up, seeing the gently arching oriental bridges here and there. Around the railed balcony I walked until I came to one of the little footbridges, crossed over to the dining area and sat down at my favorite carved oak table in the very center. I manifested a cup of herb tea. And as I was sitting, sipping the tea and thinking of how much I loved this place and my aunt and uncle, I heard Aunt Arena call.

The moment she saw my face, as I came down the stair, she realized there had been a change. I went up to her and embraced her. We held

* Sheila wept buckets of tears after coming to Earth and facing the trials of her Karma in this physical density. This manuscript was originally titled "Angels Don't Cry."

each other sobbing quietly. Arena must have been experiencing tears for the first time too. We stood there in silence.

She pushed me back at arm's length and looked into my eyes. I said, "Aunt, you have taught me so much of the beauty of life. You made me understand that my father really loved me. You have taken care of me, and I am sure that you are better to me than you would have been to your own child. I have learned from you a great deal of compassion. You have given me emotional stability which will carry me through my hardships on Earth, as you have explained will come to me there. Through you I have learned to look at things to see their beauty and quality, and to pity those who are not as fortunate as I in their awareness and station in life. I have yet to experience this fully, and I know that I will need a great deal more compassion for others. But through your loving face, which I will hold in my memory forever, and through your beautiful hands, and your words, I have learned a great deal more than most people I know. I am thankful for all this, Aunt Arena, and I will never forget you. You have given me life, and for this I know my mother is eternally grateful."

Just then Uncle Odin walked up. I went to him and I hugged him strongly saying, "I hope you heard everything I said." He nodded. "That goes for you too," I said, "because without you I would not have learned to laugh when things go wrong. I would not have learned my sense of humor. I learned from you to pass things on instead of getting upset, to shrug sadness off, to reap great joy out of the small things in life, to be unaffected by what others would call disaster. Yes I have learned much through you, Uncle —strength, how to keep going when life does not work out right. I have learned to make things useful and to not waste time.

"I am thankful to both of you for these great gifts you have given me, and I am thankful for your sharing your home with me and teaching me the unchanging Laws of the Supreme Deity, and for making me aware of what I really am. You have prepared me for the Karmic burden which I have on Earth. I have nothing to give you except my love. Thank you very much."

We stood together for a few moments in silence. Arena said that many friends were gathering outside to see me off. I walked out our arched front door for the last time to see all the smiling faces —Rimj, Zemura,

Vonic, and many others whose names have been lost in my consciousness now. We never really did go by names. I had created these names for them so that I could remember them separately.

Not much was said out there on the lawn. Each of my friends gave me a special goodbye, where they passed their hands slowly over their heart before clasping my hands and pressing them to their lips. Or they would lean over and kiss me softly on the third eye.

I felt very sad. I hated to leave Rimj. This was not a goodbye, were his last words to me, but he would see me again. My aunt hugged me and said she loved me, that I should remember that her strength was always with me and she had great faith in me. I would do OK on Earth. My uncle said that I would not be doing well in a material way for a while, but that I would be doing well in a material way later in my life there. We all knew that for a time our lives would go in separate directions, but one day in eternity we would see each other again as Soul.

I saw in each of their glances so much love and real warmth that it shall fill me for the rest of my days, as long as I can close my eyes and visualize all this. I knew that whatever I suffer on Earth is worth it if anyone else will be able to experience all these beautiful things. This I remember about my last day there on Venus.

I stepped into the bubble-car with my uncle, embracing my aunt for the last time, feeling her cool lips on my cheek, as I glanced into her beautiful sea green eyes. My uncle would be joining me on the journey to the physical plane in order to be able to finish his scientific work. Another man, who had brought the ship, would also be joining us.

I later learned that Aunt Arena would he leaving the astral plane to join Uncle Odin on the Venus physical (at the level equivalent to our upper etheric in the Earth physical) after he had escorted me to Earth.

As we sped up and away I waved goodbye, looking down at their upturned faces and waving hands. One last time I saw our beautiful home among the flowers and trees. For a moment I wished I had not made the decision. I cupped both hands around my eyes to try to keep that view a few seconds longer.

We sped over the mountains so familiar to me. Off in the distance I could see Teutonia, the great Temples of Learning which had been my home away from home.

I could see the gold sand of the beach where I played and loved to sink my toes, and the sparkling sea that I could always hear in the distance from our house. All of these things I took in for the last time, from the sky as I had never seen and appreciated them before.

As we entered the clouds I pulled myself from the side of the ship, took a deep sigh, and realized all of this was forever gone in this lifetime. I prepared myself for my new life and put my mind to thinking about these things, and about what my uncle would be telling me. The ride to Sahasra-dal Kanwal was swift, and it was near the Mountain of Light that we landed.

I waited outside while my uncle went inside to meet the Master and receive permission for using the special zone. Only the spiritual travelers, their initiates, and those who are at least one thousand years old on the astral plane have the privilege of meeting with this Master. It is easy to understand how people who live such long lives in this city can believe they have reached the ultimate Heaven.

We were escorted on foot to the special zone. I am not allowed to reveal its exact location. Few on Earth know of the existence of such a zone and it is better that it remain secret. Almost anything can be brought down to the physical plane through this zone, such as gold and powerful inventions of the future.

A greedy person could misuse this zone for his own purpose. This is the same zone through which a person travels upward after death of the physical body. Here Karmic debts are weighed and the individual is then placed on the plane he has earned in a spiritual sense.

Within this zone we entered a special room, a round room with blue lights so bright that I could barely see anything. All of us, my uncle, the other man, and I sat cross-legged on the floor and chanted a secret mantra. Mantras are words which are very powerful instruments on any plane because they have to do with sound current (vibrations), the basic fabric of all creation. On the astral plane we normally chant to raise our vibrations for Soul Travel. Now we were doing just the opposite — lowering our vibrations to manifest a physical body.

For a person who is totally at comfort living in the astral body, manifesting a physical body is a shocking experience. I had the same feeling of distress and discomfort that most people have in leaving the astral plane. The whole experience is not easy to explain.

A few minutes after chanting this secret word with our eyes closed, it happened. The world seemed to cave in all at once. I remember a brilliant white flash and fireworks inside of me, a pssht sound and a ringing in my ears, and a curious jerking motion of my body, as if all my muscles were tensed at once. All of this happened in the same single moment of shock. I felt dizzy and disoriented and could barely breathe, and my whole body felt uncomfortably warm. Then I realized that the shell enveloping me was the physical body!

I opened my eyes. We were sitting in the grass near a small shiny metallic circular vehicle that was shaped like one of your saucers upside down, and had a dome on top. Off in the distance, miles away, was the city of Retz on the physical plane of Venus.

It was frightening, this being inside of a physical body. I continued having trouble breathing because I had never done it before. And instead of the wide vision of my astral eyes, I was looking through two little holes, my new physical eyes. To help you understand how miserable I felt, imagine yourself suddenly being encased in a suit of armor feeling restricted and clumsy, and knowing there is no way out.

When I tried speaking for the first time my voice sounded foreign to me. I told my uncle I didn't like it, this being in a physical body. He laughed. He said that I had to grow accustomed to it. How was I supposed to grow accustomed to something like this, I wondered aloud? Odin replied that a person can get used to anything.

"But you have to turn your head to see!" I protested. I was not accustomed to turning my head in order to see because on the astral plane we have an awareness of what is all around us. We also have an ability to change our form and appearance. Here I was stuck in a body that was unchangeable except for the facial expression.

My uncle agreed that it was limited, that I would have to learn to keep my balance and walk properly. Walking turned out to be most awkward. I was used to gliding or simply appearing wherever I wanted to be. But the physical body did not work that way. It had to be moved inch by inch, step by step. I was the only one having much trouble getting up and stretching my new legs. After all, I was by physical standards only a seven year old child.

The Venus physical (at this upper density) looks much like Earth's Nevada and Arizona. In the distance I was able to see mountains and interesting vegetation. The weather seemed dry and hot but not at all uncomfortable here. Retz was in a secluded valley here just as on the astral plane. My uncle had explained a few days earlier during our journey through the astral, that Retz is a city existing fully on two planes at once. The physical city is the spiritual of the physical planet. The astral city of Retz existed first and the physical city is a duplicate, while in the Great Transition the reverse happened. The people recreated cities on the astral plane as duplicates of the physical cities they had left. Retz is truly unique.

My uncle and the other man and I tested our new limbs. I noticed that Odin had not changed in form, but his body was less radiant. In fact, everything around us lacked the wonderful quality of being luminous.

I was not sure how I myself looked. I would not be seeing a mirror until I landed on Earth, but I surely did feel clumsy and heavy. With my first steps I felt as if I was walking in a suit of lead.

Before we walked toward the ship, my uncle told me about my special gift. My memento of Venus was to be a sample of the plants and flowers that grew nearby in this physical level of Venus. Together we collected about two dozen of the most interesting ones and prepared them for transport to Earth. These together with my ring and jewelry were my only possessions. Taking me by the hand, Uncle Odin led me to the Venusian "Convoy" (the saucer-shaped spacecraft).

This was my first experience with the convoy at times seen in Earth's skies. On Venus alone there are several models of this space ship, all of which run in the same way. Advanced planets have their own versions and there are many sizes and shapes.

The ship I was about to enter looked very much like two saucers fitted together with the bottoms up. A raised glasslike dome on top housed a coil, and just below and all around were snail portholes. The ship had three metallic hemispheres evenly spaced underneath.

The outer surface of the ship was made of a specially treated titanium material so that it can withstand the friction and heat of atmospheric flight. Though it was very shiny and metallic-looking, it was not like the titanium to be seen on Earth. It had the translucent quality of fiberglass.

We entered through a circular opening in the lower half of the craft. This door really amazed me. My uncle showed us how it opened and closed. First a tiny hole appeared in the surface where there was no sign of any door or opening, not even a seam. The opening grew larger and larger much like the shutter in a camera, until it was large enough for a tall Venusian to walk through unimpeded. When it closed, the circular opening became smaller and smaller until it disappeared, leaving no trace of an opening — only a blank surface. My uncle tried to explain to me scientifically how it worked, but I didn't understand. It had something to do with the separation of molecules.

Inside he showed me where to sit. In the very center of the ship was a pole several feet in diameter reaching from the floor to the glass dome above. Surrounding it on the floor was a big lens, through which I was able to see the ground during the flight.

All around the lens, at intervals, were curved cushioned benches for the passengers. Here I sat down with our companion pilot while my uncle took a seat at the control panel, which was opposite the wall where the entrance had appeared and disappeared. Uncle Odin started the ship. There was a low hum.

I imagine my uncle had been trained to run this sort of ship before we left Teutonia as he seemed to know what he was doing. I was not very observant at the time because my attention was on my new body and how uncomfortable it felt. I do remember seeing all kinds of glowing screens on the walls of the circular compartment, with flashing colors, grid patterns, and wavy colored lines appearing and disappearing. The charts, Uncle Odin explained, helped him guide the ship. They depicted the various atmospheric and magnetic conditions around planets and in space.

The control panel looked very simple. My uncle sat in a swiveling bucket seat facing a slanted panel with four buttons and a lever. Above the panel there were two screens. One had what looked like a grid pattern of little squares covered with colored zigzagging flashing lines. Each square was numbered and was a different color.

All of the screens must have in fact been very important. One of the pilots was always watching them very carefully. Another screen facing the pilot showed the actual view of where the ship was heading. This screen was hooked up to a number of tiny lenses located around the rim of the ship. It was not until later that I was told how the ship worked. Uncle Odin explained that, after we landed and went into Retz for a few minutes, we would be boarding and traveling in a larger mother-ship which carried many of these smaller ships during deeper space travel.

The amazing thing about flying on board this craft is that there is not the slightest sensation of movement. In all my flights I have never felt the slightest air turbulence or feeling of acceleration, or of ascending or descending. When this ship makes a 90 degree turn at thousands of miles per hour, the passengers feel as if sitting in a room on the ground. A passenger must look out the portholes or through the viewing lens to see whether the ship is moving.

Until I saw the ground receding below us, I did not know we had taken off. The city of Retz passed below and we landed on the opposite side, near the main gate. Space ships are not allowed within the walls of the city.*

The three of us disembarked and went on foot toward that main gate. Although it was not easy, I did succeed in walking for a short while, while Uncle Odin held my hand. At times he carried me. We were on our way to the Temple of Golden Wisdom to receive the blessings of the Master, one of my favorites.

---

* The convoy described here by Omnec closely agrees with the description and diagram provided by Leonard G. Cramp, M.S.I.A., member of the British Interplanetary Society, as published in his book, "Space, Gravity, and the Flying Saucers". Before I ever heard of Cramp's book, I had already been given a similar detailed sketch of the inside of a similar ship operated by Venusians, by William Clendenen, then a telephone linesman working in Washington State. Bill Clendenen was taken aboard such a ship near Seattle and again in Tennessee. When he asked the occupants how such a ship was powered, he was given a conducted tour of the craft and explanations, which impressed him so much that he spent the rest of his life trying to understand and describe what he saw to scientists in an effort to duplicate it. His story alone would fill another book. To my knowledge, Mr. Cramp never heard of Bill Clendenen nor Clendenen of Cramp at the time the book was published. When I later showed Clendenen Cramp's drawings he said it was near enough to what he had observed to believe that the source of Cramp's information had seen a ship very much like the one he had been on, and been inside.

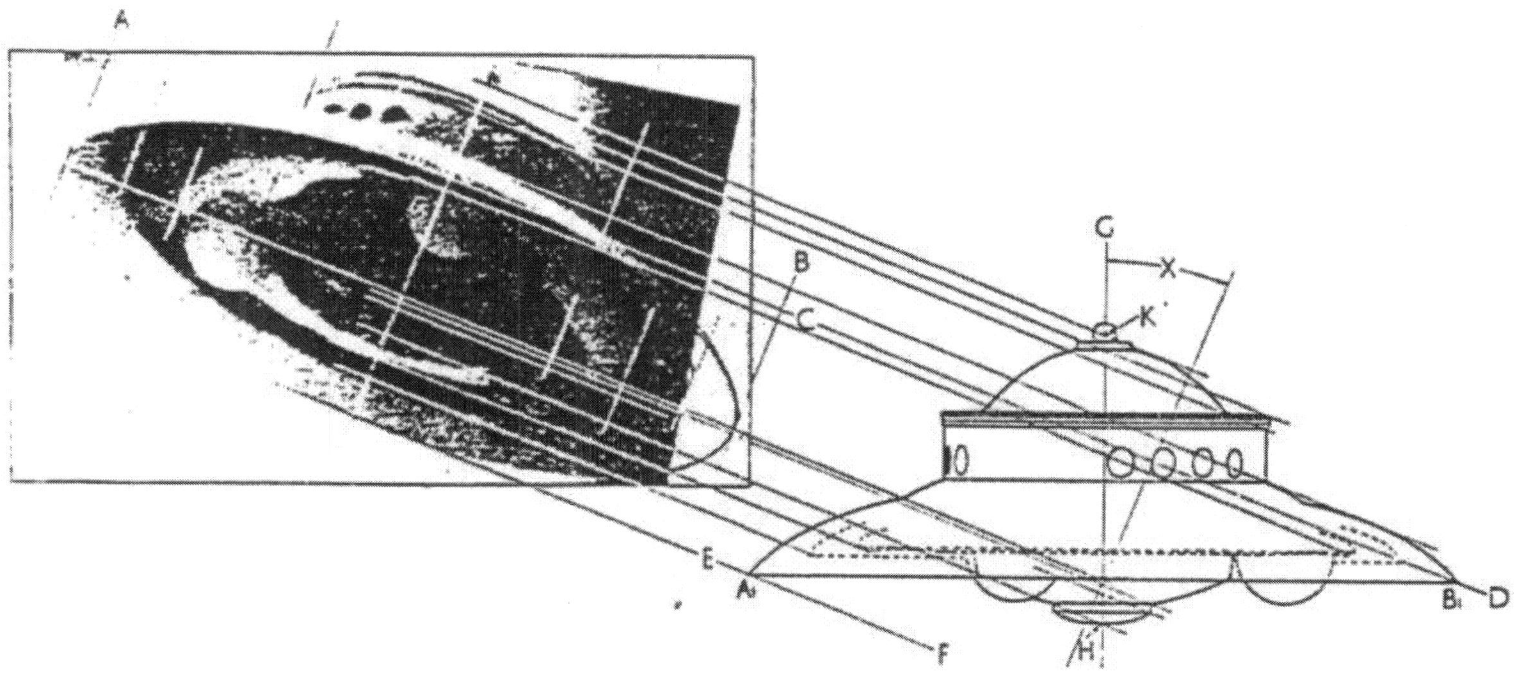

This drawing from Leonard Cramp's book, "Space, Gravity, and the Flying Saucers", was developed by orthographic projection from the photograph of a Venusian ship made by George Adamski on 13 December 1952 at Palomar Gardens, CA, through a telescope.

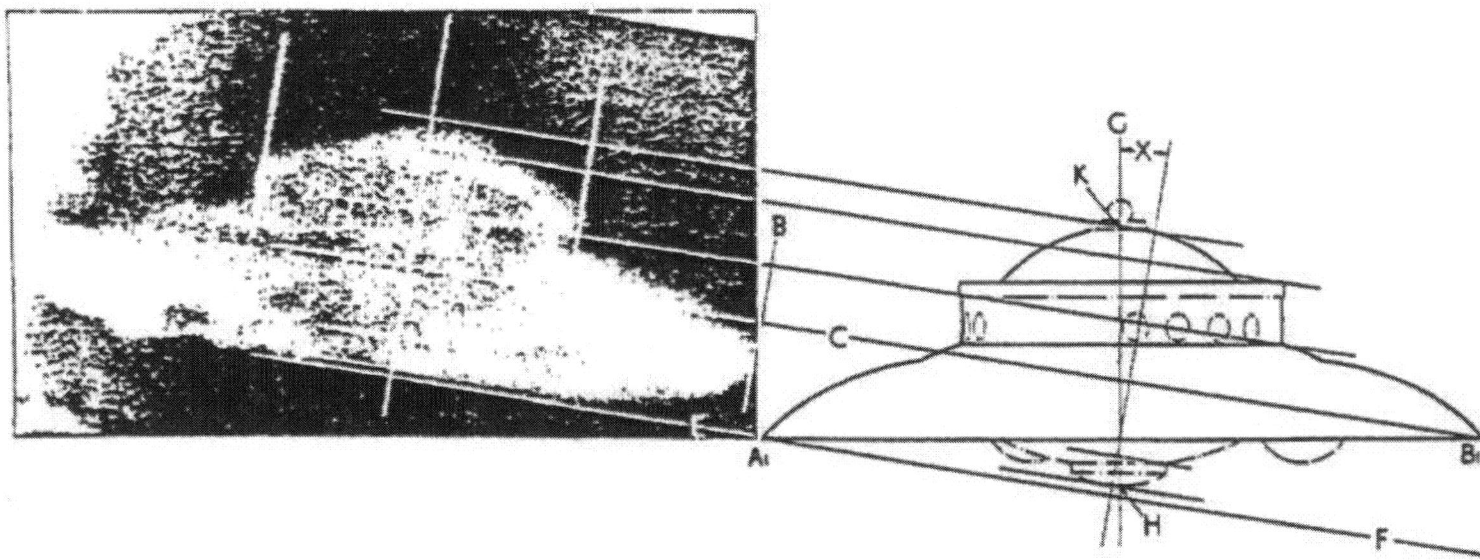

This drawing, also from Leonard Cramp's book, was developed by orthographic projection from the photograph of a strange flying machine made by young Stephen Derbisher and a cousin with a box camera at Coniston Hill, England in 15 February 1954.

Retz on the physical plane was almost identical to the astral city. I noticed this as we passed the gate and walked on. Having been there so often before, I had no desire to explore the city any further under these conditions. I had little desire to do anything.

Retz is heavenly by Earth standards, but compared to the astral city of Retz its beauty is limited. The colors are not clear and bright, the buildings are not luminous and the overall feeling is not the same. I could easily feel the much lower vibrations.

The Master was just as beautiful as ever. I must explain that a Master can very well work with people on a number of different planes. This is one of the reasons he is called a Master. At the temple we spoke to him, and he gave us words of wisdom. I do not remember what he said, perhaps because the message was not for other people to hear.

Aboard the ship once again, my uncle started it up with the familiar hum. Again I would not have known that we had taken off, but soon I could see Retz below us getting smaller and smaller as we shot directly up. After a moment we shot off at an angle through the upper atmosphere of Venus. The sky became darker as we continued on, for it had been close to dusk when we left Retz.

There was little conversation on this trip. I was so busy looking at the features of Venus below us, I hardly noticed as my uncle and his companion exchanged places to do different things.

Odin explained as he sat next to me that this ship was only used for short distances within a planet's atmosphere. Space travel would actually be on board a much larger, cylinder-shaped space ship that could hold up to fifty of these smaller craft. The mother-ship rarely landed and it drew its energy from space itself —not elements mined on the planets. The smaller ships, called convoys, needed to be recharged regularly on the mother-ships.

As I looked around I saw that this craft was very simple in design. In the center was the large circular cabin where we were sitting. Above was a storage compartment for supplies and repair parts. Though our technology is advanced, we do have breakdowns and we do need regular maintenance. We therefore carry special equipment for emergency landings. Usually these small ships carry only a few passengers, but in emergencies a larger number can be safely carried aboard.

There was also a walk-in room much like a pantry off to one side. This was the circuitry room containing fuses and wiring and flashing lights. Little children such as myself were not allowed to go in.

I noticed in both of the pilots a sudden interest in the charts, that something important was about to happen. Then, through the viewing lens, I saw a huge dark shadowy mass below us and off to one side — the mother-ship. Dots of light, the portholes of the ship, were very well visible.

Slowly we floated closer and closer to the blunt nose of the long cylindrical ship. Toward a slot of light we descended until I felt a noticeable jar — the first in the flight aboard this vehicle.

Odin explained that the rails of the mother-ship had caught the rim of our circular craft, upon which we will glide down to the spacecraft bay deep inside. All sensations of dropping ended and the door of the ship opened against a small platform with railings. Then I saw a beautiful woman, whom I recognized as a Martian, and man who looked Saturnian, there to greet us as we stepped out of our ship.

Two attendants attached cables to the ship as the platform elevator took us upward. At the entrance of a long passageway we came to a stop and our two companions took my hands and led the way.

First we came to the ship's lounge, a huge, long room that was very simply decorated and could well seat over a hundred people. Clusters of chairs, couches and tables were arranged here and there. The color scheme was also very simple. One area had blue carpets and yellow furniture of muted colors, while the other end of the lounge had beige and earth-tone colors. The room looked very pretty, very elegant.

The lighting here and in fact all over the ship was the same strange lighting that we had had on the ship. A soft subtle light filled the air as if the air itself was giving off light. There were no light fixtures and no shadows.

Along the walls of the lounge at intervals were perpetually running drinking fountains. I also noticed a portrait of the perfect balance between man and woman, simply called, The Deity, which I understand many ships have. I was told this being is called Elam, Lord of the physical plane.

The drawings on the walls looked so much like photographs that I could not tell the difference. There were scenes of various planets, their cities, and a number of their spaceships. The land and sea panoramas looked much like those which can be seen on Earth, so universal are nature's creations.

There was hardly any clutter in the lounge, and not a single magazine or newspaper. A few sculptures sat here and there, but that was all.

Beyond the lounge we came to the ship's dining room. A long table set with delicious-looking foods waited for us. All but a few seats had already been filled. At the head of this table sat the Master of the ship, not the Captain but the Spiritual Master. Every Venusian mother-ship by custom carries a Master.

On both sides of the table sat men and women in equal numbers. They were from various planets. Although this ship had been built on Venus, it belonged to no single planet. It was shared freely by all members of the Brotherhood of Planets. I recognized people from Saturn, Mars, and Jupiter in addition to Venus. The Master of course (in this case) was Venusian because this was a Venusian enterprise.

No introductions were made as we seated ourselves at the table. Rather than using names we all recognized each other's presence in silence. Our people usually do not even have names, but rather their own unique vibration.

My own name and my uncle's were introduced later, after dinner. They called me Sheila, as I would be known on Earth.

All of the people said a blessing. Then we ate in silence. Whenever a person had something important to say, we would all stop eating and listen out of courtesy. Our dinner began with a salad of raw vegetables and a cheese preparation. As an appetizer I was able to have a piece of my favorite fruit, yunya. We did not have meat. Instead we had a slightly cooked vegetable topped with a melted cheese sauce. The bread was rather strange by Earth standards, dark brown, thin slices with a slightly sweet taste like pancakes. The water we drank was unlike what people of Earth are used to. It had a slightly heavier consistency, like thin oil and was completely tasteless. Such water is common on our planet. All of the food was delicious, even for my delicate new taste buds.

After dinner the Master spoke to us and said that my trip to Earth was unique in the way it was being arranged because I would be arriving as a child with my full conscious memory. One reason was Karmic, but there was also another mission which would be revealed later.

The Master went on to say that later in my life more light would be shed on my real reason for being on Earth (and for coming in this way). My trip was special because I was not going only to fulfill my own personal Karma. He concluded with this thought, "Later in life people will admire her for her courage."

The mother-ship was an interesting place. The crew always seemed to be busy. There was piloting navigation, maintenance and repair, food preparation (now that manifesting was being given up), supplies control, and servicing of the shuttle craft, not to mention the many scientific projects. I learned that two crew members worked each job for two days before being rotated to another job. This meant that everyone was able to work every job on the ship from piloting and navigation to operating the cooking machines.

At the end of every period a general meeting of the ship's crew was held. I was able to watch two sessions, one on the first day after the special dinner and another on the second day just before entering Earth's atmosphere. The trip to Earth lasted about two days.

After dinner I was fitted into a special space-wear which looked very much like a ski-suit. Then I watched and listened as the meeting was held. It was really more of an informal discussion where reports were given and new ideas were shared. Problems were always shared with all of the crew to help generate creative solutions. There were reports of the ship's progress and the latest developments in experiments that the scientists were constantly conducting. *

One of the main reasons for these ships roaming in space is for the sake of learning. A crew of scientists was always on board to study conditions in planets' atmospheres and analyze changes in and on the

* If this sounds a lot like a space shuttle mission, remember that this manuscript was written in 1972, over 10 years before we had a space shuttle.

planets in space. Our people are attracted to space because we do not know everything.

If the scientists learned something new then this was shared with the rest of the crew. And every day the results of tests and experiments were made known — what had been learned and where the continuing problems were.

I did not remember any of the specifics from that meeting because my interest only went so far. I had been given a present of an art kit, and I finished all the coloring with the help of two women crew members.

That evening my uncle mentioned the various things children on Earth can play with because they could not create their toys as on the astral plane. Coloring books and crayons were among them. This was similar and I liked it but was not allowed to take it along with me.

My first experience with sleep came upon me unexpectedly. At first I was not aware of the need for sleep because on the astral plane this was more a resting of the mind. As long as my mind was alert I did not need to rest my astral body. Since manifesting a physical body, my experiences had been so new and strange that I never once thought of sleeping.

I was in the lounge, just sitting and listening to nearby conversation when all of a sudden I felt my head drop, klunk. I jerked awake frightened, not knowing what this all meant. My physical body is behaving very strangely, I thought.

It kept happening over and over again until someone walked up to me. He explained that I had a physical body now, and if I did not take rest then my body would do it on its own. Even if my mind was alert, he said, my body would fall asleep. That was the way it worked. The conscious mind would just completely go. With that I went to sleep.

Next day I had a tour of the mother-ship. First I went to see where the small ships entered on rails and glided down to the hangar area below. Each time that a ship needs to be recharged, a man attaches clamps to the rim and pulls a lever. The red coil then glows for the entire recharging period.

I was also shown the lower level at the opposite end of the ship where the saucers exited through another airlock. The mother-ship had three levels. The bottom level had the actual hangar area where up to fifty shuttles could be stored.

The middle level contained the lounge, dining room, and the two pilot rooms. One pilot room was at each end of the ship. I did not get a look at these rooms because my interest was not there. My escorts explained that they were not much different from a shuttle's control area, only larger in scale and more specialized. The pilot's compartments also had a viewing lens set in the floor, much pure powerful than those in the shuttles.

Almost every room, especially the lounge, offered a clear view of space through the portholes. This is where I eventually had my first glimpse of Earth.

The upper level of the mother-ship was divided into sleeping rooms and storage areas. Each of the rooms was like a motel room with beds that let out of the wall. In daytime they were sitting rooms with desk and chair. Each room also had a fountain and washroom.

Vonic had taught me about sleep and elimination and the other functions of the physical body, but at that time I didn't understand the concepts, having had no physical body in this lifetime.

One of the women on board explained what the toilets were and how to use them. I had wondered aloud on that.

Though each room could sleep two people, a crew member customarily had his own private room with a space view. Every two rooms shared a porthole. There were about 60 rooms in the mother-ship, but not all were occupied.*

---

* Again we must refer to Adamski's often disputed photographs. The disputants are never identified and their arguments are never substantiated by any form of proof whatsoever. Mr. Adamski's pictures of the Venusian cigar-shaped mother-ship launching smaller disc-shaped craft is a good example. Anyone who has seen the original negatives or prints of that series would have to agree that faking those particular pictures would be most difficult, and in fact nobody has been able to duplicate them since. The one, two, up to finally five smaller lens-shaped ships seen emerging from the belly of the mother-ship are actually horizontal formations of spots of light around the rims of darker lens-shaped objects clearly seen in space. Nearly all prints released show these spots of light run together by overexposure of the print, making the smaller ships look like daubes of light without detail, and this is the way they have always been printed. Any "experts" who make other claims should have detected this in their technical analysis. Nobody has ever duplicated even one of these pictures in this series.

Time passed quickly aboard the ship. It was toward the end of the second day that one of the crew members motioned for me to join him at the porthole. There was the Earth, a blue and white ball against the dark background of space!

The blue areas, my friend explained, were oceans. The swirling clouds made strange but pretty patterns over the oceans, I thought. A part of the globe was dark, where night had not yet been transformed into day. So this was the planet where I would soon be living.

The mother-ship entered only so far into Earth's atmosphere. Our convoy was to take us the rest of the way. At the hour of our departure everyone gathered in the lounge to say goodbye. Some gave a handclasp as a farewell and others gave an embrace, depending on their own cultural backgrounds. My uncle and I and our companion pilot walked through the hallway and doors toward the spacecraft bay. Again we stepped onto the platform elevator as two protective railings swung into place behind us.

The same shuttle in which we had arrived was waiting for us. Odin took the controls and I sat down around the viewing lens. In a moment the door closed and I could feel the ship gliding smoothly and silently down the rails to the airlock and hatch below.*

Then I saw the Earth getting larger and larger as we descended and approached the border between night and day. Soon after that a giant range of mountains came into focus. My uncle pushed an inconspicuous button near the viewing lens. One lens slid away as another took its place. We no longer needed such great magnifying power. Our best lens is so powerful that the passengers aboard a craft like this can see people walking down the street while the ship is still so high that it is barely a speck in the sky. A protective cover slides over the lens to protect it from grime when the ship lands.

---

* Once more we may refer to adequate material already produced by others. Though they existed, there is no evidence that Omnec had seen these drawings before she wrote this part of her manuscript. Her descriptions, in fact more detailed, tally in nearly every respect, except the drawings done by Glenn Passmore reveal more external detail not noticed by Omnec. (see diagrams)

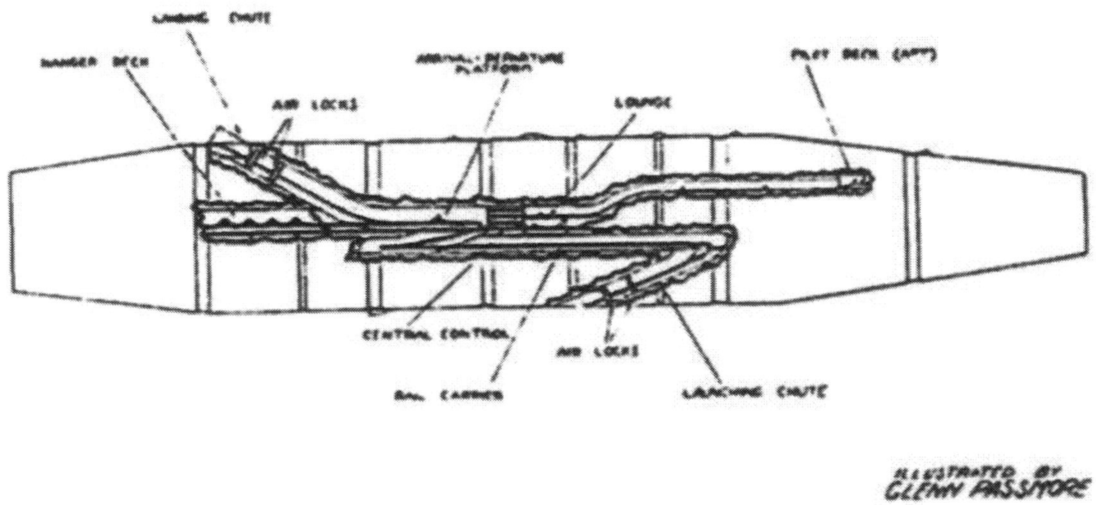

VENUSIAN SPACECRAFT
(MOTHER-SHIP)

This drawing by Glenn Passmore for "Inside The Spaceships" by George Adamski represents Omnec's description of the inside of the mother-ship very well. More and more evidence is coming to light to support those original claims of contacts with Venusian spacemen.

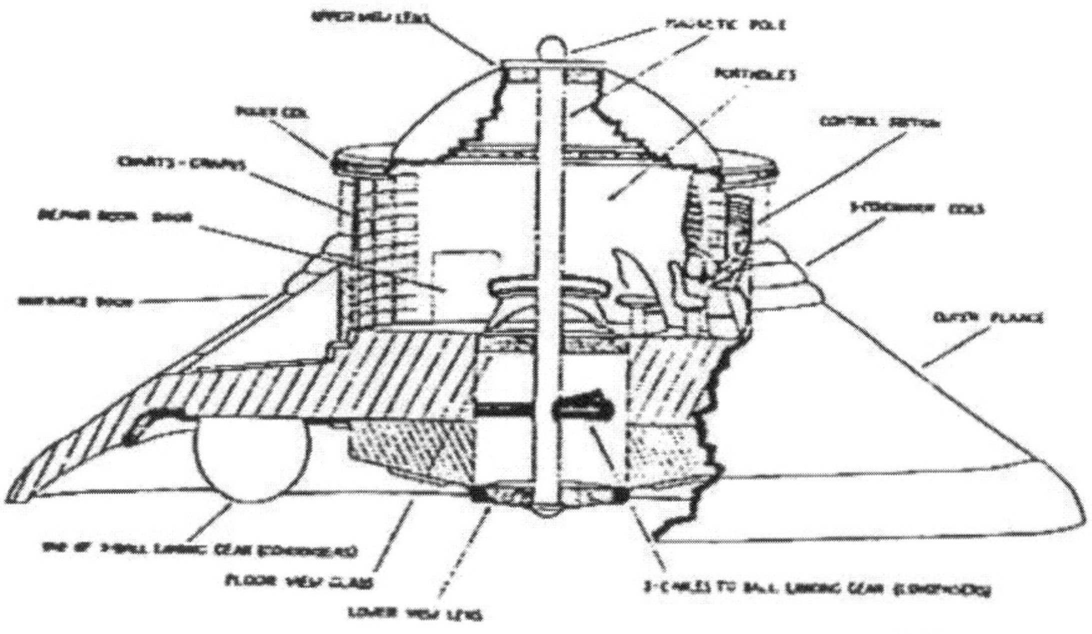

VENUSIAN SCOUT SHIP

ILLUSTRATED BY GLENN PASSMORE

We skimmed the tops of those mountains and the lights of villages in the valleys below flitted past. The country we were entering looked magnificently beautiful. As our ship approached the light side of Earth, I was awed by the huge mountains and lush green valleys. Our destination, my uncle said, was a spiritual city in the Himalayan Mountains known as Agam Des. Most of the space people first arrive at Agam Des to grow accustomed to the lower vibrations of the planet Earth.

Another drawing by Glenn Passmore shows much of what the author of this work has described. Here Passmore shows more exterior detail while Omnec furnished more interior detail. However there is no important conflict. Please note also Bill Clendenen's description in Appendix II attached to this document by the publisher.

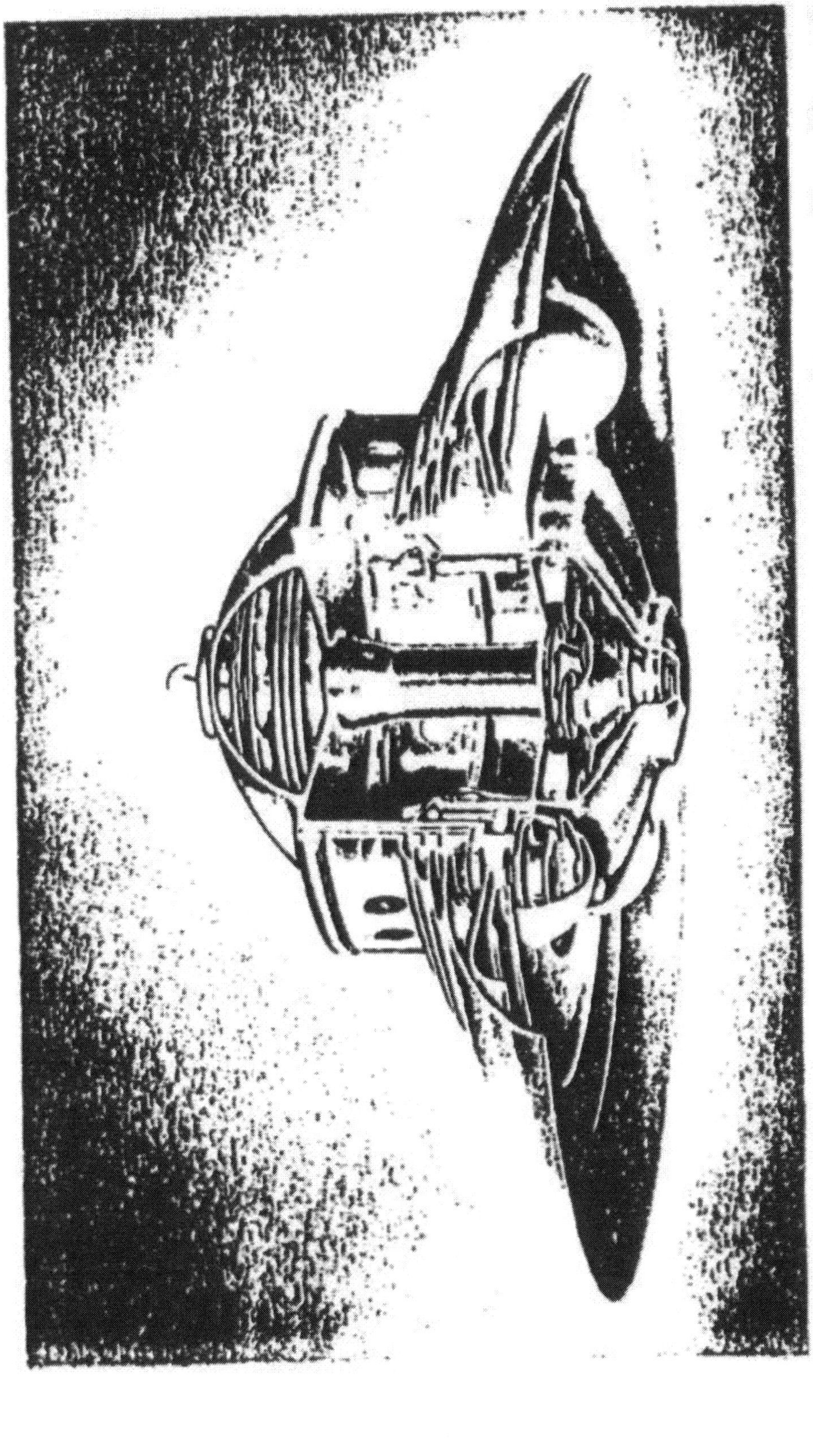

This cut-away drawing of the inside of a Venusian spacecraft appeared on the outer dust jacket of Leonard Cramp's book, SPACE, GRAVITY and the FLYING SAUCER. This is very similar to what Omnec describes and shows more interior detail than Passmore.

Chapter Nine
Brotherhood of Planets

1. A Brotherhood of Planets
2. Each planet unique
3. Evolution of planets
4. Non-interference
5. Spaceships
6. Teleportation
7. Space travel
8. Earth's moon a spacebase
9. How our spaceships work
10. Scientists from Venus

When the day comes for Earth's astronauts to land on Venus and Mars for the first time, they will find signs of human life. The same is true of the other planets of the Brotherhood. The Brotherhood is of course well aware of Tythania's astral civilization (as well as others). For some time our people on astral Venus have been manifesting physical bodies to re-colonize the physical level of Venus, or to live on Earth.

I cannot say how life on the planet has changed since I left Venus. Perhaps other people of the Brotherhood who now live on Earth will be speaking about their lives on other planets.

Trying to learn about the many varieties of culture on other planets is like counting the grains of sand on a beach. Studying Earth's many different cultures would be kindergarten work compared to studying life in this vast Brotherhood.

It is the spiritual maturity of the Souls inhabiting a planet which determines, to a great degree, what its life will be like. The more spiritually developed the individuals become, the less complex their life becomes and the less dependence there is on material technology. More dependence is placed on the natural power of the Soul working through mind.

At first the life on a planet is simple and primitive but it isn't long before a technology emerges and becomes complex. Then the planet reaches a point where its technology is much like we find on Earth today — somewhat advanced but very complex. A final stage is that which can be found on the more advanced planets, where technology has become more simple again and at the same time more advanced.

For example, walking is a simple yet limited method of transportation. A more complex way of getting around may be to ride a horse. Still more complex and more advanced is the use of automobiles. But traveling in the Soul body is even more advanced still, yet much simpler than any other way of traveling in the lower worlds. Other planets are all at some point on this scale, on their way to a simple but technically advanced way of life, all depending on their spiritual progress.

Some planets experience a greater lag, such as Earth. Then everyone in the solar system becomes concerned. Whenever technical progress outruns spiritual maturity, great difficulties lie ahead.

As I mentioned before, Venus, Mars, Jupiter, Saturn, Uranus, Neptune, and Pluto do have human life in their appropriate form. I also learned that the Planets beyond Pluto are uninhabited and are yet unnamed. This may have changed since I left Venus.

Originally there were only four planets — Mercury, Venus, Mars and Jupiter. The remainder of the twelve were formed since then through a continuous natural process of creation and dissolution. Planets are constantly forming and being destroyed, contrary to what many Earth scientists seem to believe.

Atomic testing on Earth can be a serious matter because what happened on Mercury can happen to Earth. A shift in the orbit sent the planet closer to the sun and the people were forced to leave. Fortunately Saturn was uninhabited at the time and space travel on Mercury was advanced enough to make an evacuation possible. Earth may not be so fortunate.

The truths of the Laws of Supreme Deity (natural law) are well known and accepted on other planets of our solar system. All that these planets have in common as opposed to Earth results from the population living under spiritual law and making these truths the most important part of their lives.

We do not see fellow humans as the physical body or mind, the state of consciousness, the attitudes, or any lower qualities. These are only temporary masks. Each living form is Soul expressing itself, and therefore we understand all of life instead of judging it.

The people of the spiritually advanced planets are all very well aware of the Law of Karma, how they will meet face to face with all deeds and misdeeds. As well, they know that death is not an end, but only a transition to another world. An awareness of the Laws of Life makes a huge difference in how people act.

Life on Earth would be transformed if alone the Law of Karma were understood and accepted. Only the inner unfoldment of individuals will bring Earth out of its ages of wars and tyranny. You have it because you still want it. When you are fed up with it you will grow.

The common enemy of Soul is of course the Kal power, which flows through the consciousness to control the mind and emotions and thus create fresh Karma. Since thoughts and feelings are always cause in this world, then a control of thoughts and feelings is a control of destiny.

The negative flow through man appears as one or more of the five passions — greed, anger, vanity, lust, and attachment to material things. When these passions are not in control in the people as a whole, then life improves greatly and is much like what exists on Venus and some other members of the Brotherhood of Planets.

Through such inner control there would be no conflict and war. The last interplanetary war in this solar system took place before your society even existed. The outer conditions of life always reflect the inner control of the mind and emotions.

In trying to recognize people from Earth's neighboring planets, something that is very noticeable beyond our physical appearance is our attitude toward other human beings. We accept other people not on our terms but through the awareness that each being is Soul and the lower worlds are only a school.

If we meet someone on Earth who is prejudiced or who feels badly about something, this is accepted because it is a result of that person's level of consciousness; this is all that person has learned. We realize that no one is wrong because each person can only know so much until having the experiences that change his attitudes and level of consciousness awareness.

We Venusians are known to give out a feeling of love for all life, and we have a look of peace and serenity about us. We are happy with any situation and accept it as an experience to help us grow, rather than thinking of it as something negative, no matter how negative it may seem to be. It is very easy to get along with people from other planets. There is some inner quality which draws others to us.

We are not better than the people of Earth. We have only had an opportunity to be born this time in an environment that then was at peace with itself and that made spiritual truths of life available. Many of us have also experienced life on Earth in the past.

Each man has within himself the power to change whatever he does not agree with, simply by visualizing what he would like to have.

Most of Earth's people are not aware of this power within, so therefore you tend to worship those people who have experienced and learned to see it. We have an opportunity to realize who and what we are, whereas man on Earth does not realize the great potential within himself as an individual. Each individual must choose the path he will walk.

Balance and noninterference are areas of life where our people have shown much improvement over the centuries. These are crucial to spiritual development in the lower worlds on Soul's journey to Self-realization and God-realization. They are lessons which many people on Earth yet need to learn.

Noninterference is a spiritual law of freedom for each individual. No two people think alike, feel alike, react alike, or have the same attitudes and viewpoints, or are the same level of spiritual unfoldment. Each individual has his own personal universe which according to spiritual law must be respected.

This is not recognized or understood on Earth, which is the underlying cause of many of today's problems. If people paid more attention to directing their own lives, then there would be fewer troubles in the world. The more you interfere in other people's lives, the more others will interfere in your own. This is the Law of Karna in action. Believing that another should be a certain way, or should have certain standards and attitudes leads to interference. The ideal is to accept others as individuals, at their own level, and going through their own lessons as Soul.

Interference includes pushing ideas or viewpoints on others, helping others or giving advice without permission, or even thinking that what another person is doing is wrong.

To try to understand why others act, think, or feel the way they do is much more beneficial than merely judging. It also helps each individual to understand himself better. We do not dispute. We seek understanding and feel that what the other has to say is the more important because one already knows what he has in mind.

Balance is so important in life, so universally important that beings throughout the lower worlds are trying to master it. To not enter any extreme in life is one of the ways Soul can be released from the lower worlds of time and space. Unfortunately, very few on Earth are learning the lesson of balance.

To be balanced as Soul means being balanced in every way. Even in eating, a person must try to reach a balance between positive foods and Kal foods. Sadly enough "civilized" people on Earth eat mostly Kal foods.

Regarding desire, a person must always be able to walk away from any thing or situation, otherwise he becomes a slave to the things of this world. One must be neither for nor against anything.

This treading the middle path sometimes seams like walking the razor's edge. Spiritual man is at times a channel for spiritual power, and at other times for the Kal power. The self-centered man is almost always the channel for the Kal forces.

Completely eliminating the five passions of the mind would mean being unbalanced toward the positive polarity which is not so good either because he is not learning the lessons of control. As long as a person is human he will be able to enjoy the things of the physical world, but hopefully not become a prisoner of them. One of the purposes of these revelations is to help man achieve a balance in his Earthly life.

Balance must also be observed in man's dealings with nature. A great deal of damage has already been done on Earth to delicate ecological systems and continues to be done. Ages ago people on Venus and Mars awakened in time to realize that by destroying nature they are destroying themselves. They began to respect nature by replenishing what was taken from the soil and not destroying everything to build cities and villages.

Unless the worldwide poor soil conditions on Earth are remedied and the use of chemicals to grow and protect foods is stopped, man will not survive another century on Earth.

On other planets there is no disease and average life-spans are many hundreds of years. Our people show no signs of aging beyond their twenties and early thirties. Many causes are at play here, ranging from mental attitudes to planetary influences.

If the people of Earth knew the truth about nutrition and applied it, then you could expect the same excellent health that we enjoy. Most diseases known and feared on Earth are actually caused by the food people eat and do not eat. Expecting good health after eating poisoned and deficient foods is like expecting your car to run on milk instead of gas.

Diseases are nothing more than symptoms. The causes lie at three levels — thought, emotion, and physical action. Negative thoughts and emotions will eventually reflect in the physical body's ailments.

Transportation of things on Venus is done with energy-matter converters. The sending unit converts matter to energy while the receiving unit converts the energy back to matter. Levitating machines had been used extensively before then. Their development came at about the same time magnetic power was first used for space travel.

Space travel has been tightly woven into the fabric of our lives for many centuries. Our motivation in leaving the surface of our planet has always been to learn more about the Universe and its natural law.

A great number of scientists and professional men crew our ships, both the mother-ships and the convoys. Since change is such a basic reality in the lower worlds, we always find something new to observe and learn.

There are many advantages to belonging to the Brotherhood. All of the planets but Earth joined in a common bond for the same reason that any two people with common interests and concerns join together.

We are always prepared to assist another planet or spaceship in distress, or to share minerals arid plants not found abundantly on a neighboring planet. Our scientists work together on common projects to bring into existence the wonders of imagination.

In every solar system the Kal Na-ar or negative child, as we call the planet Earth, causes much concern. (The Venusian name for Earth, using English letters to create the sound, is Jhlata Geum) Often in its growth it becomes a menace to its own survival and that of nearby planets.

Ages ago the Moon became a base of operations in our work with Earth. Here we built elaborate colonies and transportation networks in secluded valleys and craters. Much more will be made known about this fact in the near future. Among our facilities are huge hangars where our mother-ships can be safely serviced and stored.

Your public has been totally misled in its understanding of the Moon. Moons are not dead satellites but small planets just as carefully designed as the sun-orbiting planets are. Earth's Moon does have an atmosphere and suitable human life, and its surface does have water, vegetation, bacteria, insects and small animals.

Most of the Moon's surface is desert and the temperatures become hot. Yet our people as well as other visitors can and do survive in the open air without environmental headgear. Over time the human body can adjust to the rarified atmosphere. Not only was I taught as a child that Earth's moon was inhabitable, but during an out-of-body experience I saw this for myself.

During the time we were on the mother-ship, my uncle sat down with me to explain some of the secrets of space travel. Our tremendous technical growth is a result of our harnessing the nature forces instead of working against them.

Our spaceships, both the mother-ships and the saucer-shaped convoys, are able to perform what seem to be wonders by using the natural energies of space — solar and magnetic energy. Not only are our ships unaffected by gravity and friction, but they also can maneuver at tremendous speeds.

Observers on Earth have clocked our ships on radar at incredible speeds. They have seen sharp-angled turns at thousands of miles per hour, and unbelievable rates of acceleration and deceleration that theoretically would crush all the occupants on board.

The secret lies in the use of magnetic power and magnetic fields, as well as solar power. Every mother-ship and every small shuttle ship contains within it what appears to be a central shaft or pole. In the mother-ship this pole lies lengthwise, whereas in the convoy it is visible in the central cabin, running from top to the bottom. This shaft acts as the magnetic pole of the ship and it helps create a magnetic field like that around and within any planet. Just as Earth has a north pole and a south pole, so do our spaceships have positive and negative magnetic charges.

The power needed to create a strong gravitational, magnetic field is derived directly from the sun. In the convoy, under the glass-like dome atop the ship and atop the magnetic pole, sits a coil coated with a rare kind of crystal.

This crystal material very efficiently converts solar energy into magnetic energy. Together with the solid gold pole the necessary magnetic field is created. Gold is one of the very best conductors of magnetic power.

Once it has been properly adjusted, the magnetic field makes the convoy or mother-ship an independent being unlike your aircraft and spaceships, which are subject to Earth's magnetic field and the atmosphere. Thus our ships are like tiny planets in themselves. This independence of a planet's influence is called weightlessness.

In flight our ships are in a state of balance with the planet itself. When the power is turned on, the ship has become weightless. In order to fly to or from a planet's surface, very little push is needed. Friction with the atmosphere is effectively eliminated by the magnetic and high energy fields surrounding the ship. It is as if the ship were deep in space, unaffected by planetary gravities and atmospheres.

The polarity of the pole in the convoy is reversed in going to or from the surface. Horizontal flight or push is created through three charged metallic spheres which make up the understructure of the convoy. They are basic features of the machinery of this type of craft just as the magnetic pole is a normal part of the machinery and operating apparatus of all versions of these ships.

The spherical understructures of these ships also have magnetic poles and are electrically charged.* Rotating the undercarriage on which they are mounted shifts that ship to another magnetic line of force. The speed of our ships is limited only to the activity of space, not to any arbitrary speed of light. Extremely high velocities are very dangerous in a planet's vicinity.

There is not the slightest feeling of movement or acceleration on board, no matter how severe the maneuver. In a split second our ships can come to a stop without causing the least bit of strain on the pilots or passengers. The interior feels like a motionless room.

This is because the ship is independent of outside forces. Braking the ship to a stop would at the same time brake the pilot to a stop, and relative to the ship he feels nothing.†

The fields around our ships also prevent midair collisions. Ships bounce off each other without jolting the passengers. On the other hand, Earth's aircraft do not have this protection. We also run when our ships

---

* Bill Clendenen, when shown the inside of one of the three hemispheres seen underneath the typical Venusian convoy, described the mechanism as looking like an inverted Christmas tree of vertical and horizontal black carbon-like rods in a closed chamber filled with mercury vapor. This rod-like structure could be raised and lowered and could be rotated within the chamber. It had a heavy cable-like connection running from it into the floor from which the pods were suspended.

† Anthony Serantitis, formerly of Dow Chemicals, in his Unified Field Law, describes electricity, magnetism and gravity as different aspects of the same phenomenon and says that these aspects all work at right angles to each other. In his equations he showed that an artificially generated force-field could be either electromagnetic or electro-gravitic in nature, and that an electro-gravitic field of lesser density would "float" in another field of greater density. If this were generated around and through a body such as a space vehicle the craft could be made to float in the existing gravity field. Because such a field reacts directly with all the electromagnetic fields within every atom in the field, no inertial forces are experienced. Hence high speed right angle turns are possible with no physical sensations being felt. His sudden illumination and full understanding of his new Unified Field Law came after a personal experience with an Unidentified Flying Object.

are shot at because the bullets bounce back to Earth. This has been confused by some to the idea that our ships have shot back.

Our force-fields protect against friction within atmospheres as well as bombardment by meteorites. Although the titanium hulls of the mother-ships and convoys are a help, most of the protection comes from energy fields. This is not ordinary titanium, but titanium treated with a certain ray which also creates the translucent effect.

Only the mother-ships are self-sufficient. Some of the energy needs of the convoys are recharged within the mother-ship's maintenance bay. Convoys are not intended for long journeys. Mother-ships draw all their energy directly from space.

Life on Earth would certainly be revolutionized if the secrets of magnetic power were introduced. Imagine for yourself the changes that would come about if energy were free and magnetic powered ships were available to every man.

However, the negative powers have a strong hold on Earth. Anything which may give more power and freedom to the individual is considered a threat, and this includes the Laws of The Supreme Deity.

In areas of technology, inventions which are good for the people but bad for those in power are usually locked away or destroyed, or at least discredited.

Earth owes much to the electrical inventor Nikola Tesla. Without him Earth would not be where it is today. At one time he worked with Thomas Edison in designing electric motors and generators. It was Tesla who was responsible for the power system at Niagra Falls. By the time he had reached his 70s, Nikola Tesla had more than 700 inventions to his credit.

But Tesla was too advanced for his time. Even Edison turned against him and tried to discredit his more brilliant ideas. Tesla pioneered in tapping the unlimited energy available from the Earth itself, and understood that energy does not need to be generated at great power plants.

Those who knew what Tesla was talking about at that time succeeded in discrediting the man and his ideas, and in that way kept the secrets of magnetic power from benefiting the world. Tesla's own words tell us what he was aiming at, "The most valuable application of wireless energy will be the propulsion of flying machines..."

Upon his death, Tesla's laboratories were locked up and over the years, the memory of his greatness has all but faded away. Few people on Earth know that he ever existed, and fewer still know that he came here from the planet Venus to help you. *

* In 1950 Wilbert B. Smith, B.A., M.A., of Lethbridge, Alberta, was contacted by Venusian extraterrestrials who reminded him of Nikola Tesla's advances in electromagnetic technology and offered to "fill in some gaps" in understanding. They worked directly with Smith for several years trying to develop the Tesla projects for operation in Earth's physical density, ultimately cooperating in Canada's Project Magnet established to study UFOs and the physical principles which might be involved. Unfortunately the program was plagued by well-meaning but misguided journalists to an extent that those involved in the project, and the sponsors, found themselves in embarrassing positions and Project Magnet was officially dropped in 1954. Smith did not stop though, but continued working alone with the Venusians and developed, among other things, an entirely new concept of matter and energy. It was published in 1964, after his death, by his wife. (It was titled "THE NEW SCIENCE.")

Chapter Ten
Again Des

1. We land at Agam Des
2. The spiritual city and its people
3. My stay at Agam Des
4. We travel to Nevada
S. Landing
6. My first impression of Earth
7. Little Rock
8. The Bus Accident and Sheila's Death
9. On to Chattanooga
10. Knocking on Grandmother's door

Our ship landed deep in a valley among the towering peaks of Kashmir. Through the porthole I could see in a distant valley the tops of buildings of an Indian City. It was early morning and the sun was shining brightly, illuminating the steep faces of the mountains. From this first view I decided that Earth certainly looked like a beautiful place.

As we walked from the convoy, I looked back to see that it was sitting neatly in a clearing within a wooded plateau. For what seemed like hours, we climbed up the steep slopes ahead of us. Walking had been difficult enough, but this was almost unbearable. The feeling of being inside a suit of armor persisted and my legs were painfully heavy.

I had not yet glimpsed my new body in a mirror, but I felt so clumsy that I was certain I looked grotesque.

The hillsides around us looked very strange. Blotches of snow covered most of the grass and yet it was not the least bit cold. My uncle explained, in answer to my question about it, that the air was very thin so high in the mountains, therefore, it could snow without being so cold.

Ahead of us we saw a wooded plateau upon which stood a giant fortress of wood and stone. This was the physical counterpart of the spiritual city, Agam Des.

Stairs of stone led up the hillside to a wooden gate and fence that surrounded the fortress. Inside we came upon gardens of flowers and vegetables and an assortment of farm animals. My uncle and I and the companion pilot walked up a neat stone path and approached the huge wooden door with iron rings.

Just then the doors silently opened inward and a hooded figure in a monk's robe stood before us. He was a stately man with long flowing beard and blue eyes. He greeted us. "Your rooms are waiting." He led us to our sleeping quarters which I, within my fatigued body, welcomed very much.

Agam Des is the greatest spiritual city on the planet Earth, headed by the Master Yaubl Sacabi. From all outer appearances, Agam Des is much like any Tibetan monastery, yet here live some of Earth's greatest spiritual giants. Yaubl Sacabi is among those adepts who have chosen to immortalize their bodies and whose age is beyond human belief. He is reputed to be several thousand years old within the same physical body.*

For centuries space travelers have arrived at Agam Des to adjust themselves to Earth's coarser vibrations. Agam Des also has one of Earth's Temples of Golden Wisdom, the other one being the Katsupari monastery in Tibet. †

---

* One teacher in the School of Wisdom at Agam Des has occupied the same physical body for over 500 years. We are reminded of another UFO contact case in Japan where a high ranking Buddhist priest in his 80s is the contactee visited by the ETs. This priest had scores of contacts and was once taken to the ET home planet for two weeks where, in an accelerated process, he learned the history and culture of the ETs and how to read and write their language. In his 30s when he sought illumination, he went to the Himalayas to study under a Master. This teacher, though looking young, was known to be over 500 years old. That was 50 years ago and he still lives.

† The Katsupari Monastery in the Thanglha Mountains lies near the old site of the Voice of Akisvasha, an oracle still active in wild Northern Tibet. It is near an unexplored site called Timer. It is headed by an Abbot called Fubbi Quantz.

These temples hold the ancient teachings we call Laws of the Supreme Deity as respected on Venus since long ago.

Physically Agam Des is one giant square building with stone floors and dark, dark wooden walls. Candles provide the lighting. They are set in candle-holders at intervals along the walls. In the middle of the building is a large dining hall with a fireplace. Adjoining it is a large cathedral-like meeting room for spiritual chanting. Just inside the gates is a courtyard with animals, gardens of herbs, vegetables and flowers.

Along the perimeter of the building are the individual sleeping rooms - about 50 in number - very simply furnished. Each has a single bed with a nightstand that holds books and a few personal belongings. There is also a picture of a spiritual Master in each room. No one at the temple enters another's room unless invited.

Everyone at Agam Des rises with the sun, I learned on the first day. I had been told the night before that a bell would ring to summon me to breakfast.

A rooster was crowing in the yard as I heard the bell ringing in my sleep. I noticed that the robe I was to wear, with its rope belt and hood, was woven of a coarse material like potato sack. I also noted it was too big for me.

Looking out the window, I saw a sea of mountaintops below us stretching to the horizon, and the rising sun in an orange-pink morning sky. A warm breeze caressed my face. The window was nothing but a square opening in the stone with wooden shutters to each side.

The dining hall was already filling as I entered and took a seat at one of the long tables. Each table could seat about twenty-five. At the head of the middle table sat a Master, and at the heads of the other tables sat the higher initiates.

Our breakfast was a piece of fruit, a bowl of rice and herb tea. That was all. The meals at Agam Des turned out to be very simple events, twice each day. In the mornings we had brown rice and a root plant from the mountains, together with herb tea. Every other day, a piece of fruit and Yogurt was served.

In the evenings, we ate a salad of fresh greens without spices or dressing. Meat or fish was served every other day. Alternately, we had a combination plate of a vegetable and a starch. Throughout each day we drank herb tea and fruit juices, and sometimes I was treated to goat's milk.

The food was very bland but good. Gradually during my stay at Agam Des, spices and other additives from the village were added to my diet. This was so that I could adjust little by little every day to the American food I would soon be eating. As it turned out, during my first years in Tennessee and Arkansas, my system reacted violently to practically everything I ate. Food in America is so depleted, processed and poisoned, that we can rightly call it a tragedy.

During breakfast that first morning, I noticed that my uncle and his friend were not there. I assumed they were off somewhere together, perhaps arranging to have the ship taken back to the mother-ship.

After we had finished eating, I was given the chore of working in the garden, gathering vegetables for the evening meal. Every visitor and monk at Agam Des pays for his stay with a daily chore. This is how the place is maintained. On some of the days, I fed the animals or milked the goats. I did not speak with the monks very much because they had rules about not talking unnecessarily.

In the mid-morning, I sat with the monks and listened as they had their music hour, when they practiced their various instruments. The ones who did not have instruments chanted in a song-like way.

Chanting took place every day in the chanting hall, where the men gathered to sit on benches, or on the floor. I loved the chanting. It was so beautiful and musical that I felt as if I could just be carried away on it. The monks chanted every morning arid evening, each time with a different mantra, for the purpose of having an experience on the higher planes.

I soon learned that life at Agam Des was very balanced and orderly. As a matter of fact, the men had strict habits. Everything was done at exactly the same time from day to day.

After noon, everybody had a free hour to run personal errands, visit the villages, take a nap, or do whatever the individual desired. During my free hour this first day, I did not wish to take a nap, even though I was very tired. I wanted to look around. I walked outside through the gardens for awhile and then sat down by a little stream. I was deep in thought when the bell rang signaling the lesson time was beginning.

For the chelas (students) who lived at Agam Des, this was a time for lessons in the Laws of the Supreme Deity. For visitors like myself, it was time to meet with a tutor. My teacher, this first day, covered quite a few subjects. We talked for awhile on how mathematics in the western world worked, and how the American school system was set up. He explained what kindergarten was, and the fact that each child was expected to go to school from the age of five or six. He also explained to me what report cards were.

His comment was that it was not a very good system, but that nothing better was available. It would not be like what I was accustomed to. He taught me to spell a few words and to write the ABCs and read a few passages. All this was rather easy.

He explained what I had been told so often before. I would not find my spiritual teachings anywhere, and I would not find anyone who would understand them until later in my life.

People's attitudes toward other races were not what I was accustomed to. The darker races were considered inferior. I had a hard time accepting this, remembering the royal race of Jupiter. I supposed that I would live with it and try to understand why this happened.

The monks at Agam Des did not make known their names, because at the time, the spiritual teaching was very secret. This was for their protection because people in the villages harbored negative attitudes toward any teaching which was not an accepted Indian or Tibetan path. I would face these kinds of prejudices a lot more as I grew up.

In the following two weeks I learned many new things about Earth. Sometimes the tutor and I would sit in the room with our books, or we would go out into the forest to learn about the different plants, trees and flowers. In the herb garden, I was shown various herbs and their uses, and why certain kinds were taken in teas at certain times of the day.

I spent many days practicing walking, sitting, climbing stairs, and doing all sorts of physical exercises. I had only two weeks in which to lose all my self-consciousness and the haunting feeling of being in a suit of armor. Every day, I had a lesson in balance, where I practiced standing on one foot, hopping on one foot, walking and running. In our walks outside, I would jump over puddles, or climb trees while one of the monks watched my progress.

During my stay at Agam Des, I worked with several of the teachers, one for each subject. It was always same— one who was interested in the field and had studied it in depth. I was taught the history of the United States as well as the present situation. The Cold War was explained to me, how the people were afraid of being bombed by an enemy.

When I told my first teacher how clumsy I felt, he arranged to borrow a mirror for me from one of the villages in the valley. No one at Agam Des possessed a mirror. I was very excited about this because I had not yet seen my new body, and it helped my attitude to see that I was not as coarse and bulky as I felt. The monks told me that by Earth standards, I was actually very delicate and beautiful. I must admit, I looked all right and felt less clumsy afterward.

After lesson time on my first full day at Agam Des, we enjoyed a treat of herb tea and a dark bread with goat cheese. Afterwards, we made our way to the forest for an outdoor chant, and by the time we arrived, our food had been well digested. We sat down.

The chant was explained and I was told what plane it was from. Then we chanted. I can only say that my experience was exhilarating, enlightening and indescribable. To bring us back to Earth, the initiates spent the next half-hour with us in a question/answer period.

Next on the monks' schedule was recreation time, a time of exercise classes and sports that I was not allowed to join. My uncle and his companion suggested that we go for a walk toward one of the villages. Odin told me all about the street markets of these villages, which I found very interesting. Here were sold all sorts of handicrafts: rugs, jewelry, pottery, clothes and more.

I was rather excited about going into the village and seeing all these things, but my uncle explained that this would not be possible. Our light skin and hair may attract too much attention because the natives were very dark people. A number of the villages were Communist-controlled or had authorities that would want to see papers and credentials.

Along the way, my uncle pointed out various interesting buds, plants and animals. I was especially fascinated by the pheasants and wild peacocks. We arrived back at Agam Des shortly before dinner, and I went to my room to rest from our walk. There I looked at the plants from Venus and the jewelry from my mother, all the time wondering about my new life in the United States. The ringing of the dinner-bell broke the silence.

During my stay at Agam Des, I saw Yaubl Sacabi about three times; once during chanting time and twice for dinner. Once every week the Master gathered with his children, as he called them. Most of the time he was on journeys through the mountains into the villages, or in contemplation by himself to work in the Soul body on missions here on Earth or somewhere on higher planes. Yaubl Sacabi looks very much like an Indian, with huge dark eyes and a dark olive complexion, and a beard. His hair is silvery gray. He is a very quiet man and always carries a smile. Rarely does he speak about spiritual matters unless he is giving a talk.

The other Masters that I know of, Rebazar Tarz and Fubbi Quantz, have also retained their physical bodies for spiritual missions on Earth. Rebazar Tarz was directly responsible for training Peddar Zaskq and Dap Pen for missions in modern society. He taught the Laws of the Supreme Deity. He will work more openly in the spiritual awakening of Earth within the next few decades.

At dinner Yaubl Sacabi blessed the food and told of the purpose it was serving us. He welcomed Uncle Odin and me and our companion, telling us that we were very welcome at Agam Des. Speaking for all the monks he said that they were honored to have us visiting Agam Des. The Master did not say much more. All the monks did not know we were from Venus; only my teachers and Yaubl Sacabi knew this.

I liked to be close to the Master because of the way I felt when he was around. His presence made me feel good. That is the kind of person he was. And always when he was at the table, he broke bread into a dish and passed it around the table as an honor paid to his students.

All the men at Agam Des wore robes, and hoods which they never let down in the presence of anyone else. They were not beautiful by physical standards as society knows, but beautiful in the feeling I got from them and in the evenness of their features. The monks and adepts at Agam Des struck me as being pure of countenance, very pure beings. I was honored to be in their presence.

Agam Des is the home of an ancient line Masters all of which are adept at Soul travel and have great responsibilities in the spiritual evolution of Earth. Students of this ancient science live here as well. All of the inhabitants were men, mostly Indian men and a few westerners. Some of them were very young, only twelve years old, but the ages ranged up to several thousand years. It was impossible for me to tell their ages from their physical appearance. Most of them did have an ancient quality about them.

They were all very quiet, and did not talk unless it was absolutely necessary. All of them had even, gentle voices, and followed the same custom we of other planets had; not interrupting another while he spoke. No one would begin to speak until the other had finished.

The newest chelas of the spiritual teachings paid by two years of service at the Temple. These were the people who filled the water dishes (for washing) in each room, and helped with the maintenance. In this way the monks always had help at the temple, and they always had new chelas.

After dinner on that first day, everyone helped with the cleaning up. Some washed the dishes, some swept the floors, and others cleaned the tables. Then everyone retired to his room to attend to personal business, read, or sleep. The first Earth book that I read, which one of the monks had loaned me, was "Heidi." I enjoyed it very much.

Saturdays were spent gathering food for the next two days and storing it in a spring house. This was a small wooden structure which stood directly over and in a cold mountain stream. Bathing was done in a small bath house in the woods. Here was a large wooden tub with a cast iron bottom that could be heated by a fire underneath. We also had the choice of bathing in a cold waterfall at the stream.

On Sunday there was not much work for us to do except prepare the meals. The rest of the day was free. I slept very late into the day and then went to play with the chickens and baby chicks.

I sat and listened to the monks singing and playing their instruments, and I loved to join them in the singing. One of the songs they taught me sounds like this when translated into English:

I am a happy Soul today,
I'll be happy all the way.
Even if the sun don't shine,
I will shine all the time.

I'm a happy soul today,
I'll be happy all the way.
Won't you be happy with me too,
I'm a happy, happy Soul.

The monks at Agam Des always kept busy with their favorite hobbies. They loved to sing and play musical instruments, and quite a few of the men painted, but I do not believe they ever sold their work. Some of the monks had small herb gardens or helped in keeping the flower gardens beautiful.

The weather was always pleasant. I enjoyed going out and looking over the mountains down into the valleys. The air was always clean and crisp, and the sun was always shining here at the top of the world. Here I would stand, and, closing my eyes, breathe deeply.

I learned a great deal from these two weeks at Agam Des. I learned to live more comfortably in the physical body and to do everything with grace. As the days went on, I felt less and less awkward and heavy. I learned much about gravity, and I had to be very careful and adjust to physical laws safely.

I surely had to watch my feet to see that they were always firmly grounded, and I had to be very careful with objects, to be sure that when I set them down, they were sitting properly. On the astral plane, I could afford to be much more careless. I suppose that throughout my life on Earth the reason I am always getting bumped and bruised is that I have never quite become used to physical laws. When you bump against something here it is going to be painful; you cannot think something out of your way. It is probably a good thing that most people do not remember past lives on the higher planes, because the limitations of the physical world would seem quite unbearable.

After my first few days at Agam Des, my uncle suggested that I try to dance. This seemed to be a good idea, but I wondered how it would work out, considering the trouble I had had in walking. At first I practiced my movements in slow motion and day by day, they improved. I enjoyed myself very much. The monks lent my uncle and our friend a flute and a peculiar ancient-looking stringed instrument, so that I could dance to music.

Dancing with a physical body was a strange experience. The freedom of my astral body was gone. Dancing is much more limited here on the physical plane. For when you go up, you must come down. Instead of dancing gracefully with the power of thought and more or less floating, here you must physically keep a balance and control each muscle. And instead of creating music instantly with the power of thought, here someone must physically play an instrument. Nevertheless, it was an exhilarating experience, one I continued to enjoy.

My Uncle Odin spent time with me, sometimes to read me a story, or relate funny incidents about when I was a child. I could sense that he was sad about my leaving, but he was a master in not letting it surface.

He answered my questions about things that I may have missed under Vonic. I was told to watch my thoughts here on Earth because, although they do not manifest instantly, thoughts and attitudes do make the world what it is.

Children, I learned, play a lot of imaginary games, but they could not manifest what they were imagining as we did on the astral plane. Earth children played house and dressed up just as we did, but less elaborately.

After the monks found out that I was learning to dance they requested that my chore be to dance for them after meal-time. They rarely had any kind of entertainment, and since my dancing was oriented toward spirituality, they enjoyed it very much. This was a chore I loved.

Being from a higher plane, I was well aware of the high spiritual vibrations at Agam Des. For years after leaving this spiritual city, I wondered whether it really existed on Earth. It seemed more like a place that could be found on one of the spiritually advanced planets. Of course, the whole idea is to provide a real crossover point for visitors from other planets and the other planes.

Anyone on Earth who studies what we on Venus call Laws of the Supreme Deity receives most of his truth and wisdom through inner channels. He is taken in Soul body to one of these Temples, be they on Earth, Venus, or higher planes, to learn from the Way of the Eternal, the most ancient and complete scriptures on this planet.

Normally a student progresses from one Temple to the next, beginning, for Earth students, with the Katsupari monastery in Tibet. The first book of the Way of the Eternal is kept there, and the students learn under the Master Fubbi Quantz.

The second book of the Way of the Eternal is kept at Agam Des, which I physically saw in my stay there. It appears as a huge book enclosed in a glass case, very simple in appearance, but holding some of the deepest secrets known to spiritual men. Much has been written about the nine unknown and secret masters who are in charge of the wisdom contained in these books.

A third book is kept in the House of Moksha in Retz, and the next is in the Temple of Golden Wisdom in Sahasra-dal Kanwal on our astral plane, under the care of Master Gopal Das. This man took the Soul Travel teachings underground in ancient Egypt several thousand years before Christ, when he yet lived on earth.

Additional chapters of the Way of the Eternal are kept on successive higher planes for more advanced students of the Laws.

Our last day at Agam Des was very special. We began the day with a delicious breakfast of tea and honey cake with sour cream. Our rice dish was mixed with herbs and chicken, a rare treat for everyone at the Temple.

During the afternoon, a special program was held in the chanting room, a session of spiritual poetry, music, songs and chants. In a way, it seemed like a spiritual seminar, because at the very end the Master Yaubl Sacabi gave a short talk. Since the message was for his students, I am not allowed to repeat here what he said.

That evening for dinner we were surprised by a feast of lamb and brown rice and a cooked vegetable. A huge salad and herb tea completed the meal. Once again, Yaubl Sacabi broke the bread and passed it around. It was a royal end to a royal stay at Again Des.

We went to our rooms to gather our things, and all the monks walked to the gate with us to say goodbye. We waved and walked down the stairs, through the wooded plateau one last time. My walk down the steep slopes was much more graceful and comfortable than before, and it seemed to be only a short while before we reached the familiar level clearing where we had landed. After a short wait, our ship appeared in the early evening sky.

My uncle had waited until dusk to travel, because we could easily blend with the stars. We flew so high that the cities below looked like sparks of light. Our trip to the western United States would last less than an hour.

I was busy during this flight (east), looking at the stars and the surface below, and watching the flashing charts. My uncle was trying to tell me more about the people of Earth, about the things a child should know. He told me again about the world of children, their attitudes and their place in society. They were not allowed to make decisions as on other planes, and were not considered to be complete individuals as Soul.

As we approached the state of Nevada, I changed into Sheila's dress. At Agam Des I had worn a robe and sandals; these I gave to my uncle, and he gave me the package with my flowers and jewelry. Around my neck I wore the ring. The dress did look pretty, but I was not used to wearing such short clothes. My hair was combed as Sheila's would be, and my Uncle Odin helped me put the hair barrettes in the proper place. With my patent leather shoes and white socks, I looked almost identical to the way Sheila would look on the bus to Chattanooga.

A few hours after midnight our ship landed among the mountains and desert wilderness of Nevada. We waited inside for about 10 minutes while the energy field dissipated and the peculiar humming sound died down; then we got out to see the headlights of an approaching car. The timing was perfect!

My uncle and our companion pilot went over and clasped hands with the driver of the auto, speaking together for a few moments. Then I was called over and given a warm smile and a pat on the head. My uncle's Earth contact wore an American suit and tie, and lived somewhere near here. He would be giving us a ride to Arkansas. We got aboard his auto and drove off.

As we bounced along over rocks and bumps, I had trouble understanding what was going on. This feeling of movement was new to me. Convoys feel motionless in their flight, no matter how turbulent the air or how severe the maneuver. Traveling in such a small vehicle as this auto was frightening. Not only did my physical body feel like a robot, but this robot was inside another machine which was not too graceful either.*

The exhaust and the smallness of the car were irritating because I was unused to such things. But everything was probably exaggerated in my mind; in fact the auto we were riding in was quite luxurious by Earth standards—it was a Cadillac Fleetwood. While I complained about the bumpy ride, the men tried to explain Earth's antique methods of travel, that fuel was used instead of natural power. That explained the smell and the terrible noise. At least it seemed to be noisy and smelly to my sensitive nose and ears.

I was sitting forward in my seat enjoying the beautiful sunrise when suddenly our vehicle revolted against us, with two trumpet blasts of anger. I let out a yell and covered both my ears, falling back into the seat. "What's wrong? What is it!"

My uncle and the driver glanced back to see my eyes wide with fright, then broke out laughing. "That, my child," Uncle Odin said, chuckling, "was the horn. It's a sounding device to warn other drivers."

"Oh." I said, relaxing, "I thought the vehicle was revolting against us."

We traveled well into the morning before stopping for gas. My uncle explained that the auto's tank had to be refilled every so many miles or the auto would stop. The tank held only so much. He showed me the washrooms and reminded me that I had to keep my body plied with liquids and food, especially liquids.

Many people, he said, ate purely for the pleasure rather than for proper nutrition. That is why the gas station had so many snacks and soda beverages.

I had a royal initiation to American food. Odin began by buying me potato chips. I noted that they were salty and crunchy, and made a lot of noise when I ate them. Next they wanted me to try a carbonated drink. I

* As this trip to Arkansas could easily have been made in the convoy, we may conclude that the familiarization to automobile travel and all these strange inertial forces were also a part of the conditioning program so as not to have the effects develop for the first time with Omnec alone in her first Earth vehicle.

should have guessed that something was up when I saw the Martian* and my uncle sort of laughing to themselves before handing the bottle to me. With my first gulp, I knew! It was as if fire had rushed down my throat into my stomach; it was so strong I almost choked. As my eyes opened wider, and wider filled with tears, the men just couldn't hold back their laughter any longer. My new taste buds had not been expecting anything like this. It was like giving a bottle of pop to a newborn baby. Then I began to laugh too, realizing that my uncle had succeeded in playing another joke on me.

Until sunset we traveled on what seemed to be an endless highway. The cars which rushed past us, going in the other direction, frightened me for some time. I was afraid that one of them would hit us. Sensing my fear, Odin pointed out that the painted line on the highway was a divider, but that sometimes, if a person was not careful, then autos did collide. There was no barrier to protect the cars from collisions. Auto accidents caused a great number of translations (deaths).

There was also a certain beverage, my uncle went on to explain, which the people drank for pleasure. Alcohol and certain chemicals, called drugs, sometimes caused accidents because of the way they affected people's mind and perception.

My first experience with trucks shocked and frightened me. I just about had a heart attack when I saw the monster coming toward us in the opposite lane — it was so big and noisy! "What was that?" I yelled, "What was that big thing?" Laughing again, they said I would be seeing a lot more of those.

Uncle Odin explained that larger vehicles called trucks were used to carry supplies to and from different cities. One city would have a factory

---

* Another extended and ongoing UFO contact case involving human beings arriving from Venus and Mars (and some even being conditioned to live here) began in 1920 when A. Coe was contacted and subsequently visited regularly by extraterrestrials arriving in disc-shaped metallic flying craft. Please note that this began 27 years before the word flying saucer was coined for this phenomenon. Those contacts continued right on up through 1980 with Mr. Coe, and later his wife, still in contact with the ETs. Albert Coe frequently had meetings in various cities around the country with the Earth-based representatives. He released a summary of those early contacts in a privately printed report called, "The Shocking Truth," back in the early 50s as the UFO phenomenon became popular. He described Martians and Venusians too driving Earth automobiles, and knew that these two societies worked closely together. Omnec makes a casual reference to the Martian man as though everyone knew this.

while another may not, so the trucks were used to supply other cities with whatever was needed. People were paid with currency to drive the trucks.

Periodically, we made stops to eat, where I ate such things as hamburgers and other foods very new to me. For dinner I ate a steak, and I liked that, but I did not care for the cooked vegetables because they were always overcooked. Green salads were delicious also.

I found that cow-meat was difficult to chew at first; some of it got stuck in my teeth, and we stopped to buy a toothbrush. My uncle suggested that I keep my teeth very clean else they would decay.

He explained to me what restaurants were. People who did not care to cook for themselves or who were traveling would stop and have the food already prepared. In exchange, they had to part with a certain amount of currency.

My uncle ordered the food and the waitress asked him questions. He had, of course, changed into American clothes before leaving the ship. Our driver was a Martian who lived on Earth and had a job which was certainly a well-paying job because he had a great deal of currency.

They told me that a large number of people from other planets were living on Earth and had jobs here. Some of them were married but most were single, unless they had brought a wife along from the home planet.

Near the end of our first day in the United States, we stopped to sleep at a place called a motor lodge or motel. These were for people to spend the night, Odin explained, because most autos did not have sleeping accommodations as convoys do. I noted that we again used our currency in exchange for staying at the room.

My uncle was very helpful in taking the time to explain all these new experiences to me. Many of my lessons about life on Earth could not be given in lectures but had to be experienced, so these first two days of traveling in the auto were very important for me.

Early the next morning, we were on our way again, and my uncle and his friend took turns driving. Autos, they said, were difficult to operate because the driver had to rely more on the machine than himself. Often these autos would break down, and the places that sold fuel would also fix cars in exchange for more money.

Toward the afternoon of the second day, we were approaching Arkansas, and there were more houses, more buildings, more clutter, and more people. The more I saw of people, the less I liked them. It made Tibet seem like Venus because of the great difference in the consciousness of people. Someone should have told me that Agam Des was not like America.

Truly, I was worried about myself, feeling sorry for myself for having to live with people like this. I could feel the negativity as we passed through small cities and towns. I could sense the greed and anger, and the bad auras and feelings. As I picked up their thoughts, I found that their attitudes were all very strange to me. Whoever had said that parts of Earth were like the lower astral plane was right!

I sensed an overall feeling of nervousness, of mistrust and fear. My uncle explained that the cause of this feeling was currency, because currency was responsible for inequality and caused mistrust as well as all the other big problems in society.

Money was the basis for most problems, Uncle Odin said, because it was the tool used by power-seekers to dominate and control. Without currency this could not be done. Society could not exist as it does now.

The cities and towns I saw looked terribly unbalanced, helter-skelter, and not very clean. Builders seemed to have made all structures square and stacked on top of each other. I could not understand why people would live like this. Why didn't they have gardens and spacious grounds? I never imagined Earth to be so very different from the world I had grown up in. Uncle Odin told me that many people did have gardens, but this was difficult to have in a congested city. He told me about farms too, which made me feel better about being here.

I could not understand how some of the people could walk around looking the way they did, not caring if their clothes were clean or their hair combed. I just could not understand how they were able to look at themselves and not see it. Clothing styles were abhorrent, I thought, and everywhere were totally unaesthetic sights. But the real problem was actually within myself, in my attitudes.

I did not know any better because I had been protected and led a different life. And of course one of my reasons for being here was to learn compassion. As I looked around more and more, I began to have feelings that I had made the wrong decision, because I would be living in a city like the ones I was seeing.

My Uncle spoke about the attitudes which a good number of the white people had toward the black race, that the attitudes stemmed from ancestors and parents rather than from each individual.

There was little individuality on Earth because of the dominance of parents over children, not letting them be recognized as individuals. In other words, children were just an extension of the adults with the same thought patterns. Only if they left the home at an early age, or established themselves on their own to have their own experiences, could their attitudes about black people (or any other prejudice) change.

Especially in the South, I was told, were these attitudes about black people strong. I was to be careful about prejudiced people because at times they take a violent stand for what they believe.

Odin reminded me about the soon-to-happen bus accident. In taking little Sheila's place, I was to try not to be too frightened amidst all the confusion. It was getting toward evening when we entered Little Rock. Approaching the outskirts, we noticed that it had begun to thunder and rain. Suddenly we slowed down, and my uncle announced that we had caught up with the bus. The huge vehicle had stopped at a restaurant; we remained at a little distance.

The bus proceeded on its way through the pouring rain. My heart was pounding away because I knew it would soon happen, the bus would crash as Kanjuri had predicted.

The night got darker and darker, and then it happened! The bus driver must have slammed on the brakes as the car ahead of him skidded and slowed. In an instant, the bus skidded sideways on the slick pavement, turning over and slamming into the muddy ditch. Sheila had been sitting behind the bus driver, and in all the chaos, the door ripped open and Sheila was thrown out into the darkness. She was among those who were killed!

My uncle stopped the car to let me out with my little package of things. My goodbyes were said. His last words to me were about the rescue service that would be dispatched to help the injured. I didn't need luggage because hers was on the bus; and the driver had a note with grandmother's address, because Sheila was going under the care of Traveler's Aid, which helps children who travel without their parents.

In all the confusion, people were scurrying around and the sirens were getting louder and louder as help arrived. The driver was trying to help people out of the ditch, and others were climbing out of the bus windows they were forcing up, for the bus was lying on its side.

In the meantime my uncle and the Martian got out to find Sheila's body in the mud and bushes. Darkness had fallen and the storm persisted, and the police were having trouble finding the injured and the dead with their flashlights. I can only assume that my uncle was successful — Sheila's body was never found by the rescue workers. That was the last I saw of my uncle and my people for some time. I was trembling and felt very alone, despite all that was happening. I was crying too, for Sheila, hoping that she had not felt any pain.

I stood for over an hour in the rain and thunder and lightning. People were shouting and running, and sirens came and went. In the shuffle, I was knocked down into the mud and skinned my knee. I looked just as if I had been one of those involved in the accident, but had luckily not been badly injured.

Finally, the bus driver walked up to me out of the darkness. "Oh, there you are!" A lady said, "Weren't you on the bus with us?" "Yes," I said nervously. I told them that I was Sheila.

They helped me into one of the ambulance vehicles together with the injured. Everyone was to be checked out at the hospital because of the matter of insurance. As we were racing through the city with sirens screaming, the man in the white suit asked me if I was okay and he bandaged my knee. In the hospital, I sat in silence.

Chapter Eleven
Sheila

1. Donna's Early Life
2. Sheila is born
3. The first years
4. Meeting C.L.
5. Traveling with C.L.
6. A miserable life
7. Sheila is sent Little Rock to Chattanooga
8. Death at Little Rock

Sheila's mother was born in the early 1930s in Falling Water, Tennessee. Being the only one with blond hair and blue eyes, Donna was the strangest child in her family. Everyone affectionately called her "Cottontop," a name her father had given her.

Donna's father was a gentle and kind man, a man she adored and loved with all her heart. Every morning, when she was barely three years old, Donna would go into her Daddy's room to dance and sing. Daddy loved his little girl. To see her dancing so daintily filled him with joy, and he told her not to mind her aunt who warned that the excitement would kill him. Donna's father had spent many years working in the coal mines, and was now bedridden with a serious illness.

Every morning before her performance Donna ran up to collect a kiss; hut one morning was different from all others. Something was very wrong — Daddy was cold. She didn't know what to think, seeing him lying there so still.

In all the commotion that followed, Donna remembered only one horrible thing. The words her aunt screamed as she ran into the room left a scar in Donna's heart. "See, I told you if you kept dancing you would kill him!" Horrified, the little girl ran out of the house in tears, believing she had surely killed Daddy.

Under the old wooden house she crawled and hid, and wailed and wailed until her oldest brother Otto came to soothe her. He coaxed her out and hugged her, trying to convince her that she really had not killed Daddy. The whole experience was only a beginning of Donna's life of suffering and pain.

She and her family grew up in a life of poverty. With seven children, her mother Jane could barely scrape together a living now that her husband was gone. The poor family did not have much of anything.

Donna was married off at a very young age because her mother (who would become my Earth grandmother) did not have the means to care for her much longer. By the time Donna was fourteen, she was married to a man who was supposedly the handsomest guy in the county. All the other girls were crazy about him.

Two months passed before Donna reached puberty. And shortly after that she became pregnant. She was certainly excited about having a baby, but her husband never became a providing father. Back at his home before this, every penny from his job had gone to support the family. Now that he was out from under his parents' wings, it was the perfect time to buy everything he always wanted.

The money went for his pinball games, for soda pop, for hot dogs, for movies, for everything except necessities. The family's bills were never paid. The dinner table was a wooden box, with orange crates as the seats.

Donna was much too young and immature to be married, not to mention raising a child. She continued to sleep with her favorite doll, and even put cold cream on its face at night, and her husband would have to give it a goodnight kiss.

Some of the things I am saying here about my Earth mother's early life did not come to me through Vonic. I learned a great deal from what she herself told me during my life with her.

Donna was deeply affected by a fishing trip she had made with her husband during the eighth month of pregnancy. As they walked down a steep slope toward the river Donna tripped and fell, rolling down the slope bumpity-bump with her big belly. The dough balls she was carrying for bait flew in every direction.

Running behind Donna, her husband could think of nothing but his dough balls. "Oh, my dough balls! You've ruined my dough balls!" Never once did he show concern over whether Donna and the baby had been hurt. She never forgave him for that. He wasn't being cruel; he was just young and inexperienced.

On August 20th, her husband's birthday, Donna gave him a living birthday present. It was on this day in 1948 that Sheila was born. Yet all that he could think of was that she had forgotten a birthday present.

Donna knew very little about taking care of a baby, and her husband never bought all that little Sheila had need of. This was partly because of his low income and partly because he also knew very little about babies' needs. The result was that in a few months the baby was near death, and there was little the doctors could do. Her intestines showed through the skin, and she had bad diarrhea and infected ears and throat.

Donna prayed and prayed to God that if He would let the baby live, she would live right. Little Sheila did live, but Donna never lived up to her promise. For this she suffered a great deal later in life.

Soon after the little girl was well again, Donna decided that she wanted a divorce. Instead of sitting down with her husband and trying to work things out between them, she simply divorced the man. She knew little about trying to make a marriage work. They were both immature and not ready for family life. At the age of sixteen she was on her own with the baby girl.

My people at this time had been following the pattern of Sheila's life to see when I had to come on the scene. This was all arranged by a Master in charge of my spiritual unfoldment. He knew Sheila was not going to live to maturity, but the exact time of her passing had not yet been pinpointed.

Meanwhile, Sheila's father married a girl named Peggy. He brought her over one day and introduced her to Donna to gain her approval. This seemed strange to Donna and disturbed her a great deal. But Peggy was indeed a wonderful wife and a beautiful person; both she and little Sheila's father were very good to Sheila in the years to follow.

Donna at that time began seeing an older man named Ed, who had a daughter about Sheila's age. He was so kind to Donna and Sheila that she finally did marry him, at the age of seventeen

Donna and Ed then moved into an apartment building in which her older sister lived, whom she idolized. Donna enjoyed living there with her sister and brother-in-law and their little boy. The boy was only a few years older than Sheila, and the two children enjoyed each other's company.

Then Donna became pregnant and gave birth to a boy, Edgar Vernon, named after her husband. They lived there for a few years; Donna was rather happy with her little baby boy, her little girl, and Ed. What she never realized was that her husband was very much interested in her sister. Donna's love for her left little room for jealousy.

Donna visited her mother Jane one day, taking along Sheila and leaving behind her little boy Eddie at her sister's apartment next door. Returning late, she discovered her little boy was gone, her husband was gone, and her sister was gone. Donna and her sister's husband didn't realize until about two days later that they had actually run off together. It was a terrible shock and hurt Donna deeply because she had placed so much love and faith in her sister. As time passed, however, feelings changed and all was accepted.

This was Donna's second marriage gone down the drain. For the second time, now at the age of nineteen, she was alone with her little girl Sheila. She knew nothing of the legalities of getting her son back.

During the time Donna was married to her second husband, she had met a man named C. L., who happened to be Edgar's uncle. C.L. was a Cary Grant type of person with his moustache, arched eyebrows, and widow' s peak, and the very particular way he dressed.

C.L. was a jack-of-all-trades and a very good construction man, but completely untrustworthy. He could talk a man out of his last five cents; he was a conman and a deceiver. But C.L. was an irresistible sort of person with lots of personality and a way of charming people to do as he wished. He was a complex character and very inte lligent. He grew up with a very religious mother, and respected Christianity, but he drank heavily.

Even his mother spoke of how very "messed up" C.L. was. At eleven he had started drinking, and from the age of five he had always been terribly cruel. It all started, she claimed, one night during the time they were living in a boxcar. A vicious storm was raging. Suddenly C.L. let out a scream of agony; afterwards he was never again the same person. She said that it was as if some kind of evil energy had taken over his body.

C.L. was an unpredictable person. One minute he would pat you on the head, and the next minute he would knock you clear across the room. No one knew what he was going to do next, or how to react to him. He was certainly a strange man, but in spite of this, Donna fell for him. People always seemed to want C.L.'s attention and approval.

Often during their courtship, he brought food as well as clothes for little Sheila. Donna was sympathetic to the hard-luck story C.L. told about his wife, and being so young she didn't realize what kind of person he actually was. It was true that his wife was an alcoholic, but later Donna would learn that C.L. had brought it on.

After she lived with him for about a week, Donna realized C.L. was an alcoholic too, but it was too late to matter. Although she herself did not drink compulsively, he kept pushing it on her. She finally did start drinking, but mostly to escape his meanness. His cruelty affected the little girl as well. Whenever he was drunk, C.L. had a habit of beating Donna, while Sheila looked on in fright, terrified of the man.

Donna and C.L. never lived in one place for more than a few months; they traveled all over the country and lived mostly in motels and rooming houses. At one time, they owned a small restaurant in Virginia and C.L. was very successful. But he could never stay in one place for long. He always had an itch to run off with all the money and goods he could lay his hands on. From state to state he ran, in and out of trouble with the law while Donna tagged along. They managed restaurants and motels across the country, and when legitimate jobs didn't pay off he would turn to hijacking trucks or making moonshine.

Little Sheila was being dragged around with them. She was not a very happy little girl. C.L. terrified her, and she was confused as to why mother loved him.

When C.L. was sober he was charming, but when he was drunk he was extremely cruel. There was one particular instance when little six-year-old Sheila tried to protect her mother when C.L. was beating her. Enraged, he smacked Sheila across the face, giving her a black eye. The little girl saw through him and was perplexed as to why Donna put up with so much trouble.

The whole situation was very sad because C.L. could not help himself. There was something very wrong with him mentally, aside from the drinking, or perhaps caused by it. Donna drank more and more just to tolerate her lot. She began to despise the man as much as she loved him. Many times she ran away from him with Sheila, but he always managed to win her back through cajoling or by force.

The day came when Donna again tried to leave C.L. Taking Sheila along, she hitchhiked with a truck driver who took them along to his home in Indianapolis. He and his wife took good care of Donna and Sheila, and their own twin boys.

Then Donna made the mistake of calling C.L. so that he would be able to pick up his car keys, which she had taken along to prevent him from following her. She did not realize that C.L. had spare keys. Upon arriving, he cried and carried on about how sincerely he meant to change his ways. He wouldn't be mean anymore and he was going to stop drinking, he promised. Donna believed him.

On the outskirts of Indianapolis, C.L. suddenly left the highway, much to Donna's surprise. He drove on into a forest preserve. There C.L. stopped and threatened to kill the both of them for betraying him. Waving a pistol, he accused Donna of having an affair with the man. He even tried to force Sheila into saying that she saw them together. As fate had it, they were saved by a patrolman who pulled alongside warning C.L. that he was parked illegally.

This calmed C.L. down somewhat, but it was then that Donna decided this was not the kind of life Sheila deserved, that these kinds of things were happening too often. She could see that her little girl was unhappy living with C.L., and since she loved Sheila more than herself she decided to send her away to grandmother for protection, and for her own peace of mind.

Donna reasoned with C.L. that Sheila would have a much more stable life in Chattanooga; she could go to school and have friends. C.L. agreed, but only because he would rather be rid of her. At this time, C.L. and Donna were on the road to the West from Indianapolis; they stopped long enough to put Sheila on the bus under Traveler's Aid, with a note to Donna's mother Jane. This then is how Sheila happened to meet her fate on that rainy night in Little Rock, Arkansas.

When I arrived at Grandmother's house in Chattanooga, I became a part of the whole karmic chaos. Donna became my mother and C.L. became my stepfather. Living with him later in my life was all the nightmare it had been for Sheila, and more.

Chapter Twelve
My Earth Family

1. I arrive at the housing project
2. First days
3. David and Peggy
4. Church and School
5. Contemplations on the new life
6. Donna
7. Playing
8. Adults
9. Grandma
10. Donna again
11. Illnesses

At last the lights came on and the door opened, and I saw inside an elderly woman in her nightgown. I recognized her immediately; this was my Earth grandmother, Jane. Vonic had been right when he described her as a sickly woman. The floating tumors in her stomach made her look eight months pregnant.

"Sheila?" she asked, peering into the darkness to see who was there.

"Yes, it is me," I said. I stood there in silence, awaiting her reaction.

"Well, what are you doing here? And where is your mother? Where is everybody?" she asked. It was obvious to me that she couldn't believe her own eyes, waking up at three in the morning to find Sheila at the door. As it turned out Donna had not called ahead to say that her daughter would be coming to Chattanooga.

"There's nobody else," I answered. "I'm here by myself."

"What do you mean you're here by yourself?" she demanded. Then she held the door open for me to enter.

Vonic had well prepared me for what I was to say next. "Well, my mother sent me here because her and C.L. were fighting, and she didn't want me to stay there anymore."

I showed her the note and told what C. L. had done, how he tried to kill Donna and me, and how Donna asked C.L. if she could send me to stay with her mother Jane.

"How could they do that without even letting me know?" Grandma looked upset. As we walked through the living room toward the stairs she said worriedly, "I just don't know what I'm going to do with you."

I felt a bit uneasy as Grandma took me upstairs to her room and put me to bed with her. But it wasn't long before I fell asleep, listening to the gravel roof crackle and pop as the temperature dropped. It had been a long, eventful day to say the least.

This was to be my new home for the next several years. Grandma hadn't completely moved into the housing project from her home in the country. Some of her furniture was already there, but her daughter Ellen still lived in the apartment. Grandma was staying there to recover from her recent coma, when doctors discovered she had sugar diabetes and heart dropsy. Aunt Ellen was planning to move into a nicer neighborhood.

I awoke in the morning to find that everyone was already downstairs. Quietly, I walked into the kitchen and sat down at the table, only momentarily interrupting Aunt Ellen and Grandma's conversation. It was about me.

Ellen's idea was to send me away to a foster home, mostly because my grandmother was very poor at the time, living on welfare and supporting the two boys.

I was dumbfounded! "Is this for real?" I thought, and yet they continued with their discussion as if I wasn't even there. It just broke my heart to hear how little they seemed to care about Sheila, so soon after I had arrived.

When I sensed how serious they were about sending me away, I burst into tears. "I don't want to go to a children's home," I cried, running up to put my arms around Grandma's legs. Tears were streaming down my face. "Please don't send me to a home," I pleaded.

Grandma looked at Aunt Ellen. "I just can't put her in a foster home," she said, reminding Ellen that I had probably suffered enough, living with C.L.

"Well, maybe I can take her until you can make some arrangements," Aunt Ellen suggested.

Grandma decided to keep me. That very morning she made a call to someone on the telephone to arrange a court date for the custody proceedings. I was relieved.

After breakfast I met my cousins Donny and Jim, Aunt Ellen's two boys. They had been outside, playing. Donny was a few months older than I, and Jim was about three months younger. Their butch haircuts intrigued me.

Almost immediately they began telling me all about the school I would be going to, which made me very happy. It was not that I was anxious to go to school, but I was happy to be accepted and liked.

I had already seen Merle and Ben the night before, when they came downstairs to see what all the commotion was about. These were the boys who were each other's uncle, although they were both high school seniors.

As we were sitting together in the kitchen, Donny and Jim were both trying to tell me everything they knew about the neighborhood, and all the things they were going to show me. Just then two girls came into the kitchen. Both were about my age. One of them, the one with the brown eyes and brown hair in bangs, and a very pretty face, I recognized as my cousin Lynn. The other had long auburn hair and green eyes — Andreia.

Grandmother introduced me to them; they were Donna's brother's two girls whom I (Sheila) had not seen in along time. They lived nearby in the housing project. Not long ago they had moved from their home in Falling Water, where Grandma still lived.

Most of my cousins, I noticed with satisfaction, were close to my age and would probably become good friends. And they looked exactly like Vonic had described them.

On this same day, Grandma and the two boys and I moved back to her home in the country. It was the first of many sudden moves, which kept me from feeling at ease during these first few months on Earth.

Falling Water was the most primitive place I had ever seen, although very lush and green. We were amidst the wooded hills of Tennessee, not far from Chattanooga. Our home was a nine-room frame house set up on masonry block and the toilet was a patch of woods beyond the clearing. Our water supply was a mile away at a mountain creek.

Animals thrived in the wild and I enjoyed them, except for the wild boars that occasionally came out of the woods to chase me into the house.

I wondered about all this. I loved the crisp smells, and playing in the woods, but I had never imagined Earth to be so primitive. Of course, by modern standards Falling Water was indeed primitive, and I had not seen much of the city of Chattanooga.

We did not stay long in Falling Water.

My grandmother and I sat up late one night, talking. "Grandma, you aren't going to let me go home, are you?" I asked.

"No, I already talked to this judge that we will have to go and see in the city. I guess he's going to let me keep you."

"What's the matter, Grandma?" I asked, suddenly aware that she looked sick. "You don't look too good."

She answered with a sigh. "Yeah, I don't feel too good either. I'm pretty tired." Then she started talking to me about the Bible. I laid my head on her lap, and by kerosene lamp she read a beautiful story about Jesus and the woman at the well. It was very late, and Merle and Ben had not come home, when I fell asleep.

I opened my eyes with a feeling of apprehension. "Where am I?" I thought to myself, seeing the strange walls surrounding me. "Is this real?" Electric lights burned overhead in an adjoining room. On a mantle I saw a picture of a pretty woman and a nice-looking man. At the other end of the mantle was a picture of a baby.

Just then I heard footsteps nearing the room. Closing my eyes I pretended to be asleep.

A woman's voice said, "Well, I don't know where we'll put her. I guess we'll just make a pallet somewhere."

She decided. "David, I think we'll put them over here. We'll put the baby here and Sheila there."

Then the photo on the mantle flashed in my mind, and I remembered Sheila's father was David. "That's my Father," I thought, "my Earth Daddy." I opened my eyes and stretched.

"Hi Honey, how are you?" said David as he walked up to the bed, smiling.

"Daddy!" I cried.

"Yes, it's me," he said merrily as he bent down over me. I reached up and hugged hm, sincerely glad to see him. It felt really good to hug this man's neck; he was such a sweet person.

"We're going to put you in the baby's bed," he explained, "and let the baby sleep with us. All right?"

"Well, that's okay with me, but I could sleep on the floor."

"No, you don't have to do that. We have room. You know, we've got a little boy too. He's about four years old."

Peggy came in from the other room. "Okay, let's go eat. It's time for supper."

"Supper?" I blurted out. I was sure it was morning.

"Sure," David said, "You slept here all night. And you really must have been tired, because you slept all day, too."

"I did?" I could hardly believe it.

"Yes," he repeated, "Your uncle brought you here and you'll be staying with us until your grandmother gets better."

I assumed that Grandma had gotten very sick again and that one of her sons had taken her to the hospital. She did get sick quite often I was told.

I stayed with my father and Peggy until Grandma recovered and moved into the housing project. I never went to Falling Water again, except for short visits to other relatives still living there.

During these first weeks on Earth, I never was nervous that one of my relatives would say, "You're not Sheila!" I knew enough about Sheila and looked enough like her that I had plenty of confidence to carry it through.

Peggy and David were very good to me, and I enjoyed being with them. It never bothered me that she was not my own mother, because none of the people I would be living with were my own relatives. Peggy was a sweet and wonderful person and treated me equally as one of her own.

After dinner that day we visited Peggy's mother Rose and her children Jimmy and Janice. I thought Janice was simply beautiful with her long blond hair falling to below her shoulders. She was only five days younger than I and we got along together very well.

"Hey Sheila, let's go play movie stars," she suggested.

"What?" I asked. This was new to me.

"Movie stars. Don't you know anything about them?"

"No," I said, "I've never been to a movie."

"Oh, that's right. You lived out in the country," Janice remembered, thinking of Falling Water. "I'll be Doris Day. No... I want to be Janet Leigh. You be Doris Day."

"Okay," I said. "Who's Doris Day?"

"Over here is a picture of her." Janice fumbled with a magazine and finally pointed to a photo.

"Oh, she's cute," I said, "but can't I be Marilyn Monroe? This one right here?"

"No, you can't be her, you don't look like her. You be Doris Day."

"Oh, okay." I said.

"Tony Curtis is my boyfriend," Janice explained. "and I guess you can have Dean Martin."

I said okay once again. Then we started to play. "How do you do this?" I asked.

"First you have to fix up. Here put on one of my mother's dresses."

Janice must have wondered why I was so little. I guess she blamed it on my stay out in the country, in Falling Water.

I felt silly in the long, flowered dress and high heel shoes. Janice put lipstick on my lips and then stepped back, looking satisfied. "Now you look pretty."

"Well, thank you," I told her. "You look pretty too." Then we played movie stars. I learned that you sing, you have big cars, you go out to restaurants, and you spend lots of money.

Janice's eyes lighted up. "I'll tell you what!" she exclaimed. "I'll see if you can go to the movies with us tonight. We're supposed to go to the movies."

"What are we going to see?" I asked excitedly. This sounded interesting. Playing movie stars was a dull game.

"The Blob!" Janice said. "It's supposed to be real scary. Let's see if you can go with us."

Janice and I ran into the living room. "Peggy, can Sheila go to the show with us tonight?" she asked. Peggy was Janice's elder sister.

"Well, I don't know." She looked at Daddy.

David spoke up. "Yeah, you can go. It's all right. Here Janice. Here's a couple of dollars. You can take Sheila to the movies with you."

"I don't need that," Janice said. "We get in for free!'

"How do you do that?" Daddy asked.

"Well, Bobbie stands outside the show and we duck under her arm when she pays for herself." Bobbie was Janice's fourteen-year-old sister.

"No, that's not honest. Now you girls pay," Daddy said. "Here's the money. Get Sheila some cashews, she'll like those."

"I never had them before," I said.

"Yeah, I know, because your grandmother doesn't let you go to the show, right?" he asked.

"I don't know."

"Well, she doesn't believe in movies, so never ask if you can go," he said.

I didn't understand. "Why doesn't she believe in them?"

"Because she is a Christian, honey, and they don't go to shows."

It still didn't make sense to me, but I said okay anyway. My favorite word was okay because it kept me out of trouble. I was a very agreeable little girl.

This idea of religions telling people what to do just seemed absurd to me, and I remembered that my Aunt had once spoken about this subject.

When we started to leave, Janice held me back. "Wait a minute. You can't go to the show looking like that."

"Like what?" I asked. I felt fine.

"You have to take off the lipstick, and the dress, and the high heeled shoes first," she said.

I laughed. "Oh yeah, right."

Bobbie took us to the show, and there I had the second soda pop in my life, and popcorn too. Popcorn! I really liked that, and the cashews especially.

The Blob was about a flying saucer that brought all sorts of havoc and terror to the people of Earth. It landed one night in a secluded woods. A couple of teenagers were the first to see it, but when they reached the landing area nothing could be seen but an eerie glowing blob.

Curious to see that would happen, the boy poked into the blob with a stick. Suddenly the burning mass covered his hand and crept steadily up his arm. The boy's girlfriend screamed and ran off, while he tried desperately to fling the blob away.

At the hospital, the doctors were perplexed. Whatever the thing was, they agreed, it had to be stopped soon. As they stood discussing the boy in the next room, they suddenly saw before them a gigantic glowing and pulsating blob of energy. It had consumed the boy and was now moving on to its next victims.

Until the very end of the show, the blob absorbed people and houses and cars, and it had become even wore gigantic. People panicked and flew from their homes.

Quite by accident, the heroes of the show discovered that the creature could be killed with low temperatures; when it tried to hide in a freezer, Earth was saved.

My problem was that through the whole show I couldn't stop laughing. Everything was so funny to me. And the blob was the most hilarious of all.

"How come you are laughing?" Janice said. She had trouble understanding me. "It's really scary!"

"I don't know," I said. "It just looks funny to me." All along, I was thinking, "This is really strange. Why do people have ideas that such weird creatures come from space?" And with people's consciousness as it was. They often formed conceptions from what they saw right there in the movies.

I realized then the wisdom of my people's warnings, that I was not to speak of being from another planet. Those people who would believe my story would probably remember the terrible creatures of science fiction movies. Either way, the negative powers had made sure that our people would not reveal themselves too soon.

It was a strange coincidence that this first movie I saw on Earth was about creatures from outer space. Janice was still terrified when we left the theater. "Wait until you see Dracula!" she said. "You'll like that."

"Yeah, I probably will," I said. But when she started telling me about Dracula, who he was and what he did, it was my turn to be frightened. I had reason to believe that such creatures really existed on this Earth planet.

Daddy was waiting to take me home when we returned to Janice's house. "Well, tomorrow we're going to have to enroll you in school for a couple of weeks, until you can go live with your grandmother."

"Do I have to go back to her?" I asked. "Can't I live with you?"

My father pulled me close to him. "Honey, you can't stay with me because your grandmother is getting custody of you. That means the law is giving you to her and you can't stay with me."

"Well, I don't understand why," I said.

He tried to be firm with me. "Because that's just the way it happened. If you would have come to me first, then I would have gotten custody of you. But it really would be hard on me. I have my own family, my kids to raise, you know. You are my first child and I love you very much, and you'll always be special to me. But it's just the fact that I don't have enough money to support everybody right now."

"Okay," I said, "but then is my grandmother going to get well?"

"Well, I don't know. That night you went to sleep in her lap she got real sick. She has sugar diabetes, you know, and a bad heart. She should be home pretty soon."

"Back to the country?"

"No, she's going to be living in the city, at the federal housing project."

"Oh yeah, that's right," I remembered.

My father went on to explain, "I guess she's going to live there because it's real cheap, only twenty five dollars a month rent."

"And I'll be going to school there?"

"Yes," he said.

"Will I ever see you again?" I asked. I had a great deal of affection for David.

"Oh sure, I'll come and get you sometimes and bring you to our house, if your grandmother will let me," he answered me.

As I was lying in bed that night, I thought of all the wonderful things that had happened. I had enjoyed myself with someone my own age, and I had seen my first movie. Movies were a popular form of entertainment, Uncle Odin had once told me.

Playing in the country was fun, but this was an adventure, going to a show and seeing a creature from outer space. I suppose there are such menacing creatures as the blob on the lower astral plane, but I don't know of any on the physical plane.

The next morning my father woke me to get dressed for school. First he showed me something special.

"For me?" I asked, as he handed it to me.

"Sure," he said smiling.

It was a writing tablet, with Gene Autry and his horse on the cover. "It's beautiful!" I exclaimed, but I did not understand why the black pencils he gave me were so fat. And the lines on the pages were so huge. Children were expected to write big, I guess.

In school that morning I was nervous. Janice was already there to introduce me to her friends, but she was in a different class.

My teacher was a beautiful woman with big brown eyes and short, curly black hair. She introduced me to the class, saying that my parents had been traveling a great deal. Therefore I was beginning first grade at the age of seven.

I was surprised and happy to see how nicely the other children treated me. Some of them could not resist their taunting me because I was older, especially the boys. But everyone quieted down after a while.

Mrs. Lewis was a wonderful teacher. She was sincere about helping me learn, and I grew to love her. I already knew what she was trying to teach me, but I surely couldn't let her know. I pretended to be learning.

At first she worked with me while the other children were busy, teaching me the ABCs. I caught up with the class in very little tine. Soon she didn't need to make special trips to my desk to explain what the rest of the class was doing.

When she saw how quickly I learned to spell and count, and write my name, I was passed on to the second grade. It was only two weeks since my father had enrolled me. Sheila herself had never finished first grade, and my father and Mrs. Lewis couldn't possibly think anything but that Sheila was a bright child who was done an injustice by C.L. and Donna's traveling.

I entered the second grade class just as our teacher, Mr. Reed, was introducing subtraction.

He said, "Now, today we are going to learn subtraction..."

"Subtraction?" I blurted out.

He looked at me sternly and spoke. "You're not supposed to talk unless you raise your hand."

"Oh, okay," I said. So I raised my hand and asked, "What's subtraction?"

Mr. Reed sounded impatient. "I'll be explaining it in a few minutes." But the more he talked about it, the more I became confused.

"That's really strange," I said. "Why do you want to take anything away from something?"

"I don't know," he said.

This disturbed me. "You don't know? You're our teacher. What do you mean? You take one from two and you get one. Why would you want to take a one from a two?"

"Sheila, those questions don't make any sense."

"Does this make sense then— one take away one is zero. How can you take something from itself? You can remove the object and have nothing, but not take it from itself." I persisted in trying to make my point; these new mathematical ideas didn't agree with what I had been taught.

"Sheila, if you don't stop asking questions I'll send you to the principal."

"Oh, okay." I said quietly. "I won't ask any more."

Subtraction never made sense to me, and it never will. I do not like it because it is too mental and doesn't follow the natural laws of expansion. In Teutonia I was never taught to take anything from something else. We only changed what existed.

I also had a problem with Earth's base ten number system. On the more advanced planets the zero does not exist because of its very nature. In following the laws of nature, we have learned that the base nine number system suits us best of all. Incidentally, governments of the Earth have investigated crashed flying saucers over the years and have found that their dimensions point to the use of a base nine number system.

To make everyone happy, I learned subtraction. That evening I went home and told Daddy what I had learned, that one from two is one.

"That's very good!" he said.

"I also know what ten take away five is," I said.

"What's that?"

"Five."

"How did you know that?" he asked. "Did they teach you that?"

"They taught me two take away one, and I just figured the other one out."

"Yeah, you're pretty good at that, aren't you?" He smiled. "I really am proud of you because you are my first little girl. You look a lot like your mother.'

"I do?"

"Yeah."

"She's pretty." I said, remembering Vonic's description of her. "She looks like Marilyn Monroe."

"Yes, she does," he agreed, laughing.

I wondered if I would ever meet Donna, and when it would be. I had heard so much about her from Grandma and Aunt Ellen, but I hadn't seen her myself. It wouldn't be until a year had passed in my life on Earth.

We were seated at the dinner table on Friday evening, having the usual hot dogs and chili, which I learned to love. The phone rang and Daddy went to answer it.

My grandmother was coming home, he announced, and my heart sank. I would be going back to her in a week.

I didn't like the idea of leaving; David and Peggy had been so very good to me. And what would happen to all my new friends at school, I wondered?

"Do I have to go back?" I asked.

"Yes, Honey," Daddy said. "I told you before that you had to go back to your grandma."

"Okay," I said quietly, with a note of sadness. Peggy was real sweet and rolled my hair for me. I thought she was so beautiful with her blue eyes, wonderful skin, and long, wavy-brown pony tail. I would miss them.

"Monday we'll have to go down to school with you, or send a note, and tell them you'll be leaving at the end of the week. Then they can send your records to the new school."

"Okay."

But instead of going to school on Monday, I had to say goodbye to Daddy and Peggy. Tears filled my eyes. Grandma wanted me home early to help her straighten out the house and unpack. I wouldn't even be able to say goodbye to my friends.

Grandma was waiting for me when I once again knocked at 1821 Southern Street. Everything inside was a mess, and even with Merle and Ben's help there wasn't much any of us could do to make the place beautiful. The apartment itself looked new and shiny, but Grandma's furniture was so old and horrible-looking that I was quickly depressed.

Grandma, I had learned from Vonic, had separated from her husband on account of his drinking, and was living alone with the two boys.

Looking down from the ridge in Chattanooga, the apartments of our housing project took the shape of a huge horseshoe facing the railroad yard. Southern Street bordered our end of the project, and behind us were rows of two-story brick buildings with flat roofs of white gravel. Each family had its own backyard, an upstairs and a downstairs, and garbage cans marked with the house number.

The inside walls of our apartment were plain masonry block painted mint green, and the floors were covered with dark brown asphalt tiles. In the front was the living roan. A hallway on the right led to the kitchen, and the concrete stairs to the bedrooms led to the left from the hallway.

Everything was electrical; our apartment had a new refrigerator, a range, and electric heaters installed into the walls. Next to the kitchen and behind the living room was the utility room. Here were two huge washing sinks, as well as plenty of shelves and cupboards.

Upstairs were three bedrooms and a modern bath room equipped with a low built-in tub.

For the twenty five dollars per month Grandma paid, this was luxury even by modern standards. Exterminators came every month to spray for bugs, which I learned was a service many people in large cities did not have.

A few days after we settled down, Grandma hauled all of us to a pretty white wooden building near our house. I soon learned what Vonic meant when he said she was a devout Christian in the Church of God.

The novelty of going to church wore off pretty quickly as we went every Monday, Wednesday, Friday and Sunday. Sunday School was fun. We read stories and sang songs. So was the singing in Church, and listening to the guitars and piano. One young man who sometimes sang in front of the congregation was especially well-liked. His name was Elvis Presley.

The rest of my experiences in Church were lessons in tolerance and understanding. The Church of God made it very difficult for a person to remain an individual. Just as Vonic had explained, women were not allowed to wear pants, cut their hair, get a permanent, wear makeup, or wear jewelry. It seemed as if most of the rules were for women.

The men were forbidden to drink or smoke, which was actually good for their health. But it bothered me that they did it only because it was a rule.

The preaching bothered most of all. The ministers always preached directly from the Bible, beginning by telling a story and then explaining the moral. Often they repeated the same idea four or five times, using different examples. And it was always a highly emotional, and sometimes shouting-type of preaching.

Whenever an evangelist was in town, the preaching and singing came to a heavy boil. Grandma insisted on taking me along to these revivals; the meetings were held every night.

The members would bring newcomers with them to be saved and prizes were awarded to the one who brought along the most converts. I didn't know what to think about all of this.

The evangelist pleaded and begged for the new people to come up and be saved now, before it was too late, as hymns were sung in the background of his charged voice. Meanwhile, the vibrations of the church often reached a strange level. People started crying and went up to kneel down. Others started jumping up and down, shouting in high-pitched voices and speaking in tongues. With their Bible open to a certain place, they went around emotionally pointing it out to others, speaking in a mysterious tongue.

The ones who were being saved fell to their knees, crying and wailing at the long wooden bench which served as the altar.

The preacher and his associates promptly came along and knelt by each person. "Are you willing to ask God to forgive you for your sins? Are you willing to be a holy person? And let the blood of Jesus wash away your sins?"

This business with the blood of Jesus often worried me because I took things literally.

When it was all over, the saved people stood in front while everyone came by to shake hands and welcome them as members of the Church.

Revivals usually put me to sleep if I couldn't draw pictures or play. Sometimes I tried to listen to what was going on, but my interests never lasted long. I loved the singing and the clapping; that was about all.

I saw and understood that these people were very sincere, and it all had a very deep spiritual meaning to them. My reactions were based on my own experiences and teachings.

On Venus I had learned and come to understand that the Bible was a diary of special people who lived on Earth long ago. It was little more than a history book. This is very difficult for people on Earth to accept. At one time there was great Truth in the sayings of religious leaders, but after centuries of rewriting and retranslating, the words of the Bible cannot be considered of absolute truth. I do agree, however, with the commandments.

It is known on Venus that many individuals have used the writings of spiritual leaders for their own good, or to get some special point across. If there was a difference of opinion with what was written, or if something was not understood, then that section of the Bible was rewritten.

Different denominations have different Bibles for this reason. The writings have been changed according to their understanding of the Truth.

The Word of God or Truth must be experienced, not read in a book. This is done by actually seeing the Supreme Deity and communicating with it in the Nameless World beyond the Soul plane. Only Soul itself can experience It. It is not a physical experience.

In order to control the people, religious leaders have created the "Believe or be damned" gospel — a religion of fear. A postulate was created that a certain collection of writings is the Word of God. By manipulating and interpreting the book, the people can be controlled. Such are the works of Kal, although most of those who are involved are not aware of it.

The man-made law bothered me, and I often got into arguments with Grandma about why women couldn't wear pants or lipstick. It just didn't make sense to me that a Church was able to tell people to do this and not do that.

According to the laws of the Supreme Being, I was born with the right to dress and act as I pleased. And I accepted full responsibility for my actions under the law of Karma. No Church, or person, had the right to take my rights away.

The one thing that I learned from my arguments with Grandma was that it was useless to argue. As my uncle and Vonic had told me, children on Earth are given very little freedom of individuality.

Especially in school was this true. Grandma enrolled me at Mary Ann Garber School, which belonged to the housing project and was run by the government. Elderly Mrs. Jensen, my second grade teacher, did not make much of an impression on me. I sensed she was not interested in her students or the school.

For a while, school was a fine novelty, but my own interest wore off quickly. It disturbed me that teachers taught only what they felt the children should know, which were the basics everyone should have leaned at home.

Much too much time was eaten up by the memorizing of facts, facts which would aid us very little in life unless we're quizzed on a show or in a contest.

From the very beginning I saw that testing and grading instilled in the children a sense of competitiveness, a destructive force which Earth well could do without.

The slower learners were degraded by receiving low marks or being sent to learn with the retarded children. Educators didn't seem to make allowances for the fact that each individual learns at his own pace.

I liked the teachers, the children, the recess, and the lunch hour, but class itself was boring. Many of the children enjoyed class because they felt it important to learn whatever was being taught.

A greater freedom of choice for children in what they learn and when, would do wonders.

When I wasn't in school, I often spent time by myself, alone, thinking about the different things I objected to. There were just too many routine events in my life eating up too much of my time, just so my physical body could survive. Yet very many people were fat, and unclean, or did not care about their appearance. I realized this all came from improper training and poor eating habits.

Alone in bed at night, I couldn't help but think about home, about Arena and Odin, my father, and all the creativity in our lives. It was something I could never forget, no matter what role I played. My life here seemed so strange, and how sad I was not being able to share my past with anyone.

I imagined myself back in my room and in all my favorite places. Memories of Rimj and the smiling faces of all my friends as they said goodbye to me, kept me company when I was feeling low.

There were times when I hoped someone would recognize me, that I wasn't Sheila. I was afraid of actually becoming her, from being so immersed in her life.

As Sheila I became known as a very quiet child. As Omnec I was unreserved and bubbly. Part of my quietness came from not knowing what to do, and being afraid of saying or doing something wrong.

Within my Earth family I watched, and I learned from watching, instead of asking questions. No matter how much it put me out, or how long I would have to wait for the answer, I always wanted to see for myself what was going on. Asking questions embarrassed me because it attracted attention to something I didn't know.

My people communicated very little with me until later in life. They believed in not interfering unless it was absolutely necessary. Sometimes, though, I recognized certain thoughts as not having been my own, and so I was aware of their interest and inner guidance.

I visited Teutonia only a few tires, in the dream state. I soon learned that I had much less control over my astral body now; its vibrations had been lowered when I manifested my physical body.

Most of the time, my mind was cluttered with what I was learning on Earth, and my attention was very seldom on Soul travel. I was busy feeling my way around in this new life, learning what people expected of me so I would know how to react. I listened carefully whenever comments were made about Sheila.

Doing spiritual exercises was almost impossible, with the little privacy I had. And I was preoccupied with many new physical plane experiences.

Christmas was approaching and I had been in Chattanooga almost two months. I knew the Earth version of the story of Christ, but what did the tree and giving presents have to do with it, I wondered? It was a wonderful time of year though. People seemed to have better attitudes toward one another.

On Christmas Eve we found presents under our tree, wrapped in gaily colored paper, and we could hardly wait till the next morning. Everyone claimed that Santa Claus had brought them, but until they showed me a picture of him I didn't believe there really was such a man. He looked absurd, but he did seem happy. I couldn't decide whether to believe in him or not, but it was inconceivable to me that the grownups had deceived the children. Perhaps he existed long ago!

Outside our front door on Christmas morning sat a big woven basket brimming with hams, chickens, cookies, candy, fruits and nuts. It was the first fruit and candy I had seen at out house. It was from the American Legion.

Then it was time for us to open our presents. From Aunt Ellen I received a little play stove. Mr. Dow, our neighbor across the street, gave me a toy brass bed, just the right size for the gifts from Grandma, a baby doll. Also from Grandma were gloves and tights, and a scarf with attached hood. The coloring book and crayons were from Merle and Ben. I loved drawing. It was very creative.

Donny and Jim were given toy cars and guns, and some plastic bricks and a Lincoln Log set. Building play houses was fun, but what meant more to me than anything else was that baby doll from Grandma.

Our Christmas dinner of chicken, gravy, and biscuits, and blueberry cobbler was the best meal I could remember having since I first arrived in Chattanooga.

The next few years I lived the life of an ordinary child. I was very small, and life was not very meaningful. My beloved puppy was killed in front of our house by a car; I probably went through all the things little kids go through.

I enjoyed Chattanooga. It was a beautiful, green city surrounded by lush forested mountains and hills. I soon learned that a famous Civil War battle was fought just to the east, on Missionary Ridge. Lookout Mountain as well as many other parts of the area were tourist attractions.

What bothered me most about Chattanooga were the people's attitudes toward the Blacks. All of the Negro people had their own part of town called Niggertown. And no Black family lived in our housing project. This was in the early 50s.

I knew from experience how important a part of our Brotherhood of the Planets the Black people are. They have a right to be proud of their heritage. Many times I had to keep myself from saying something if a negative remark was made. Who would understand or tolerate a young child defending a race? It would only have caused more trouble for myself. So I learned to close my ears to the blasphemy of the Black people.

I had lived in Chattanooga for almost a year when I first met Donna, my Earth mother. I often had wondered when it would be, and I actually looked forward to it. I never worried, though, about her recognizing I wasn't Sheila.

Deep in my sleep one night, I could dimly hear Grandma and another woman speaking in the hallway, in hushed voices. Was it a dream? I didn't have the energy to wake up and see.

Then I was aware of her next to me, lying beside me in the bed, and I instinctively snuggled up to put my arms around her neck. That's how I awoke in the morning.

Big blue eyes, full of love, looked into mine, and happiness bubbled up inside of me. My arms were still around her neck, and I knew she waited for me to wake up, happy to have me so close. She loved me!

"Well well, you finally woke up, sleepyhead!"

"Mommy!" I cried. I hugged her and buried my head in her neck.

"How's my baby?" she asked in a broken voice, holding me tight.

"I'm so glad you're here, Mommy."

Donna began to cry, and so did I.

She wanted to take me somewhere special, she said, and did I have a special dress to wear?

I told her yes. Deep inside I felt akin to her.

"I've been looking at all your clothes," she said, "and I noticed that Grandma has really kept you dressed very well. You've got twenty seven dresses!" She had counted them, every one of them.

"I don't know how many girls have twenty seven dresses. I don't have that many myself."

I told her that Grandma goes downtown and looks in the store windows to see the latest styles. Then she comes home and makes me these dresses, using scraps of materials left over from the dresses she sews for other people. That's how I kept in style.

Thanks to Grandma I had gotten an award in school for being the best-dressed girl.

After breakfast Mom and I went downtown, shopping. A raincoat was just what I needed, she decided, but it wasn't until hours later that we finally found the one I liked — beautiful sky-blue instead of yellow or black.

Then we had lunch at a little hamburger restaurant, not a fancy place at all. There I devoured a hamburger, french fries, and soda pop. This was my first meal at a restaurant, since when Uncle Odin introduced me to this American food. It was a real treat.

I enjoyed being with Morn, and I felt completely at ease. Somehow, she made me feel as if I was indeed her own special little girl. It was a warmth and closeness I hadn't yet experienced on Earth; I welcomed it. And there wasn't a doubt in my mind that the two of us had spent many lifetimes together.

At home I went right to work on the coloring book Mom bought me—the kind where the colors are printed for each space. When I showed her my first page, she was amazed. How did I read so well, she wanted to know? All the colors were correct. Grandma and Mom talked about that for quite some time, while I, not knowing what to say, kept quiet.

Morn visited us on and off during the next few years, usually only once a year, whenever she was able to get away from C.L. for awhile. From what I heard, life with C.L. was getting rougher.

In no time I was quite attached to my new Mommy. During one of her rare visits, I cried and cried all evening when she went off with friends instead of spending the time with me. Being a child, I was unreasonable. The deep feelings I had for her, the warmth I felt whenever I was near her, puzzled me at times. What was it about this Soul, what experiences in past lifetimes had we shared that made me feel this way? Years would pass before I finally knew.

When I was ten years old, my life started changing. I suppose it was because I was becoming more aware of what was going on in the world around me. I had played until then and enjoyed myself as far as playing goes. Now I was keenly interested in life; I was in between being a child and becoming a teenager.

Life at home was beautiful and peaceful. I always looked forward to when Merle and Ben brought the band to our house to practice and have fun. Ben played the drums and Merle the bass fiddle. Then I would be able to dance. And whenever Ben played the guitar for me, I practiced ballet. Seeing me perform, Grandma was certain I would grow up to be a ballet dancer.

I discovered that in dancing I was able to be myself, my real self, for awhile. As the music played and I lost myself in its rhythm, I was Omnec again.

How wonderful it would be, I often thought, if my family were not so poor. Then maybe we would have a harp.

I enjoyed playing with the children in our neighborhood, making a club and having lemonade and cookies, playing house and circus together, playing dodge-ball and softball. During the summer there were few days when we didn't stay out very late, often until midnight, running up and down the street in part of the housing project while the grownups sat talking.

I usually avoided the competitive games, and playing only for the sake of winning. It bothered me that the winners taunted and made fun of the losers, who in turn resorted to fighting. Life was serious enough; games were supposed to be fun.

When it came to playing games, I almost always turned out to be a leader. Perhaps it was because my head was always brimming with new and exciting ideas, and being an outgoing person I loved to share what I knew and felt.

Rarely did I find myself being critical of the other children. I always made an effort to befriend the outcasts, to treat them as equals, which sometimes made me an outcast, too. And I began to feel less and less sorry for myself, for my plight. I was too busy learning many new lessons.

In playing with the children in our neighborhood, I learned a great deal about the world and adults. The children's attitudes and habits came directly from their parents, instead of from their own experiences. They cursed as their parents did, and repeated what their parents said about politics and the Negroes. Some of the children hated the president because he didn't belong to the same party as their parents. The Russians were all bad because they were planning to bomb us. And all wanted to grow up and go into the army because Daddy and Grandpa and all the uncles had gone off to save America.

The adults likewise had picked up the attitudes of their parents.

It seemed that the devout Christians weren't as prejudiced against the Blacks as everyone else. Grandma, for example, set food aside for the railroad bums who occasionally knocked on our door. She felt that as long as she was generous to others, God would be generous to her. From her I learned a valuable lesson of generosity, and that he who gives always has what he needs.

I also leaned that adults were very easily influenced by what others said or thought. And everyone interfered in everybody else's life.

I resented being told what to do all the time, but I had to accept my place as a child. How strange that the children were rarely given credit for having intelligence, and were given little freedom to choose. What the adults said became the law and was not to be questioned.

Children were expected to become extensions of their parents, not individuals. It wasn't intentional, but it came from not understanding that each child is an individual Soul. Naming children after their father or a relative takes away from their individuality. Every name has a distinctive vibration, and people with the same names are Karmically related.

As time went on, I saw how very negative people's attitudes were toward anyone outside themselves. Earth people were much more self-centered than I ever first imagined them to be.

A very common attitude was that I have to be a winner, or I have to have a lot of something— money, talents, good looks— in order to make it in the world. I didn't understand this, and it took me a long time to accept it as a part of this world. I knew that such an attitude brought a great deal of suffering.

I did not see how it mattered whether a person was beautiful to look at, because only the inner qualities really count. The physical body is only a shell.

In my life on Earth, I have never escaped the feeling of being an outsider, of living in a foreign world. As a young girl in Chattanooga, I often responded to people's thoughts in a physical way. I would run errands or answer questions before anyone asked me. This was puzzling to my family, and I had to be on guard against it. I soon leaned that many people were frightened by those things outside their understanding. It seemed that anything outside their understanding brought a negative reaction.

Because I looked at everyone as Soul rather than the physical body, I was different. I rarely reacted to other people's anger or negative feelings, because non-reaction is the only way of warding off the attack. The negative energy then has no place to go, and returns to the sender. An angry person just gets angrier.

I do become angry when someone purposely tries to hurt me or a friend. I always stood up for the persecuted and harassed children in our neighborhood, and I was often hurt emotionally and cried because I couldn't understand all the cruelty in the world.

Communication was a big problem for me. I have always had trouble with the English language, such as spelling and pronouncing correctly.

To this day I often use one word when I really intend to use another, much to my own dismay.

At first I took seriously everything that people said. When one of my relatives said to me just before dinner, "Go wash your face off," it disturbed me a great deal. People used words carelessly.

After Merle and Ben entered the Army, Grandma and I lived by ourselves and the house was very quiet. Grandma was very good to me during those years. She had become attached to her last grandchild. At one tine there had been a houseful of children to raise— now there was only one. It was a great change for her.

By the time school started again in the Fall, life at home had begun to settle down. Thanks to our new teacher, Mrs. Dodson, fourth grade turned out to be a most beautiful year.

Every day she read us a story, but first she would put on these hilarious-looking glasses. Whenever she moved her head, the eyes which were painted on the glasses blinked. We looked forward to it every day.

Then a time came when Grandma left for an Army hospital in Kentucky to have an operation. It was arranged by one of her sons so that she wouldn't have to pay. Aunt Ellen moved in for two weeks to take care of me.

It wasn't ten minutes after Grandma was gone that Aunt Ellen and the boys began to show their mean side. Aunt Ellen was always nice to me when Grandma was around. Now I wasn't allowed to do anything but go to school and do chores at home. At the same time, her two boys Donny and Jim had a great deal of freedom. They could do almost anything they wanted.

Grandma's stay in the Kentucky hospital was almost over, and I could hardly wait to see her again. I felt very fortunate that I was able to live with her, instead of someone like Aunt Ellen.

Donny and Jim early one day went to the show, while I was sent to the store on an errand. Arriving home, I found Aunt Ellen and our next door neighbor just preparing to leave for the lake with a tub of beer.

Aunt Ellen spoke. "Your Grandmother won't let you go to the show, Sheila." I knew it wasn't true. Grandma had written a note to Ellen saying that if Donny and Jim went to the show, I could go along. "And you can't go with us to the lake because we'll be drinking beer," she continued. Aunt Ellen locked the front door and left, warning me to stay on the porch.

I sat down on the porch step, head propped up with both hands, feeling low. I wasn't really surprised that this was my special treat for the day, being locked outside while Donny and Jim were at the show enjoying themselves. The whole week hadn't been much better. I sighed, wondering what I was going to do all day.

When I looked up, my spirits lifted. It was Daddy, actually Daddy! There he was, walking down the sidewalk toward me. How wonderful it was to see him, today of all days.

"Hi, Honey, where's your Grandmother?"

"Oh, she's in the hospital," I said. "She's having an operation in Kentucky."

"Well, who's watching you?" he asked.

Aunt Ellen, I told him, but she was at the lake today and I was locked out.

Daddy looked around. "Where's the boys?" he asked.

"They went to the show," I explained with a note of sadness.

"This is not nice. I'm not going to have it," he said indignantly. "Your Aunt Ellen been good to you?"

"Well, no," I admitted, "She was real mean to me for a long time...." I poured out my woes to him.

Entering through a screened window, my father led me into the house, promising that I would most surely stay with him until Grandma returned. We gathered my things and left a message for Aunt Ellen with the neighbors. I of course was elated. But this was nothing compared to my joy on Monday, after Daddy had enrolled me in his neighborhood's school.

All of us children wore marching over to the play park on Cherry Street when someone sneaked up behind me in line and tapped me on the shoulder. I turned around, expecting to see the girl behind me, giggling.

"That's my Mommy!" I cried in jubilation, jumping up and down. We hugged each other. "How did you find me?" I asked. This was too good to be true. What a wonderful treat to be seeing her again!

"Oh, your Grandmother wrote me..., and I was worried about you. Aunt Ellen said you were with your father," she explained with a beaming smile. It was great to see Mommy so happy.

Our teacher walked over. "So you're Sheila's mother. We've heard so much about you." I had told all the kids that my mother was prettier than a movie star.

We continued on our walk to the play park where Mom and I sat by ourselves to talk. She asked how I was doing, how I liked school; I learned that she and C.L. were passing through Tennessee on their way East to open a restaurant.

Mom sat through the reading hour and then our teacher let me leave school early. At Peggy and David's house we gathered my clothes. Then we returned home to 1821 Southern Street. Upon hearing how badly I had been treated, Mom decided to stay with me until Grandma came home. I was greatly relieved, and thankful too that she would be spending some extra time with us.

All of a sudden, Aunt Ellen and the boys were unusually kind to me. A few days later when Grandma returned and heard the whole story, she was so upset as to vow that I would never stay with Aunt Ellen again.

As always, when Mommy left I cried and she cried, until we were out of each other's sight. My strong attachment to her was unexplainable. It was as if she had always been my mother, for whenever the time came for her to leave, I yearned to go with her.

All that year and into the following summer I was in and out of hospitals and medical clinics. According to one doctor my problem was anemia. I was a sickly little girl.

Ever since I began eating Earth food, my stomach has given me trouble. Often I had to leave school and go home because of stomach pains. Part of the problem was that we rarely had a balanced meal. There was barely enough protein in my diet to keep me alive. We ate mostly starches, no salads, and almost no fruit. Cooked greens were overcooked, and whenever we had meat it was overdone. Our family was very poor indeed.

Because I ran around barefooted, and thanks to our poor diet, I came under the attack of pinworms. Shortly thereafter I had an appendix attack. But most of my discomfort and suffering was from persistent colds, fevers, boils, sties, and terrible stomach pains. Perhaps it was all a part of my subconscious rejection of the physical world.

Physical pain never bothered me a great deal, not as much as emotional pain bothered me. It hurt me more if someone was angry with me or was mean to me than if they smacked me in the face.

I was never one for letting on that I was physically hurting. I would act as if nothing was wrong, no matter how bad the pain, partly because I felt it was degrading to have physical pain. And then, being chronically uncomfortable in the physical body made all the extra pain bearable.

It wasn't easy to live in a physical body that always got tired, and that had to be put to sleep every day whether I desired it or not. Bumping against objects was painful, tearing the skin was dangerous, and all kinds of bacteria were constantly attacking the body. "What a miserable place this physical world is," I often thought.

Taking baths, washing, brushing my hair, brushing my teeth, all these chores were a bother that I had to accept.

Cold weather was something I especially disliked; it made me more conscious of the physical body and all its pains. The discomfort and pains of the body have become a whole new dimension of existence for me.

I didn't realize it at the time, but sixth grade was my last year of school. As usual, we were taught all kinds of things that I wasn't interested in, yet most of the time I was given very high grades. My favorite school experiences were art classes, sports, and school plays.

History classes bothered me. How could so many people be proud of the wars that had been fought for freedom? Children became impressed with the idea that force and rebellion was a sure way of reaching goals. I always thought it should also be taught that there were other ways to overcome disagreements.

During this year my interest in boys began to blossom. Until now, Grandma was always after me about being interested in boys. Finally I was getting interested within myself.

My cousins and I enjoyed dressing up when I spent the night with them. Wearing long dresses, high-heeled shoes and lipstick, we paraded up and down the streets. Grandma would have killed me had she found out.

My friend Mary was most responsible for my growing interest in boys, and loafers, and Elvis Presley. I did not exactly love the music, but it was a part of our being together.

Mary's older sister Lilly influenced us a great deal about boys and makeup, and the world of adolescence. She was sixteen. They played a weird game together, Mary and Lilly. At least that's how I felt at the time. It wasn't for me. Lilly pretended to be a boy and Mary the girl; and then they made love.

It was close to August when Donna wrote us again. Everything had changed for the better. She and C.L. were no longer drinking and fighting, and were now living a delightful life on Sanibel Island, off the Florida coast from Fort Meyers. They were managing the Sandcastles Motel. From the postcard they sent, it seemed like a paradise; and I drooled over the miles and miles of long white sandy beaches and the lush tropical growth.

"Would it be all right," they asked, "if Sheila stayed with us a few weeks?"

I yearned to leave that very same day, but Grandma wasn't so sure. I begged and pleaded, and we discussed the pros and cons for days.

Finally the turning point came. Grandma said, "I know you love your mother, and you cry about her all the time, so I guess you can go see her for awhile."

I didn't know what to say, I was so happy and excited. Hurray! At last I was going somewhere outside of Tennessee!

The day Uncle Bob drove me to the bus station, I felt more grownup than ever before. All summer Grandma had been sewing dresses for me, and today I chose to wear my favorite one. It was a white dress, printed with red and orange and yellow sunset-colored flowers. It was fitted in the waist and had a flared skirt and low-cut back. And I wore the black patent leather pumps and hose that Mom had sent me.

As I boarded the bus, my cousin Andrea slipped me some lipstick behind Grandma's back. Grandma sniffled and said goodbye. I looked at her. Yes, I truly would miss this woman who had made sure I was provided with everything I needed, despite our poverty. I hugged her and kissed her. I really loved her.

The bus left Chattanooga. I was going somewhere by myself! "I hope I never see this place again," I thought. Feeling very grown up, off by myself, and wearing red lipstick, what I didn't know was that my life had been very protected during these first Earth years. But the roughest bout with Karma was yet to begin.

Chapter Thirteen
Compared to Venus

1. Education and Experience
2. Aunt Arena and the basics
3. Temples of Learning
4. A trip through time
5. Earth's many religions

You are Soul in the lower worlds for only one reason, to have the experiences which will lead to becoming a conscious co-worker with the Supreme Deity. It is a truth the Tythanians have long been aware of, and this awareness reflects in our way of life. Learning from new experiences is an inseparable part of each individual's life.

Every day we strive to learn more about ourselves as Soul, and more about the many planes which we may explore. We look carefully at experiences and situations to see what lessons they hold for us. On Earth, the inner and outer lives are neatly handled by religion and formal education. Religion supposedly takes care of the inner, spiritual life; while the educational system takes care of learning about the outer, physical life.

As a child in Chattanooga, Church and School were two very prominent areas of my life. In both I could not help but be disappointed, as they reflected the consciousness of Earth. They gave little individual freedom, and they did not allow one to have his own experiences.

Education on my home planet has resulted from centuries of evolution. Just as Laws of the Supresre Deity regards personal experiences very highly, so does our educational system. It grew hand in hand with the new Tythanian culture, after The Beginning.

Organized education was left behind with the money and industry and the decaying cities as the people moved on to their new life. They faced the bare truth that children had done little more than memorize facts and concepts, and that most of what they learned was soon forgotten. More importantly, they understood that man in the physical world must learn as Soul learns, through actual life experiences, not through being told.

As the people moved back to nature, the children became involved in life at an early age. Each family taught its own young ones. The people invented new ways to teach children the basics through participation in running the household.

When the mother prepared vegetables for the meal, she would count each one as she prepared and peeled them, thus teaching the child to count. In the garden, the child was allowed to pick vegetables to see what they looked like and how they grew, and then helped to prepare them. In that way they would have an experience directly with the vegetables instead of with artificial representations.

During field excursions the children were taught about nature; they learned which plants were edible and which were not. On special occasions small groups of children were taken into space to be taught about the planets and the Universe.

At home, not only did they care for the animals and help clean the house, but once a week a child was put in charge of preparing the family meal.

Culture was not forgotten. The children were always encouraged to create poems and songs about what they had learned, as well as to render on paper the things and people they had seen in the course of the day. Dancing, painting, acting, and all sorts of crafts became popular hobbies for young children and adults. Expressing their individuality through art became the vital part of daily life that it is today.

One particular game was especially popular. Here, all the children gathered together to improvise; each in his turn thought up a certain character, situation, and setting. Then another child would act, sing, or dance to express the idea. This went on all evening until everyone had been given a turn to create an idea and to act one out. The children thus learned to think quickly and to create stories, poems, or whatever the individual talents led to. At a very early age they learned to express themselves in many different ways and to have fun at the same time.

Late every evening, everyone gathered together within the family for a half-hour of silence, relaxing the body and mind in order to have a spiritual experience. This is the period of devotion to spiritual matters which I spoke of earlier, called Study Time.

As the people grew in their understanding, they would learn that if a child is given the freedom to develop his own attitudes and have his own experiences, then he would become an individual rather than a replica of the parents. The child would grow naturally and by his own standards with the proper guidance and discipline.

Children who were not interested in learning were not forced to do so; they were allowed to begin learning the basics of our culture at that age when they felt ready. But since all of the learning games were very interesting and enjoyable, most of the children participated. Every child was aware of his natural desire to learn and grow.

Venusian children learn most of the basics at home, and every parent was involved in the learning process. This was very natural because the home had become the center of life.

As the people of Venus translated to the Astral Plane, their approach to education of course continued the same way. During the first few years of my life, Aunt Arena taught me many useful basics. The most important ideas I learned had to do with becoming a mature citizen of the astral plane, which involved much discipline because of our unlimited powers.

She guided me in leaning to manifest things. But always, she encouraged me to learn on my own rather than rely on being taught. Most of my knowledge since the earliest years, about the astral as well as the physical planes, did result from my own individual experiences.

Very early in life I was taught the Venusian alphabet and language, and the number system. Beyond this, Aunt Arena allowed herself to be directed by my questions and interests. Every day in the afternoon we sat down together to learn the arts and crafts such as painting and carving.

The world of plants was especially interesting to me. I loved plants! I learned about herbs, their medicinal uses and everyday uses.

I learned about so many various things that I could well write another book to share them with Earth's people. My interests ranged from clothes styles throughout history, for example, to the nature of man. I learned attitudes that would enable me to make many friends and keep me from being a critical person.

As I grew older I began to visit the city of Teutonia almost every day. At the temples of learning we were not taught, but experienced with the guidance of experts in each field. The Temple of Arts was the largest of all Temples and attracted children and adults alike.

Every morning several Masters arrived at the Temple of Arts to guide the students. Most of us worked in the round center hall, seated cross-leqged on the floor with materials in front of each person.

Usually a Master would begin with an example. He would show the students the various materials to be used, and which tools were used to create different effects. He left out the history of that kind of art, or who created what techniques; this was left to the history teachers. The ideal was for the student to learn his own style, not to copy another's.

Then everyone was set to work, to learn by trial and error. The lazier students asked the Master to show them how everything was done; he was always available to those who asked for help.

Thus each student learned at his own pace, whether it was in painting, weaving, or woodcarving. And each created his own individual works of art, using his own individual style. The other temples were run in the same way. It is the students choice whether he will spend many years to master an art, or spend only a few days to learn several basic techniques.

Each individual was encouraged, after he had mastered a given technique, to lead his fellow students at least for one day. Anyone could become the Master of an art in time.

As soon as we reached some degree of adeptness, we undertook a project to be placed on display for an open house exhibition, for all the villagers to enjoy. Compared to Earth works of art, the creations I saw on display at the Temples were fantastic because only the pure imagination limits us on the astral plane.

It is a tradition in our culture that when an individual nears Mastership in his chosen field, he attempts to achieve something which has never before been done. In this way we are constantly adding something new and different to the arts and sciences.

At various times during my childhood I studied at the Temples of Mathematics, History, Religions, Horticulture and Biology. At the Temple of Biology they showed how life can be created from the basic life chemicals. They also showed how humanoids can be created. These were used at one time in the history of Venus as robots.

The people learned through a tragic lesson that this was not a good idea because humanoids could be entered and controlled by monstrous astral entities. (Venus life was physical then.)

The Temple of Biology taught the deepest secrets of life, and how every form of life was created. The secret is that life itself originates beyond the physical universe. On huge magnified screens we were shown life actually entering a physical form. Much of what was being taught at the Temple would blow apart theories which are presently being taught and respected on Earth. I enjoyed my experiences at the Temple so much that at one time I seriously considered devoting my life to being a doctor.

My visit to the Temple of Mathematics was short-lived. This was a pyramid-shaped building which had many levels above and below ground. Here I planned to learn more about the base nine number system, but my interest waned because too much mentalizing was involved. The Temple, of course, taught all the number systems, and many more mathematical subjects.

The Temple of History dealt not only with our own past but that of all the planets in our solar system, and all those which our space travelers had discovered. Knowing that I may have to reincarnate on Earth in a future lifetime, I desired to learn as much as possible about the planet while I had this opportunity. As Soul I would remember all that I had learned.

I was also interested in Earth because I knew that I had spent many lifetimes there. My favorite place and time was ancient Egypt; so much of my natural feeling and love for music and dancing came from a past life in that great cultural empire. Since that era, dancing has been a part of my being in every incarnation. My experiences have grown to a point where they are now all stored at the Soul level. I have also developed a talent of always knowing ahead of time what will happen in a piece of music; this is a great help in interpretive dancing.

The Temple of History was one of my favorites because it made the dead past come alive. The main level of the building was a time machine!

This was a dark room where everyone would sit down in the middle of the floor. On a control console the date was entered, the planet, and the exact location. Then, without warning, the walls of the room and the darkness disappeared and we would be there, viewing the actual past.

But since we lived within the astral body and were looking into the physical plane, we viewed the scenes as if we were physically dead. Those living in the past who had psychic vision would recognize us as ghosts. To us it was a very real experience.

Until we realized that everything passed through us, we found it very frightening. I had to learn that it was not necessary to flinch or move out of the way if someone walked into me.

I visited prehistoric times on Venus, an age of strange-looking huge beasts and rainforests. The age of dinosaurs on Earth was a similar period, they told us. I found this journey fascinating but a little frightening because it was so eerie.

Then I visited way into the future. It was a time when man had technical control over everything. Everything was automatic. Landscapes were strangely barren-looking; so were the cities and individual homes. Pressing a button brought out the dinner in the form of a tiny concentrated cube.

The most horrible taboo in this culture was that no person could touch another in any way. This was considered unclean and dangerous because diseases could be passed. To have children, the male semen was put into a test tube, and this was injected into the woman.

The children were raised by machines that cared for them around the clock, fed them, changed diapers, provided educational toys, and taught them from screens built into the walls. They had everything but love.

I found all of this very frightening and disturbing. I learned from the guides in the Temple that this era will last about 50 (Earth) years. Because the people were not allowed to touch one another, emotional feelings turned to hate, and murders became widespread. This planet was not Venus, but another in this solar system whose name I shall not mention.

During my childhood years I learned many things about the Supreme Deity's vast worlds, from the physical plane to the spiritual worlds above. My task is not to bring out the many facets of Laws of the Supreme Deity here on Earth. This is being done today by spiritual Masters who have safeguarded the teachings since they were last taken underground. These purely spiritual works are too vast and deep to be taken up in one book.

Instead, I am introducing the teachings I was exposed to on Tythania, and I will point in the direction where it can be found on Earth.

Remember that Tythania has only one planetary spiritual path, or religion if you wish to call it that. Earth has a confusing number and variety of religions, spiritual paths, occult and metaphysical groups, and philosophical systems. I was well prepared by my aunt to live with this change. One of my most valuable lessons had to do with the origins of these many paths.

The reason Earth has so many conflicting religions and spiritual paths is that it is spiritually immature and still in early development. Throughout history, planets in development have had similar problems. The truth is that the Supreme Deity established few of these paths. Yet these few are really different names for the same teaching.

If you were to look back through Earth's religious history, you would find that religions and other spiritual teachings are each founded by a particular spiritual leader, an individual, whose work is carried on after his physical death by devoted disciples. Most of us now recognize such individuals as Jesus Christ, Buddha, Mohamed, Krishna, and many others.

What happened in most cases is that one individual managed to have one or more out-of-body experiences on a higher plane. Whichever plane he reached, astral, mental, or causal, he came back with great wisdom and a fiery motivation to share the message with others. It may have been a salvation gospel or a social gospel, but nevertheless it all originated from contact with a higher plane.

On the physical plane, a new religion then begins to grow and prosper. Followers for centuries afterward make a very basic mistake as Soul. They try in re-experience what the original founder experienced, by following in his footsteps. They try to receive the wisdom and spiritual unfoldment of another Soul, received through out-of-body experiences on a higher plane.

Certain followers then have their own enlightening experiences from a variation in belief and method. Soon a splinter group or branch is formed, based on this follower's success. What does all this do for the individual? It makes him more of a conformist and slave to outside forces than ever before.

Each individual must seek his own Truth, his own experiences, just as the so-called spiritual giants did. Since each Soul is unique, one individual cannot follow another's path, methods or teachings and expect the same results. Each person, as he spiritually unfolds, will seek his own out-of-body experiences using methods suited to himself. Then each individual becomes a spiritual giant, learns for himself what goes on in the heavens beyond, all before physical death.

The masses of people need what religions and assorted spiritual paths offer at a certain level .These teachings cannot be condemned. Every Soul needs the experience of various religions, cults, and philosophies to develop background to help understand the higher Truths. They are steps along the way.

We must always remember that the physical, astral, causal and mental planes are prisons run by negativity. Most religions and paths are furthered by its agents. A sincere student needs to find his own Truth, which is ever the same, because it originates above the lower worlds. Just as there are agents of the Kal in the physical world, who have reached no higher than the mental plane, there are also agents of the

Supreme Deity. The individual, in time, learns to depend on his own inner experiences rather than looking up to those of someone else.

The true teaching always makes known that the spiritual essence of the Supreme Being can be seen in the inner light and heard as the inner sound. The sound is most important, for this current is used by Soul like a homing beam to reach the true spiritual worlds.

It was discouraging to learn that the Laws of the Supreme Deity were not being openly taught on Earth at the time I would be arriving. That was one reason that I might have decided not to come, but on the other hand, knowing about karma I decided otherwise.

Earth culture is young and full of many ups and downs. Spaceships were as familiar in the skies of Biblical times as are the UFOs of today. The space travelers visited here regularly to observe Earth's development.

Instead of being masters of the elements, the descendents of the Earth's first colonists had become a very frightened people. They were ignorant of the most basic Truths, about the Universe, about God, and about themselves, Physical survival and comfort was the number one concern, and death was the number one fear. Idols and gods ruled everything in life, and sacrifices were common. Having leadership and a life of ease in mind, the priests had established religions for control. Their tools were rules and rituals and fear, and their control became complete. Limited beliefs had produced a limited way of life for the mass of people.

Into this era a Great Soul was born. As Soul, he had chosen to reincarnate to lead the Jewish people because he felt close to them. One of his strongest incarnations had been with these people, but he was one of those who had led them into ignorance. As a spiritually advanced Soul, he chose to return and balance his karmic debt by enlightening them in a spiritual way.

The way in which he was born among his chosen people had much to do with the Brotherhood of the Planets. The space visitors saw what was happening on Earth and became involved. The Martians had been in Mexico and South America for some time, and influenced the Incan People. The Martians brought beautiful teachings. They were also known as the Winged Gods or Sun Gods because they came down from the heavens with great powers and wisdom.

In Jerusalem and the lands of those people, visitors from space were called Angels, which means heavenly beings. What else could they say of beings who landed in spaceships, and who had such peaceful, heavenly countenances? The people assumed that beings from the sky were spiritual. And so, Biblical history is full of tales of prophets meeting with God or the Angels, or crude descriptions of their ships as "ball of fire" or "wheel within a wheel."

If your scriptures had translated more of that available information for public examination, you would be surprised at the real identity of the legendary "Three Wise Men"; who they were and who they represented, and how they knew and arrived on scene at the time and place they did. There are great truths behind some of those events reported in your holy works — much of which has been deliberately withheld, or hidden in the translations, in order to maintain the control over the people as intended by those Earth spirits establishing and carrying out the system.

Your brothers from other levels and other planes still come, seeking experience and rebalancing of karma for themselves, and to help Earth humanity at this density of being.

Some live among you unrecognized, and some come from elsewhere to observe, and occasionally they make contact with your people.

This has always been and always will be.

Part of my mission is to help awaken you to the realities as they are, for those who want to know. It is for them only that this work was prepared.

Omnec Onec

Publisher's Comment

We elected to end this account here, though this is by no means the end of this story. Omnec spent many years balancing the Karma she came to adjust. This was also, in part, a kind of preparation for her second mission to come later in life.

The time for the beginning of the second mission has arrived, of which this book you hold is a part. Omnec's secondary mission was to offer an increase in awareness of our relation to spirit and its relation to being in the greater sense which extends beyond the boundaries of our small world.

Later in life, as the karmic trials were nearing an end and she was slowly being released from her ties, Omnec's people began renewed contact with her here and began increased face to face meetings.

These began about the time in young adulthood when it became necessary to confide the true state of affairs to Donna and what happened to her little Sheila and how she was cared for by Omnec's Uncle Odin after leaving her body, and how the body was disposed of by Odin and his companion.

Once Donna knew the facts and the true state of affairs, both on the physical and the spiritual planes, she fully accepted Omnec as her own daughter, a relationship which continues today.

Omnec says there are a number of Venusians here in Earth bodies at this time, but most have come through the birth channel. She knows of no others who have precipitated bodies by densification from spirit to physical as a young child who are living on this planet today. She is quite able to recognize most of those from her last previous plane when she meets them

Densification into the physical plane has cost her many of her spiritual faculties, but she still can perform some remarkable feats with the little control she has left

Another part of this story may be offered at a later time, when it is possible to see what kind of reception it gets and where it seems to be going. She does not want to get caught in the personality traps that so easily materialize on this physical plane.

We allow this story to stand alone, without persuasion, nor do we offer any corroboration, although some exists. It is not our intent to prove any part of it because that implies an effort to persuade which inhibits the freedom to choose. We only offer this information for those who seek. It matters nothing to us how you choose. You will do that by your own choice. Some similar information may be attached for possible reference by those so inclined.

—Publisher—

Omnec Onec's natural mother, Shawik, passed out of body on her home planet only hours after Omnec's birth. She was raised by her Uncle Odin and Aunt Elena up to the time she accepted a mission to Earth.

Omnec Onec's natural father, Deashar, worked with his brother Odin to try to perfect a means of direct transmission of matter between two planets. Odin came to Earth to work on this end of the problem.

Postscript By Publisher

Though in this business of UFO research we may all be "blind men with an elephant," the whole picture becomes a bit more clear through this autobiography of Omnec.

From the perspective of objective research this account is not supported by a great deal of verifiable evidence. While this is in fact a UFO case of a very profound and meaningful nature extending over a long period of time, exceeding 25 years of active contact, it is apt to be rejected by most, if not all, of the recognized UFO research groups, organizations and clubs because of the inter-dimensional (though also extraterrestrial) nature of the contacts. We might find however, if we looked close enough, such inter-dimensional aspects in a great many of the UFO cases already studied that have been deliberately overlooked because the phenomena were not understood by those working on the cases.

I would have been inclined to bypass a case like this myself 15 years ago when I was looking for the real authentic UFO photograph. Pursuing the photographs however got me into contactee cases including some that had real evidence of undisputed nature as well as inter-dimensional and spiritual aspects. There didn't seem to be any sharp definition between the objective physical features and the subjective inter-dimensional and spiritual features of a great many cases — maybe even all of them. I, like Jacques Vallee, was forced to study esoteric and metaphysical phenomena in an attempt at understanding.

About that time I was going through my own personal religious trauma also, finding problems in the finality of the Lutheran religious beliefs in which I was raised as well as the once-saved-always-saved fundamental

Baptist beliefs of many of my friends. I got more answers from the Catholic Chaplain in the U.S. Air Force and I found his beliefs a little broader. I undertook a study of Catholicism and was baptized again as an adult in the Catholic Church. Shortly after that I was on assignment on Taiwan where my home was on a rise just across a bamboo grove from the local Buddhist Temple. My children liked to go to the Buddhist Temple and watch the colorful activity there. When they told me they were talking to the priests I went back with them to see what this was all about. Yes, there was a temple priest who spoke to them and he spoke English well. I ended up visiting the Temple regularly where I had long discussions with the priests.

I was surprised to learn that he knew much about the Lutherans, and the Baptists and the Catholics too, and that he had answers they apparently knew nothing about. When I discovered that he was current on all the latest world news, without a radio or newspaper in the Temple (and he seemed to always be there), and that he knew about things that had never been published, I became fascinated. When he explained the symbology and purpose of various parts and articles in the temple it struck me that this belief was no more pagan than any of the Christian beliefs with which I was familiar. The symbols were only symbols of an unseen God, but this priest had an understanding of that divinity that he could discuss at great length, and he did not ask me to believe anything on faith alone. He said that Divinity was everywhere and that it is available to all to experience for themselves if they so desire. He thought that believing anything on faith alone was a lazy way of forfeiting one's own awareness in favor of an unknown other. He told me of things that would be called miraculous in the western world but which were no more than simple use of natural law once understood.

He knew all about UFOs and where they came from and why they are here. His explanations then, though I did not know it, agree now with what Omnec is saying in her manuscript. Some UFOs at least are manifestations from another level of reality perhaps equivalent to the level that angelic beings came from. Others care from different realities, and others still are from realities equivalent to ours that exist elsewhere, but all these realities are intimately connected.

When I learned from Omnec that she went through a stage of her preparation to live here in a Buddhist Temple in the Himalayas I was reminded of this. I studied the metaphysical literature on the different planes of being, and their interrelationship and intercommunication, and found approximate correspondence. This began to fit with what other extraterrestrials arriving in UFOs had told other Earth contactees.

The metaphysical literature discussed inter-dimensional relationships, and related metaphysical concepts to the physical sciences. It also discussed the interrelationship between microcosmic and macrocosmic concepts and realities, and showed an underlying unity of all of our own physical world with all beyond. We are not an island unto ourselves. We are a small part of a much greater whole which includes all the UFOs and all the planes they come from, and they are concerned and we should be concerned too.

Other UFO contacts have pointed out that we are not here alone and that we may even be greater than we think now. This idea involves a continuity of consciousness through a succession of life experiences, both here and elsewhere, learning the lessons of life on a grander scale than we ever imagined. Not only do we undertake more than one experience here but we do the same elsewhere too, and others from elsewhere undertake needed experiences here, schools of life these might be called.

Don Elkins has for years been in contact with a superior consciousness that discusses UFO phenomena and the greater realities they represent in a series of phenomenal books called "The Law of One." This Intelligence, which has no name familiar to us, says that it may be called RAMA for our identification. It said, in response to a discussion on extraterrestrial visitors, that many entities were being given priority into Earth incarnation at this time to fulfill their own Karmic needs before the close of this cycle for Earth, and that Earth entities that will not partake of the close of this cycle are already being prepared for next incarnations elsewhere. In response to a direct question RAMA said that nearly 20% of Earth humans in physical bodies now are actually extraterrestrial spirits closing their cycles here, and that some of them are being watched over and even contacted and guided by their own contemporaries.

Andrija Puharic, in his many extensive communications with an intelligence that said he could call it Spectra, has told that there are a very many extraterrestrials here in Earth bodies now.

Ruth Montgomery, in her book "Strangers Among Us," was also told that there are many extraterrestrials here in physical bodies now. She called them walk-ins.

Brad and Francie Steiger have written a documentary called "The Star People" discussing a number of cases of what they believe to be extraterrestrial spirits incarnated in Earth bodies. They should know! They even know Omnec Onec personally, whose biography is the subject of this book.

Dan and Aileen Edwards of the UFO Contact Center International in Seattle have assembled a whole organization of extraterrestrials in Earth bodies and UFO contactees in an attempt to help these people to understand and work with each other. They also ought to know all about this subject quite intimately.

More and more, as contactee cases accumulate, the evidence is tending to show that there is some special relationship between the contactee and the UFO visitors. Eduard Meier in Switzerland was told that at one time he was one of the visitors, subsequently entering Earth experience directly and incarnating into this evolution.

SMS Charles Moody of Roswell, New Mexico, said that he felt a strange kind of kinship with the extraterrestrials from Betelguese who picked him up in a gravel pit near Roswell. Bill Herrmann of Charleston said that he felt a warm comfortable friendliness toward the visitors from Reticulum who repeatedly contacted him, "almost like they were kin," he said. Filiberto Cardenas of Hialeah, Florida, did not fear his captors after the initial shock of his first abduction by them. It was almost like he knew them from the past. Pat McGuire of Wyoming felt very strongly this kinship with his extraterrestrial visitors. They actually helped him succeed where failure was certain, and remained in touch with him after that. Edwin, a South African contactee in the remarkable contacts from another solar system also felt very strongly a special kinship with his visitors, and the list goes on and on.

I am aware of several Earth humans today who have vivid recollections of lifetimes spent in the Venusian lifewave before their present incarnations here on Earth.

No, exotic as this may seem, I can't think it is any longer possible to exclude this class of report from the ever-accumulating UFO files around the world. Another situation that must be confronted is the seeming inseparability of the UFO phenomenon from long established metaphysical concepts, nor can either of these be separated from our present day physical reality. They seem to all be different parts of the same thing, neither of which can be ignored or denied.

In Omnec's story we find references to contact with Himalayan Temples and great Teachers that also appear in a body of teaching called Eckankar, a Way of Spirit. Since Omnec's awareness of this information was current in 1955, predating the popular revelation of that school of thought here in the west, we must assume that she did not pick it up in Tennessee. She in fact did meet one of her several Teachers in the Himalayan Temple, as the young Sheila was being prepared for her role, whom she later recognized here in the United States, living in the world at large as Mr. Paul Twitchell. She had several meetings with and exchanged letters with Mr. Twitchell before he left his physical body. She is known to Mr. Twitchell's successors.

This neither adds to Omnec's story nor does it detract from it, nor does it do anything for the Eckankar belief. It is simply a coincidence in fact that tends to corroborate for those who accept such levels of spirit as a reality in their own universe. Many readers will in fact find profound understanding as a result of this mutual clarification of reality and spirit. Those interested in Eckankar will certainly find vindication for some of their own beliefs about extended awareness.

I don't think that the inability of many of us to "see" the Venus lifewave until it emerges into our reality should be sufficient cause for outright rejection of the possibility of its existence. We simply do not know in a personal sense until such knowledge "touches" us and then it is quite different to those. A Canadian sportsman back in the late twenties began experiencing physical contact with some beings who arrived in his remote area in the far Northwoods in a circular disc-shaped metal flying machine. The visitors landed and held face-to-face conversations with him and even took him aboard their ship for extended conversations about our society and theirs, and discussed comparisons and some of the dangers we faced. They told the witness that they came here from Venus and Mars where there was a civilization that we perhaps would not be able to see (because they were of a different density). He was told that there was a time when they were the same as we are now but were forced to change by changing conditions, and that a time would come when we may be forced to change too. They said that their original ancestors came from another star far away and that others still lived there. They were aware of and in contact with life on Venus and in the Jupiter and Saturn systems, and even others too, and that others from still elsewhere are coming to Earth on business of their own. These extraterrestrials remained in contact with this witness off and on for over fifty years, even following him when he moved to the cities later in life.

Of particular interest in connection with this particular case is Omnec's reference to a Martian man, known and expected by her Uncle Odin, who picked her and her uncle up in Nevada, in a Cadillac automobile, and drove them to Arkansas (which may have been another form of density conditioning). The Martian had to also be aware of the coming bus accident that would take the life of little Sheila Mansel who's place Omnec had been prepared to take, because he drove right to the scene of the accident and they sat in the car and waited for the accident to take place! Makes one wonder about destiny and possibly interfering in it.

One of the biggest stumbling-blocks in this field is the seemingly "different" nature of many of the UFOnauts encountered and the craft they use. Hi-speed right-angle turns and instant acceleration of ships observed have always been clues to non-substantiality, and that is exactly what Omnec describes. That they can appear and disappear in a moment is no longer a mystery. Their dimension of reality, or vibrational rate of being, is changed by an act of conscious will.

The seeming one-piece seamless construction of certain spacecraft reported is exactly that in those cases. The vehicles are "manifested," as Omnec describes it, by a process of visualization and then densifying the visualization into our reality by slowing down its rate of vibration. This is a normal process of construction at the level of being described by Omnec and not unusual at all. The invisible openings that just appear and then disappear the same way after entry or use are, as Omnec explains, quite naturally (as if everyone should know) a result of mind control over the molecules of the "material making up the ship."

Real materials are used but they are better understood and better controlled as they are precipitated into being and slowed down vibrationally into denser levels, even physical.

This also accounts, in part, for the seemingly infinite variety of vehicles observed. The Venusian ones at least are in fact all different because they are not assembly-line built.

If there were single observers, or if all the observers of such vehicles were known to each other, we might properly charge collusion in producing such stories. But this is clearly not the case. There are not only multiple observers in a given event, but there is also a multiplicity of such cases. Of the several UFO cases involving bell-shaped craft that I have investigated, I have found only one possible case of a new witness reporting a case, knowing of another similar witness, and that was Bill Clendenen in Seattle. He had been seeing strange things in the sky, and when George Adamski's story was first published and he recognized some similarities, he wrote Adamski to compare notes. After that his sightings increased, became close-up observations, and then a face-to-face meeting, and ultimately his visits aboard the ships. It is interesting that Bell Clendenen was picked up several times in Tennessee and taken aboard the bell-shaped craft.

At the time Bill Clendenen was allowed to inspect the inside of the bell-shaped ship, and examined the structure of the hemispherical pods underneath, he described almost exactly what Glenn Passmore later illustrated in his drawing. I do not know where Passmore got his information but it is correct, and Bill Clendenen said he had not heard of him before Leonard Cramp's book with those drawings came out. Clendenen spent the rest of his life trying to duplicate what he thought he understood of the system, even working with engineers at Redstone, Alabama, trying to achieve something. He never succeeded, possibly because he did not know that the machinery was "manifested" and had unique properties of its own.

I believe I am the first to bring these drawings to Omnec's attention after receiving her manuscript. I am the one who inserted them in this book because they best illustrate what Omnec is describing.

But not only Omnec's descriptions here but descriptions by others, unknown to her, and who have never heard of her, have described the same thing. I have inserted several of the UFO cases involving bell-shaped ships in a separate Appendix to this book. Omnec has not seen my reports of these cases.

There was a series of contacts in England involving a similar bell-shaped craft and a Venusian occupant who was understood to say that he could be called "Yamski"! This was observed by a man who upon questioning insisted that he had never heard of George Adamski. It is also possible that he did not hear the name correctly at the time. This case was extensively investigated by Eileen Buckel, who ended up putting the whole investigation report in book form under the title "The Scoriton Mystery."

This able investigator and researcher was put down by the antagonists seeking to destroy the Adamski contacts, which by now had been maneuvered into popular disrepute by the agents of disinformation. Many of the UFO groups were used, both wittingly and unwittingly, to further this major disinformation effort to a point where anyone who advocated the possibility of the Adamski contacts as having some validity was considered a "nut" and a "cultist." This may have been deserved in some cases, but it is true that there are many real facts in that case that have never been told, and mainly because the disinformation program became effective before such additional information was released, and it was therefore then withheld from release for public knowledge. I know that Major Hans Petersen of Denmark and Herr. Karl Veit of West Germany, both personal friends of Adarnski, know very well what I am talking about. Madeline Rodeffer and the late Lou Zinsstag also knew. Perhaps someday, in a better climate of popular opinion, more of those remarkable experiences may be told. If the U.S. Government were to release all they know about the case, their Pandora's box would be open and we could prove the contacts beyond any doubt.

The agencies of disinformation and many at large may want to cast this story also into the "loony bin" where they think they safely have all other contacts with the Venusian cosmonauts, but there is one saving point that all the agents of disinformation in the world cannot control — and that is the <u>real truth</u> of the matter.

Adamski knew he was a Venusian in an Earth body, one of the reasons <u>he</u> was contacted. And at a certain time in his life he was awakened to a particular mission he came here to carry out. He did that well and departed.

Where did he go? Back to his Venusian heritage, just as Omnec knows in full certainty she will do. Having initiated his particular mission however, he was concerned and continued to participate in it and to observe its effect on the physical world here. That it has had a profound effect is certainly not in doubt. Now Omnec is being awakened to her mission which may take a few of us one more step on our own path. That is all it is expected to do, and for each one that step may be different.

Although this indication of Venusian contact with our Earth may be contemporary, it is certainly not new. The classic heroes of Greek mythology are almost perfect examples of the typical Venusian race-type, and their connection to Venus is certainly indicated. The Greeks even built a Temple to Venus in honor of these "Gods" who flew in the heavens and could control the very elements of our physical Earth.

But even before that, in another age, the Venusians regularly visited Earth and the great White Marble City of Light on an island in the then Gobi Sea. All of this is now under the sands of that great desert.

Some Venusians, according to the theosophists in "Man, Whence How and Whither" by G. W. Leadbeater, took up abode in that melting pot and produced offspring which became a separate race a few thousand years later and migrated to the region we now know as the Caucasus Mountains. They settled there for a time and then spread into Armenia, Greece, and central Europe, becoming the Nordics, and ultimately arrived in America where they are now known as Caucasians.

The Venusians were well known to the Brahmins of ancient India whom they visited frequently and whose vehicles are described in the Mahabarata and other ancient works. At times the numbers of these visiting vehicles "filled the skies" according to observers. The long cylindrical mother-ships were called Vimanas and they carried scores of the smaller "flying cars" of several varieties inside.

In Theosophical literature the Venusians are called "Lords of The Flame," the fire being the intelligence of higher mind brought to younger Earth humanity.

But they were not the only ones who came here. There were reported visits by intelligent men from Mars and Saturn and other planets too, and sometimes in company with the Venusians.

When George Hunt Williamson, author of "Other Tongues, Other Flesh," began channeling the space brothers of the Solar Cross, members of the Brotherhood of Planets in our solar system, the participants were amazed to learn that intelligent beings from Venus, Mars, Saturn and other planets in our solar system were working together.

Williamson was giving a voice channel demonstration to a group in a Detroit home one night after an Adamski UFO lecture, when a young man, Richard Miller, was in that witness group to observe what was going to happen. As Williamson was preparing to induce his trance condition, Miller, the younger of the group which was too big for the number of chairs to go around, was reclining on one elbow on the floor waiting for things to start. He seems to have dozed off as he waited and when Williamson jerked into trance and began speaking in a different voice, the voice of the communicator, Richard, now also in a trance, spoke an identical counterpart of the same voice saying the very same thing simultaneously, word for word IN STEREO!

After that Richard Miller continued to channel the entire solar cross group of a dozen or more communicators. I joined the group studying Richard Miller at Victorville, California, where I participated for over a year filling four notebooks on this phenomenal development at the time. Those Extraterrestrials provided adequate and convincing proof that they really existed, and that not only Venus, but Mars and parts of Saturn and Jupiter, even Neptune and others, had evolving human life-forms.

Their statement that Earth is in quarantine at this time supports Omnec's allusions to certain restrictions on Earth humanity.

Omnec has managed to bring a few of her extended faculties through with her into this physical density, although much of the acuity of these and even all of some others were lost completely. She can still read thoughts and see auras, sense previous life experiences of others and perceive future events before they happen. She is capable of out-of-body travel and telekinetic manipulation of matter to same degree, such as unlocking locks under certain conditions. She has an excellent conscious recall of many of her own past lives as well as full recall of her earlier life on Venus before being brought here. She can attract butterflies and small birds to her hand and pet them, and wild animals do not run from her. She can think and write poetry almost as easily as a letter. As she was penning a letter to me she quickly wrote the following:

There is a place we long to be.
  It is our home eternally.
We travel there when our bodies sleep at night.
  Only to return by day's early light.

Soul am I, and you as well.
  Within this cage of clay we dwell...
To experience life our lessons we must learn,
  Until eons from now our freedom we shall earn.

Sheila '83

Omnec has lived a low profile life as Sheila most of the time since coming here in 1955 except for a brief exposure in 1975 when she was finishing the manuscript of her experience. The time was not right then, she now feels, and is told by her Venusian mentors, that the time has come to reveal her real identity, hence the release of this manuscript now. She thinks we may experience an upsurge of UFO activity soon, and that many extraterrestrials in Earth bodies are about to discover, or else recall, their true identity, and that many of these will make themselves known.

Wendelle C. Stevens

Publisher

Special Comment

Finding some of Omnec's descriptions in substantial agreement with what I knew of Eckankar philosophy, I took the liberty of sending a copy of this manuscript to Mr. Ed McCabe, a responsible man whom I knew to be a senior authority on that particular belief system. He examined the material carefully, including all of my added material in corroboration of the basic narrative account, and offered some very important advice. He suggested that I delete my references to certain "channeled material" because it could be misleading to some individuals seeking their own self-realization. He recommended against depending on another entity for our truths, and suggested that they were only valid for us if we came by them in our own way through inner realization. I couldn't agree more, but, since some people do accept extrasensory contact, I decided not to delete such references, but instead, to include his comments to me verbatim, for each to consider in his own way. This is what he said:

"Although Omnec's work does <u>not</u> fall into the following category, an avid reader might have read any number of works that on the surface seem similar. There is a big difference between Omnec's writing from experience, and those of the "channeled transmissions" class. Most people doing UFO studies have, or will, run into this subject eventually. Usually, without knowing what it really is. Here is a viewpoint you may find useful. This is being included either to prepare you, or to let you know what you experienced.

"Channeled transmissions means someone acts as the mouthpiece (or writer) for someone or something else that is usually not physical. In the old days it was called being a "medium" or "spiritualism." The person who allows another energy to use his or her body for communication purposes must be careful that they are not on a tangent from the most efficient utilization of the Laws of the Supreme Deity. Using extrasensory gifts for any other purpose than furthering the acquisition of direct personal contact with the Divine might lead to trouble. Many famous occult books have come to us through these methods, and everything has its place in the Divine Play, but I am speaking of efficiencies. You don't let a grocery clerk tell you what to eat, so why settle for second hand information about Life Itself?

"Many people who are sincerely seeking answers to life's mysteries core across such mediums, or 'vehicles.' These intelligences coming through someone claim to be, or in fact are, 'space beings.' Please note that in this analysis, I exclude the class of contactees who have actually physically met an ET, and have agreed to act as a communicator. This class can be good or bad for the whole, depending on which side, (positive or negative) they are aligned with. They are, simplistically speaking, like a man with a walkie talkie. Although we can be fascinated by their ability to communicate, verbally and otherwise, how do you know who is on the other end, or why?

"So how can you tell if they have really met an ET and agreed, or are making it up, or which side they work for? This is a problem best solved by exercising caution while seeking first God Realization for yourself. In time, after training, you will acquire the facilities and discrimination to solve any such question.

"When using mediums, there usually follows a period of being fascinated by the information supplied, and/or becoming fearful of something. The result is most always the same. The participants are slowly drawn into the aura of the sensitive and/or the entity. Some form of subtle or overt control factors are perpetrated upon them, and those involved start to run to the medium to solve all their problems, or explain or predict for them. Slowly they give up their own self determination, or at the least, get their subconscious filled with fear of misinformation which may take years to overcome. The misformation is usually mixed in with 'true' things to get you believing. That's the worst case, but even those with the purest of intentions must be careful. We have to go through all sorts of experiences on our way home."

Ed McCabe

Ed indicated his satisfaction with Omnec's reporting from direct experience, as a more valid source of such information, and offered no quarrel with the nature and content of the narrative account.

Appendix I
Other Venusians

The following report was published in the Green Bay, Wisconsin, PRESS-GAZZETE, dated Friday, 26 June 1959, where it appeared on the Family Fare page under the byline of Charles House, Staff Writer:

FAMILY SEES FLYING SAUCER:
FATHER TALKS TO PASSENGER

"Somewhere along the shore of Lake Huron I found a story which I could not dateline without exposing my source to ridicule and perhaps contempt. I had halted my little canoe and hiked overland to a filling station for gasoline. As usual, I was unkempt, bewhiskered and much travel-stained. My appearance elicited from the station proprietor a little more than casual interest. He questioned me and I explained my mission. He then invited me to his nearby home for a cup of coffee and to meet his 12 year old son and his pretty wife. After a general discussion of my experiences, he asked me if I had seen any unidentified flying objects. I grinned.

"Well,' he said, "it isn't so funny. See that island out there?' and he indicated a small island a few hundred yards off shore. "That," he said solemnly, "is a frequent landing place for a flying saucer." His mien was serious, his attitude and his speech sensible. I questioned him further. I must admit at this point that I have my moments of skepticism, but that I feel it part of my duty to try to believe if my judgment tells me a statement deserves some objectivity. My informant had every indication of being a man of good sense and sound judgment.

"Yes, I have gone out to the island to watch the flying saucers land and take off. I have seen them many times and so have my wife and son," he said. I glanced at them and got a nod of confirmation from each. "Have you seen the creatures in the flying saucers?" I asked. Then he shocked me with an offhand statement. "I certainly have. I know one of them," he said calmly.

At my request he described the persons he said came so often in the UFO. "They looked like you or me. They can speak English and they do it perfectly although in a sort of singsong manner. They are tall and quite strong, and they live for hundreds of years. They are much advanced in technology and keep such equipment in their aircraft as would amaze a world scientist by its material and perfection. I am not permitted to reveal what these instruments are." "Where do they come from?" I asked.

"These particular ones care from Venus," he said. 'They have friends on Earth like me, and they visit with us. Those of us who can believe have been selected by a process only they know. Skeptics are avoided." "What do they want here?" I asked. "They want to spread the peace —everlasting peace." "Did you ever ask your friend why he did not make his objectives known to all of us who love peace and want peace?" I asked. "Of course I have. But he told me that our people are not ready to accept their word. But they are vitally interested in our aims and attempts at interplanetary travel, because anything which happens on one planet must surely affect all other planets." He continued, "If for example, we sent a party to the Moon, the first thing they would do would be to plant a flag and declare the Moon to be the property of the United States. Now, if somebody already owns the Moon, our action would be considered warlike and inconsiderate. It is just such a thing as that in which the Venus people are concerned."

"Does your friend have a name?" I asked. "Yes, he has a name," replied my informant, "but I am not permitted to reveal it. And it is not proper to call him my friend; he is so superior to me and all the Earth's people that one is inclined to look up to and revere him." "How many of these Venusian people are aboard the UFO?" I asked. "About 25," he said, "but I have not been permitted to speak to them although I have seen them many times. Only the one who has spoken to me is the one with whom I have closest contact. You may have trouble believing that I have talked many times to him, but you could believe my wife and my son. Neither of them would ever tell a lie deliberately."

The wife and son both solemnly stated that they had seen him conversing with a person who came out of a very brightly illuminated UFO which landed a number of times on the small island off the shore of Lake Huron.

Later, away from the personality of the father, I asked the boy if he had indeed seen these things. He is a very bright, intelligent young fellow and I might have been inclined to believe whatever he told me. "Yes sir," he said firmly, "I have seen my father talk to the man from the flying saucer many times." "What do they talk about?' I asked. "I don't know," said the boy, "Mother and I usually sit in our boat just off shore of the island. We have a good view and can see these people in their shiny clothes and always the same one talks to dad. I have never heard what they say. I think they talk about peace."

"Perhaps they do."

These contacts with Venusian UFOnauts, though obscure to the public at large, continued for a long time. But this is not the only other one. We have already mentioned others, and in Appendix II on bell-shaped UFOs reported, we shall describe more, some more authoritive than others.

About the same time, in the middle 1950s, there were other equally extensive contacts with UFOnauts who said they came from Venus. There were the contacts of Lt. Comdr. Frank Halsey and his wife Tarna of Salt Lake city, that took place all around their home area and even as they traveled around the country. Mrs. Halsey says that the couple was summonned to the White House for an hour and a half discussion in the Oval Office, alone, with President Dwight D. Eisenhower, after his meeting with a team of Venusians at Muroc Air Force Base in California in the early 1950s. The Venusians arrived in several disc-shaped spacecraft and remained at the U.S. airbase awaiting the arrival of the President by helicopter from Palm Springs; and then also remained overnight with their aircraft sheltered in a hangar on the flight-line. Mrs. Halsey said that when she asked the President why he didn't announce his meeting to the American people, she says he answered, "My dear, even a President cannot do all that he would like. It is out of the question." Two of those participants in the Eisenhower meetings are still alive today. I am advised that a 5-star Admiral, "Bull" Halsey, then Commander of the Pacific Fleet, an uncle to the aforementioned Frank Halsey, also had a contact with UFOnauts who said they came from Venus. These are pretty powerful statements, but I have interviewed two eyewitnesses who confirmed that these events did actually take place.

About that same time Albert Coe, camping in the Canada Northwoods, was, according to him, visited by human beings who arrived in a disc-shaped flying craft. They told him that some of them came from Venus and that we, and they, had a common ancestry back in time. They said that they were studying and reporting on Earth conditions. Mr. A. Coe's contacts went on for 60 years, eventually including the wife that he met and married after he returned to civilization. In the early years of his contacts he thought he was the only one to have such strange experiences and was reluctant to tell anybody about them. He was persuaded to set them down in detail in a manuscript he called "The Shocking Truth" that was later published privately in only a few copies for very limited distribution. Only ten copies are known to exist today. Albert Coe did not hear of Adamski until years later when he moved back to the city.

Then there were the contacts of the Mitchell sisters of Texas, which also began in the early 1950s and continued for years. Contrary to Coe, these sisters, like the Halsey's and Bill Clendennen, had heard of George Adamski and his contacts, and had their own reasons for believing that much of what Adamski was saying was in fact valid. They even appeared on the same lecture platform with Mr. Adamski and told their history. One of these lecture accounts was subsequently written up and published by a UFO promoter in a small booklet, and many hundreds were sold around the country. What escaped attention, however, was the fact that these Mitchell sisters had carefully set down in detailed chronology, a full report of the repeated ongoing contacts with them by human beings who told them that they came from Venus. These sisters were, one at a tine, taken aboard the ship and were shown some of the marvelous instruments and devices contained in the spacecraft with which the occupants aboard could tune in any place and scene on Earth at will, and they demonstrated this for one sister by tuning in the other for her to see and hear for herself. These contacts went on for years and that manuscript fills hundreds of pages.

There are other such reports also which tend to confirm the Venusian contacts. An interesting sidelight in these reports is the frequent occurrence of the Venusians, and humans from Mars as well as other planets, working together on common projects, as in the cases involving

Omnec Onec and Albert Coe, the Halseys, the Mitchell sisters, and George Hunt Williamson and Richard Miller. These cannot all be easily dismissed.

Appendix II
Bell-shaped Spacecraft

Omnec's description of the small Venusian spacecraft that brought her and her Uncle Odin from the mother-ship to Earth's surface closely fit the descriptions of the bell-shaped craft photographed in 1953 by George Adamski out near Palomar Gardens in California. Long before I heard of Omnec I had already rejected the Adamski photographs as fakes, accepting the pronouncements of the UFO group leaders at face value, until I later found that most of them were accepting still others statements the same way, and nobody was doing any real investigation or work on proper analysis. I decided to see what I could find out, and I first went to Mr. Gabriel Green of AFSCA in California who seemed to be the only one actually looking at the evidence in a properly inquisitive manner.

His efforts surprised me and he gave me leads to other witnesses who had seen similar bell-shaped UFOs. I ran some of them down and turned up several more myself, and dug some out of my letters file. In 1975 I had a whole folder of material from which I have extracted the following cases for your information.

Two of these cases I have investigated at great length personally and have interviewed the witnesses extensively and walked over the sites and examined the situation. These witnesses convinced me then, and they do now, that they are honest and sincere and really believed what they described to me.

Here then is a summary of several of those cases. None of those witnesses were in contact with each other, with the exception of Bill

Clendennen who wrote to Adamski after a news item had appeared in his local paper concerning George Adamski and his claims. Clendennen described what he was seeing and Adamski sent him a friendly reply.

The bell-shaped style keeps popping up in UFO reports with astonishing regularity despite extensive ridicule and personal and official efforts at debunking this configuration.

Ever since George Adsrnski, an amateur astronomer living near Palomar Gardens in California claimed to have photographed a bell-shaped flying object on 13 December 1952 through his homemade 6" telescope arrangement, private researchers and official agencies alike have tried to put the lie to this type.

Adamski described the strange craft observed and photographed through his telescope as deep disc-shaped with a large upper dome having vertical sides sitting on the upper surface. It was "opalescent' in color and seemed to be made of some sort of "translucent metal." He guessed it to be about 35 feet in diameter. Its dominant characteristic, however, was a strange understructure composed of three large lighter colored hemispherical shapes, evenly spaced 120 degrees apart on the undersurface inside the rim of the craft. Inside of that was a dark central core revealing little detail in the photographs. On top of the raised dome was a spherical transparent ball-like device of some kind. This was the first known description of a craft of this configuration in our modern era of reporting.

Adamski is accused by his attackers of photographing the end of a cylinder vacuum cleaner and the top of a beer cooler, and Prof. Donald H. Menzel tried unsuccessfully to show that it was a chick brooder, each suggesting that such mundane objects were photographed under controlled conditions to deliberately perpetrate a hoax. Of interest is the fact that in 32 years of searching by experts the world over, nobody has ever found a matching configuration or been able to duplicate the picture. If it was so easy for one untrained man why haven't those experts with unlimited facility been able to come up with the definitive answer?

There was one big flaw that couldn't be overcome, and that was the distance graying due to atmospheric attenuation by matter suspended in the air.

On 20 October 1957, near Winona, Missouri, Mr. Tom O'Bannon observed and photographed a similar bell-shaped craft rising out of the rear yard of his home, and retracting three hemi-spherical protrusions into the under surface as it ascended.

On 24 April 1959, Sr. Helio Aguiar photographed a huge disc-shaped machine estimated to be over 100 feet in diameter as it swept in from the ocean, and it had four hemispherical protrusions spaced evenly around the center on the underside. What these structures were was anybody's guess.

On 5 March 1961, again at Palomar Gardens, the same George Adamski successfully took five pictures through his telescope of a large dark cigar-shaped craft in the act of launching five small bell-shaped craft, one after another from the belly of the larger ship. These photos were taken in a dark sky. But on 3 September 1975, at Nagoya City, in Japan, Hirohito Tanaka successfully shot ten daylight photographs of a similar operation where a large cigar-shaped mother-ship high in the sky is seen to launch more than a dozen small bell-shaped craft from its belly, some of which descended to the surface and made low passes over the city. The profile and contours of that cigar-shaped vessel are almost identical to the one Adamski photographed 14 years earlier.

But returning to personal observations of the bell-shaped configuration, we find witnesses who have never heard of Adamski or any of these other witnesses. Around 8:20 P.M. on 17 September 1965, just about dusk at that time of the year, Mr. and Mrs. M.L. Nelson of Tucson, Arizona, were lounging in their yard at 247 South Cherry Avenue, with an acquaintance Dave Phillips present, when they heard a low whispering whooooh sound, and looked up to behold a bell-shaped craft passing almost directly overhead in a straight line from northwest to southeast.

It was a dark silvery gray metallic color with an orange corona-like glow around the middle. It had three hemispherical protrusions from inside the flange under the bell rim. They projected below the trim-line of the bottom of the ship. Above the disc flange was a cupola with windows or panels of a darker color. The orange glow surrounded the craft above the rim and below the window-like features. The glow was not painted on the ship but it seemed to be definitely a part of it.

The height of the craft above the around was estimated from familiarity with the Davis-Monthan Air Force Base air traffic, which also passed almost directly over the Nelson's home. They guessed this strange ship to have passed over about 2,000 feet above them. Its apparent size from that distance was 3 to 4 inches measured at arm's length, about twice the size of the jet fighters that they see flying over every day, as they land at the airbase.

This ship was flying at about 130 mph in a slight tilt of 20 to 30 degrees, with the lower edge forward, like it was gliding, but it did not descend. The speed was about the same as the traffic speed for the jet fighters.

The hemispherical understructures were all full half-spheres with the other half seemingly buried in the understructure around it. The under-rim area shaded from dark grays to midnight black. No center structure of any kind could be distinguished — it was just black.

The craft disappeared in the direction of Davis-Monthan by entering a puffy white cloud, one of many in a layer at about 1,500 feet above the ground that day. It would have come out the other side, not visible to them, and was lost in the cloud layer.

Before that, in the evening of 4 October 1951, Bill Clendennen of Seattle, Washington, had an experience with a bell-shaped UFO that changed the course of his life. From his home near NW 55th Street and Roosevelt Way, he could look to the west across Green Lake and Elliott Bay toward Seattle, where the World's Fair was in progress. In the direction of Port Townsend, 40 miles NW, he saw a smoky vapor making a staggered trail in the sky. Then suddenly a brilliant white light popped on at the head of the vapor trail, made a quick zigzag movement and turned south. The vapor trail disappeared. The light continued south until it was due west, just north of Bremerton. It then made a sharp 90 degree turn without slowing or curving, and came straight east, passing almost over the Space Needle monument just south of its course and continuing over Green Lake. The light was now changing from sharply outlined to a fuzzy-edged ball in a pulsating sequence.

"The ball of light grew to about the size of a tennis ball held at arm's length as it came towards me over Elliot's Bay and Green Lake. It was now about dusk, but still light enough to read a newspaper outside."

"The ball of light faded out and became a dark orange colored glow which shaded into shadow. The light pulsated in intensity in a regular sequence. As it came closer it appeared to be distinct bands of light with a small ball of bright light on the top and a little ball of light on the bottom. Distinct bands of rusty orange all pulsated together."

"As it got closer, I could see 'windows' or ports in the cabin superstructure, and the orange pulsating light resolved itself into a circular bell-shaped craft similar to the one Mr. Adamski had photographed, except I saw four 'ports' in a group.

"The cabin didn't rotate, and the ball on top and the outer flange didn't rotate, but the rings underneath inside the flange rim were all moving. The first and darker ring inside the rim flange was rotating clockwise, and was not flat but concave cupped, as a 'U' ring with the open face down. The next inner ring was white with white half globes on 120 degree spacing, and it rotated counterclockwise. The half globes mounted on this lighter ring seemed to turn also, and there were sparks or pulsations of light coming from the point where the half-spheres met the lighter flange surface, and seemed to surround the half-spheres at that point.

"A darker midpoint convex structure with a lower center cone having a pulsating point of light on its tip was also revolving clockwise, but the lower center cone with the light was stationary. The entire upper surface of the craft was flat white in color, not silver. A band of orange light or halo surrounded the outer stationary flange, and also the upper cabin above the 'windows,' or whatever they were. These orange halos and the spherical ball of light on top of the cabin were all pulsating together. There was a space between the halos and the surface of the craft. The color of the halo was a rusty orange."

The craft flew away in the direction of Sand Point Naval Air Station and disappeared from view.

But back to 15 February 1954, a little over a year after Mr. Adamski had made his famous photograph through his telescope, two young English boys suddenly photographed an almost identical bell-shaped craft with a very cheap pin-hole camera.

It was about 11:00 A.M. when 13 year old Stephen Darbisher, son of a doctor, while walking on Conniston Hill with his eight year old cousin

Adrian succeeded in getting two photographs of an unidentified flying object of almost identical size, shape and proportion as Adamski's version. The following statement was written by Stephen half an hour after the incident:

"Adrian and I were walking on the fell (looking for some birds and good scenes to photograph) when suddenly Adrian slapped me on the back and told me to look at a queer round object which was gliding down slowly from a gap in the clouds. The object was shining a silvery-white as the sunshine caught it. I quickly pulled out my camera and took one photo, turned the film and took another. Just as I finished, the flying object shot off up into the clouds at an alarming rate and disappeared. As it flew off it went out of the sun's rays and I could see it was made of a plastic-like metal which light could travel through but I could not see through it. It had three landing wheels or domes and a cabin with portholes in it. The bottom came to nearly a point. Adrian and I were down in a small valley, so the rising in the foreground of the photo is due to the position we were in. Some grass is shown under the object. It made no sound whatever, except for a swish as it went by."

Except for different words the descriptions of these several witnesses were remarkably similar.

In his book, UFO, PIECE FOR A JIG-SAW, Leonard Cramp made a very careful comparison of the Adamski photo and description with the two photos and description by young Stephen Darbisher, and also extended both pictures into the same plane by orthographic projection, and found the two different sets of images to be identical. Cramp prepared a cut-away drawing of the Adamski ship, prepared from verbal descriptions, and that cutaway very clearly shows a number of the features mentioned by Omnec in her description of the interior of the ship that brought her from the mother-ship to Earth.

Is this pure coincidence?

Why My Interest In This Case

I met a young woman ten years ago who had remarkable psychic faculties including extended perceptions such as clairvoyance, clairaudience, far memory and precognition all very natural to her. She was very artistic in sketching and painting, but particularly so in creative dance. She could pick up almost any musical instrument and be playing it in a few hours. She could get out-of-body easily and did frequent astral travel. She created poems and lyrics for her own music almost as easily as writing a letter. She could remember past life experiences, one of which she believed was on Venus some time ago. She described scenes of the Venus life to me which I listened to at the time as interesting if verifiable, knowing very well that our scientists had already discovered the great inhospitality of the surface of that planet and its atmosphere, rendering it completely uninhabitable.

As the years passed and new information came in I began to wonder if we were going about our assessments the right way. Other cases seemed to indicate a scale of lifewaves of which the physical realm is only a part but somehow connected in the scale. More research and more information began to expand my ideas of the true realities. Maybe we were looking at our universe through a long straw and seeing very little of it. Other UFO cases involving totally unassociated witnesses who knew nothing of each other continued to build on the developing idea of a multiple level universe on very different planes of being, though somehow related.

Then I encountered Omnec's story, which now did not seem so far out, and even fit a considerable amount of the data I had collected. I was constantly reminded of the earlier Venus story as I got deeper into research on Omnec's manuscript and the other Venus UFO cases. As you have seen from this book, there is a definite thread of continuity.

Wendelle C. Stevens

Available Now—The Collected Works Of

TIMOTHY GREEN BECKLEY

FREE CD OR DVD WITH ORDERS

Some Have Called Him The "Hunter Thompson" of UFOlogy—Others Just An Ordinary "Mad Man!"

( ) UFOS AMONG THE STARS

—First person Interviews with punk queen Helen Wheels on her abduction. Wm Shatner's MIB encounter. Muhammad Ali's 21 sightings of "Mothership."
—Jackie Gleason Saw Alien Bodies
—Also: Buddy Rich, Sammy Davis Jr., David Bowie, Charles Bronson, Jimi Hendrix, John Lennon, Dick Gregory, Ronald Reagan. - $15.00

( ) SUBTERRANEAN WORLDS INSIDE EARTH

Is our planet honeycombed with caverns inhabited by a mysterious super race? Are the legends true about the earth being hollow? Have cave explorers encountered, and even fought with frightening creatures from the abyss? Is it possible that flying saucers originate from beneath our feet? What of the tales of the wee people, the giants from Atlantis and the mysterious disappearances of explorers?

Nine editions – A real treat! - $15.00 (includes free CD)

( ) FLYING SAUCERS IN HOLY BIBLE

Angels? Demons? ETs? A sign of the "Second Coming? What your minister is afraid to tell you about UFOs and aliens! God once walked the Earth in physical form. Tower of Babel was a spaceport. Parting of the Red Sea was a miracle performed by ETs who befriended the Israelites and "levitated" them across the Red Sea. Several Biblical figures may have gone for UFO rides. And members of the Royal Family believe they have a "direct link" to Higher Realms (gives reason why).

Large format – Lots of previously unpublished material - $16.95

( ) MJ-12 & THE RIDDLE OF HANGAR 18: THE NEW EVIDENCE—Is the craft that crashed at Roswell stored away along with the remains of its alien occupants? According to Beckley and assistant Sean Casteel, the last 8 presidents have been in on this deception. Describes over 60 UFO crashes (one in Central Park), the existence of the "secret government's" MJ-12, and an alien "space glove" kept under wraps. Includes CD of Prof Carr's personal "inside" story.

Over 200 large size pages. Illustrated – Special price, $22.00

( ) OUR ALIEN PLANET: THIS EERIE EARTH

Following in the tradition of John Keel and Charles Fort, this fully illustrated work tells you how to enter other dimensions and possibly enter time loops in your own backyard. Ghost Lights. Glowing Orbs. Energy Fields. Interdimensional Life Forms. Crop Circles. Ley Lines. Invisible Phantoms Of Myths & Illusion. Mysterious Messages From The Soul Of The Planet Conveyed in Signs and Symbols and Freaky Weather. Co-authored by Sean Casteel. Includes Audio CD Interviews with Joshua Warren and Phil Imbrigno. - $22.00

( ) STRANGE SAGA—40 years in the making. The amazing lifetime journey of Tim Beckley containing his early (mid 60s) columns from Ray Palmer's famous Flying Saucers magazine, as well as clippings from his scrapbook, world journeys and interviews and full length articles. Reprints from Saga's UFO Report includes: Invasion of the Space Giants. The Mind Manipulators. Town Haunted by UFOs. Wyoming Hunter Kidnapped by Aliens (Carl Higdon story). UFO Base Miles From White House. Canada's Secret UFO Program. Astronauts UFO log (from Apollo missions). - Includes free DVD—$25.00

( ) THE UFO SILENCERS: MYSTERY OF THE MIB

Accounts based on first hand conversations with terrified witnesses. From Albert K. Bender's shocking confrontation with three men dressed in black suits and dark sunglasses, to those whose lives may actually have been "compromised," here are tales too chilling for most to accept – but all are true. Inside story of the untimely death of Dr. M. K. Jessup, as well as the MD who was threatened in no uncertain terms to keep his mouth shut–or else! Sale price - $20.00 (Note: 3 set audio CD containing lectures by Keel, Barker, and Bender just $20.00 more!)

( ) STRANGE ENCOUNTERS: BIZARRE AND EERIE ENCOUNTERS

Tim's favorite Top Ten stories from the "Twilight Zone" of UFOlogy UFO witnesses who "mutated." Undersea saucer that sank an American sub. How HAM operators are being inundated with voice messages from "aliens." The WV man abducted by vegetable-like humanoids. The UFO base hidden in the California foothills. Remarkable healings attributed to space beings. Two women have "craziest" UFO encounter of all time (bar none!). Crawling lights in Oregon invade home. $17.50

SUPER TIM BECKLEY BOOK SPECIAL - All items listed for only $139.95 + $10.00 S/H. Includes 8 books, various CDs, DVD and additional UFO PHOTO ALBUM containing over 400 photos of "space ships," aliens, orbs, monsters, and other non human oddities. How to Order: We accept VISA, Master Card, Discover, Personal or Business Checks, Money Orders, Western Union. Add $5 S/H for up to 3 items. $7 for up to 5 items. Or $8.50 for super special. Canadian & Foreign customers double shipping. NJ residents add sales tax. Or at: **MRUFO@webtv.net**

Check Desired Items

24/7 Automated Credit Card Hot Line: 732 602-3407

Global Communications, Box 753-U, New Brunswick, NJ 08903

Available Now—The Latest Works From The UFO Review And The Publishing Arm Of

TIMOTHY GREEN BECKLEY

Some Have Called Him The *Hunter Thompson* Of UFOlogy... Others Just An Extraordinary Mad Man

FREE CD OR DVD WITH ORDERS

HOW TO CONTACT THE SPACE PEOPLE—Was Ted Owens the soothsayer of the space generation? When published, readers reported "miracles" and supernatural experiences while carrying one of the "Space Intelligence" discs (FREE bonus). This book asks: Have we been sent-and ignored-messages from Spacemen? Does the Saucer Intelligence control our weather, civilization, our very lives with their advanced technology? Was TED OWENS really selected to "relay" their warnings and predictions?
—**$20.00 Large Format ISBN: 1606110012**

SON OF THE SUN: SECRET OF THE SAUCERS—by Orfeo Angelucci. Introduction by Tim Beckley. One of the most dramatic contactees of the 50s, was Orfeo caught in a simulated life Matrix? Was he under "Programmed Control?" Journey with Orfeo as he enters an alternate reality of "Infinite Entities," travels to other dimensions, and experiences moments of illumination. Comes with 80 minute audio of Orfeo, Adamski, Fry, Van Tassell, Long John Nebel speaking about aliens visiting earth.
—**$22.00 ISBN: 106110047**

THE ALLENDE LETTERS AND THE VARO EDITION OF THE CASE FOR THE UFO—Rare Reprint of Dr. M.K. Jessup's annotated manuscript some say may have caused his death. Probes time travel and the mystery of the Philadelphia Experiment. Originals of this banned publication have sold for up to $2500 to "true collectors." Were the mysterious annotations made by three men, who may have been gypsies, occultists, hoaxers or ETs living among us?
—**$39.95 ISBN: 1892062410**

UFOS, NAZI SECRET WEAPONS: CONSPIRACY JOURNAL BOOK AND AUDIO CD—Not endorsed by the publisher, any legit UFOlogist or Conspiracy buff or the "Space Brothers." Banned in 22 countries, the author claimed to be a political prisoner for over 20 years because of his strange belief in Nazi made flying saucers. Mattern Friedrich claims the discs are being constructed by secret societies and that Hitler escaped to the South Pole.
—**$25.00 ISBN: 9781606110348**

BEHIND THE FLYING SAUCERS - THE TRUTH ABOUT THE AZTEC UFO CRASH - Sean Casteel offers 50 new pages of details to important reprint of the famed early 50s work involving the crash of a UFO in Aztec, NM, reported on by Variety columnist Frank Scully. Were I6 alien bodies found in the desert? What happened to the downed craft? FBI involvement? New evidence? Stan Friedman, Scott Ramsey, Nick Redfern, Art Campbell—**$20.00 ISBN: 1606110209**

2012 AND THE ARRIVAL OF PLANET X—Commander X, Diane Tessman, Tim Swartz and Poke Runyon call on "confidential sources" to probe the concept that the world will come to an end on Dec. 21, 2012. There are those who claim that certain world leaders and the rich are making secret plans to leave this world – and here is a hint: we are NOT INVITED!
—**$20.00 ISBN: 1606110144**

UFOS, TIME SLIPS, OTHER REALMS, AND THE SCIENCE OF FAIRIES—Little Men do not come from Mars! Beckley, Sean Casteel, Brent Raynes and Tim Swartz (along with occult historian Edwin Hartland) espouse the theory that UFOs are not visitors from space,but, that the occupants of these craft could be more like specters, phantoms or spooks, rather than flesh and blood ETs.
— **$20.00 ISBN: 1606110101**

Check Desired Items

MIND CONTROLLED SEX SLAVES AND THE CIA—Tracy Twyman — with additional material by Nick Redfern and Commander X —Did the CIA turn innocent citizens into mind controlled sex slaves? What do devil worship, human trafficking, mind controlled experiments and sexual abuse have to do with the U.S. government? Includes expose of mind controlled "Stepford Whores," and sacrifices at Bohemian Grove.
—**$24.00 ISBN: 978-60611-018-8**

Check Desired Items

Please allow adequate time for us to process your order (up to 21 days)

Ask Tim Beckley for his new 2008 book special. All items listed for just $169.95 + $10.00 S/H. Includes 8 books, various and companion CDs, or DVD.

How to Order: We accept VISA, Master Card, Discover, Checks, Money Orders or PayPal to MRUFO8@hotmail.com. Add 5.00 S/H for up to 3 items. $7.00 for up to 5 items. Or $10.00 for this super special. Canadian double the postage rate. Foreign e mail for rates. NJ residents add sales tax. eMail address: MRUFO8@hotmail.net.

24/7 Automated Credit Card Ordering Hot Line: 732-602-3407

Global Communications • Box 753-U • New Brunswick, New Jersey 08903

FREE CATALOG UPON REQUEST MRUFO@webtv.net
Global, Box 753, New Brunswick, NJ 08903

The Incredible Cities of the Inner Earth

by David H. Lewis

Ancient Mayan and Aztec maps lend support in proving the legends of Utopia buried far beneath the Earth's exterior in vast cities that exist throughout the planet. The author pinpoints the seven land openings on our surface that, if explored, would lead one to the almost forgotten civilization that has existed below our surface for more than one hundred centuries. The book's contents is based upon an actual expedition which began in April of 1979 that took these explorers on a journey into the many tunnel passages that eventually led to the very outskirts of these active inner cities.

PARTIAL CONTENTS: • The Seven Days of Creation • Time in Relation to Being • The Seven Living Planets Below • Seven Years of Devastation and the Seventh Hour • Power of Telekinesis • The Astral brain • Reincarnation Beyond Our Galaxy • Esoteric Knowledge of UFOs and Those Who Walk Among Us • Teleportation and Probing the Black Holes of Space. Well worth its price.

$21.95 plus appropriate shipping charges.

❑ **THE SMOKEY GOD AND OTHER INNER EARTH MYSTERIES** edited by Timothy Green Beckley

The complete text, reset in type for readability, of a rare, century-old, but all too true book which tells of a fantastic journey inside the earth by the author who meets a race of giants who befriend him. This manuscript was believed lost for all time, but is now made available again to provide important evidence that our Earth is hollow and populated by beings related to those who once lived on Lemuria and Atlantis. Additional material includes an otherwise unavailable chapter—over 20,000 words—by Ray Palmer on evidence that flying saucers come from inside the Earth and that our world is hollow. There is also an exclusive interview with Princess Sharula from Telos, headquarters for Mu beneath the Earth's surface.

Published price $14.95. CATALOG SPECIAL: Only $12.00 plus appropriate shipping charges.

❑ **RAINBOW CITY AND INNER EARTH PEOPLE** by Michael X

This is a rare and educational and inspirational course of study. The following chapters are included in this brief work: The Strange Great Valley - The Rainbow City People - Colonel Fawcett's Fate - The Sun God's Secret - What Do Inner Earth People Want? Written by an "inside source."

$10.00 plus appropriate shipping charges.

❑ **EDIDORPHA: Strange History of a Mysterious Being and an Incredible Journey** by John Uri Lloyd

Only 50 rare collector's reprints of this 150 year old manuscript exist. The story Lloyd tells is that he belonged to a secret society and, because of his heightened awareness and spiritual beliefs, he was taken on a fantastic voyage to the inner world, entering through a cave in Kentucky.

$29.95 while supplies last (plus appropriate shipping charges).

❑ **HOLLOW PLANETS** by Jan Lamprecht

JUST ADDED: THE SCIENTIFIC EVIDENCE YOU'VE BEEN SEARCHING FOR! The great English astronomer, Sir Edmund Haley, first proposed that the Earth might be hollow. Later the great mathematician, Leonhard Euler, speculated about it, as did scientist, Sir John Leslie, and author Jules Verneis. Some religions maintain to this day that a vast underworld exists inside the Earth. Scientists say all planets are solid, but could science be mistaken? This book is an in-depth review of many papers from science journals of the highest repute. Contains interviews with many top scientists in fields as diverse as seismology and astronomy. The results will send your mind reeling. 600-page reference book is packed with fascinating information and includes a 16-page color photo section with evidence that Mercury, Venus and even Earth, are possibly hollow. Published to sell at $39.95.

SPECIAL CATALOG OFFER Only $34.95 plus appropriate shipping charges.

❑ **UNDERGROUND ALIEN BASES** UNDERGROUND BASES by Commander X

A former military intelligence operative offers shocking proof that FLYING SAUCERS COME FROM INSIDE THE EARTH and aliens have established underground UFO bases around the planet. He maintains that entrance ways can be found in major cities and that serpent-like ETs are using high powered mind-altering beams to take control of humanity. Above all...some government officials have taken the side of the aliens and have allowed them to utilize our own military bases such as those beneath Area 51.

$17.50 plus appropriate shipping charges.

❑ **VIDEO! JOURNAL OF THE HOLLOW EARTH—NOW ON VIDEO!**

Well done history of the Inner Earth phenomena on VHS in color. Very dramatic, professionally narrated. Discussion of various theories and Hitler's belief.

$17.00 plus appropriate shipping charges.

AUDIO

HEAR RAY PALMER and RICHARD SHAVER in a RARE AUDIO INTERVIEW conducted by the original dean of late night talk radio, Long John Nebel. This is the only known surviving interview of decent broadcast quality exactly as it was conducted via phone in the 1950s. A real collector's item.

$14.00 plus appropriate shipping charges.

ENTIRE INNER EARTH LIBRARY — $199.95 PLUS $10 SHIPPING IN USA. Shipping for up to 3 items-$5. 4 items or more-$8.

GLOBAL COMMUNICATIONS • BOX 753 • NEW BRUNSWICK, NJ 80903

Credit card order use our safe, automated 24-hour hotline at 732-602-3407

This edition issued 2008. Price/availability subject to change.

Credit Card Automated Hot Line: 732 602-3407

An updated interview with Tim Beckley can be found at
www.conspiracyarchive.com/UFOs/beckley.htm

SOME HAVE CLAIMED THIS IS THE BEST KEPT SECRET OF THE AGES...

Visit the INNER EARTH!

Suppressed Manuscripts Available in Limited Editions Reveal The Strange Truth About The Earth's Inhabited Interior!!!

LIMITED TIME ONLY!

- Does An Underground Race Dwell In Vast Subsurface Caverns Beneath All Major Cities?
- Are There Entrance Ways To The Inner Earth At The North And South Poles?
- Are UFOs From Outer Space Exchanging Technology With These Underground People?
- Are They Friendly Or Are They Using Deadly Rays And Mind Control Apparatus Directed At Humans From Far Below?

Due to the POWERS THAT BE, we may only have a LIMITED TIME to get this information into your hands. The following manuscripts contain information on a variety of theories pertaining to the world that exists beneath our feet, unknown to the majority of people living on the surface of the Earth!

❑ **SUBTERRANEAN WORLDS INSIDE THE EARTH** by Timothy Green Beckley

Critics recognize this as the definitive book on the Shaver Mystery and his deadly dealings with the subsurface race of the Dero who the former Detroit welder established contact with, tapped into their hideous attempts to establish mind control over surface dwellers. Here is the story of the wee people, the Tommy Knockers, the elves of legend, as well as the Atlantean Giants and Nazi explorers who disappeared deep in the jungle of South America. Here also is the story of "Mr. X's" harrowing escape from a being with a birdlike tail dwelling in a "haunted mine" in the Southwest. The disappearance of Col. Fawcett while in search of a "Hidden City." The existence of the Jersey Devil said to roam the shoreline on rain soaked nights. American Indian legends of the "Hollow Hills" and the strange story of Steve Brodie who became a mental robot of the Dero. A MUST READ!

$15.00 plus appropriate shipping charges.

❑ **THE FLIGHT TO THE INNER EARTH: The Missing Secret Diary of Admiral Byrd**

Here is the most fascinating...and the strangest...story that the history books fail to relate. It is Admiral Byrd's amazing trip beyond the North Pole into the land of great mystery and enchantment, and his being greeting by a race of superhumans. For years rumors have persisted that such a diary existed. This seems to be the real thing!

$14.00 plus appropriate shipping charges.

❑ **CAVERNS, CAULDRONS AND CONCEALED CREATURES** by William Michael Mott

NEW FOR 2008! This is a serious study of subterranean stories in history, folklore and myth. Includes correspondence claiming that these 3-D holographic images contained the images of the underwork as well as the inexplicable memories for abductions, reincarnation, premonition, clairvoyance, etc. The Earth itself being a vast database, stored within its own electromagnetic field.

PARTIAL CONTENTS:
- The Deep Dwellers of Folklore, Myth and Literature.
- Faerie Lands Revisited.
- Caverns, Grottoes and Eldritch Horrors of North America.
- Hollow Moons and Hollow Worlds.
- The Fortean and Cryptozoological Connections.
- Lake Monsters, Hairy Humanoids, Chupacabras and Other "Hybrid" Beings.
- Re-Invention, Paranoia and Deception From Below.
- Our Surface Farm and Playground.
- Hamburgers From Hell and Other Nasty Dishes / or The Farmers in the Delve.

Secrets From The HOLLOW EARTH

The author concludes that there is "a definite link between electromagnetism and some types of underground beings and the connections between varied topics such as "ghosts", UFOs and electromagnetism are well documented.

$29.95 plus appropriate shipping charges.

❑ **TELOS - TELEPATHIC COMMUNICATION FROM EARTH'S INTERIOR** by Diane Robbins

Timely and fascinating messages from the people of the Hollow Earth and from the Underground City of Telos beneath Mount Shasta. Offers proof we are not alone on this planet as the call goes out from the Hollow Earth and the Underground Cities beneath us. Explore the rich family life of the people from the lost continent of Lemuria who have been underground for the past 12,000 years and who, due to their isolation from the surface population, have created a civilization of peace and abundance with no sickness, aging or death. They have mastered immortality in physical expression.

$19.95 plus appropriate shipping charges.

CHECK ITEM(S) DESIRED, ENCLOSE PROPER FEES AND RETURN APPROPRIATE PAGES OR LIST TITLES ON SHEET OF PAPER. PLEASE PRINT CLEARLY. NEW JERSEY RESIDENTS PLEASE ADD APPROPRIATE SALES TAX.

FREE WEEKLY NEWSLETTER ON NET ONLY
WWW.ConspiracyJournal.com

Manufactured by Amazon.ca
Bolton, ON

31151455R00155